Edited and scanned by Jonathan Downes, Hennis and Mr Pooter
Typeset by Jonathan Downes and Wally the Comedy Rhinoceros
Cover photo by George Ward
This edition - layout by Peanutt for CFZ Communications
Using Microsoft Word 2000, Microsoft Publisher 2000, Adobe Photoshop CS.

First self published in Canada
Second edition by Gonzo Multimedia 2014

c/o Brooks City,
6th Floor New Baltic House,
65 Fenchurch Street,
London EC3M 4BE
Fax: +44 (0)191 5121104
Tel: +44 (0) 191 5849144
International Numbers:
Germany: Freephone 08000 825 699
USA: Freephone 18666 747 289

© Gonzo Multimedia MMXIV

All rights reserved. Without limiting the rights under copyright reserved above, no part of this publication may be reproduced, stored in or introduced into a retrieval system, or transmitted, in any form of by any means (electronic, mechanical, photocopying, recording or otherwise), without the prior written permission of both the copyright owners and the publishers of this book.

ISBN: 978-1-908728-47-0

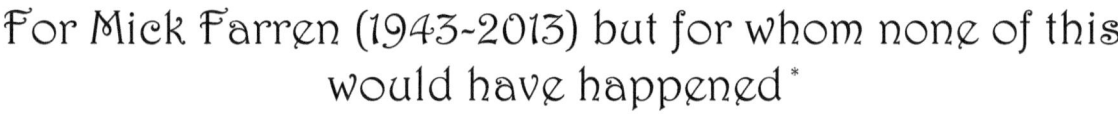

---

* And if you didn't know the quote on the front cover was from Hunter Thompson then shame on you...

The Gonzo Annual 2015

A Message to all the young Ladies and Gentlemen from the far flung reaches of the Empire who shall be reading this morally uplifting book

Hello Boys and Girls,

Welcome to the first ever *Gonzo Annual*; a compendium of interesting, thought-provoking, and above all uplifting articles from the pages of *The Gonzo Weekly* from the Year of Our Lord 2015.

Being the decent Godfearing company that we are, we are proud to bring you this unparalleled collection of articles, papers and *memento morii* written by some of the finest authors and penmen from England and Her Colonies. Yes, you heard us right! This volume contains articles written by and about Colonials. Because although they will never be a match for the good olde yeomen of Merrie England, some of those living in our far flung foreign possessions across the Empire on which the sun will never set can make some quite interesting plinky plonky sounds on their banjoleles. And being subjects of our great Empire means that they are still preferable to foreigners, because—after all—Johnny Foreigner is a rum cove.

We are publishing this groundbreaking compendium of facts, frivolity and fun, because today the Empire faces a threat unparalleled in all the years of her glorious existence. There is—and I know that you will be as shocked as I, boys and girls—a new breed of person afoot. A new, and disturbing breed of person. A breed of person who does not believe in loud amplified rock music! Yes, there I have said it.

There are people who eschew sitting in muddy fields, bobbing their head up and down to the beat of a distant drum...even when that drum is being played by a member of the Worshipful Company of *Hawkwind*. Yes, these degenerates prefer to watch their so-called reality television, and have not even *heard* of the pothead pixies of the planet of Gong. I would wager that they don't even know who the singer for Galahad is, or that Judge Smith is *not* a member of the legal profession.

Yes, boys and girls, I feel your shock and disgust from where I sit in my converted potato shed writing this upsetting screed. But there is hope boys and girls, and it is you that are that hope. If we all pull together, respect our betters, fight the good fight and make sure that we don't Bogart that joint my friend, then there is still hope that the Empire we love so well shall continue for another thousand years.

What Ho Chums,

The Editor

A brief note from Jon Downes and his increasingly infantile Orange Cat (Captain Frunobulax the Magnificent)

A couple of years ago Rob Ayling the *Grande Fromage* of Gonzo Multimedia, and my old friend of well over a quarter of a century asked me whether I would edit a weekly newsletter for his record company. I think I managed two issues before I became bored with the concept and started morphing it imperceptibly into something else; a weekly, full colour multimedia music magazine.

I have had various attempts at editing a music based magazine during my life; indeed it was whilst editing one of these magazines that I first met Rob Ayling back in the summer of 1988. When I started these endeavours it was with a manual typewriter and the school Gestetner machine. After a few more years we moved onto the high tech luxury of an electric typewriter and Letraset, and even ventured into offset litho printing for a while. But in the mid 1990s along came the internet, and the world was changed forever.

We now have the technology to put out a full colour multimedia magazine for FREE, and furthermore to disseminate it far and wide. Earlier this year the editor of the *New Musical Express*— the magazine which I read avidly from the age of 14 for the next twenty years— told the BBC that "the digital edition of the magazine sells 1,307 copies a week". Well, most weeks these days we get more readers than that, which I feel is no mean feat. OK, we are not comparing like with like, and I would never dream of claiming that we are outcompeting the *NME* who not only have a print version that still sells over 18,000 and is the hub of a highly successful brand, but it is a step in the right direction and it shows quite how far we have come.

Rob and I are both children of the 1970s and have many cultural references in common. Like me, I am sure he remembers devouring the annuals (like *The Beano Book*) which we received each Christmas, and so when he asked me to produce a 2015 Gonzo Annual I knew exactly what he wanted. At least I hope I did, or I will be sacked. Herein find a miscellany of interviews, features and general silliness culled almost at random from a magazine which I started for fun, and which is growing beyond my wildest dreams…

Slainte

An interview with Don Falcone of the mighty Spirits Burning

Spirits Burning are very much a 21st Century sort of band, and have made a complete art of long distance recording. Working mostly within the broad genre of Space Rock, and co-ordinated by digital maestro Don Falcone (born November 5, 1958) - an American musician and producer.

Originally a poet-performer in Pennsylvania, he relocated to San Francisco at the beginning of the 1980s. He was a member of Thessalonians and the original Melting Euphoria, had a solo project called Spaceship Eyes, and since 1996 has led the Spirits Burning Space Rock collective.

Falcone set Spirits Burning on their continuing mission just as the internet began to open up an index of collaborative possibilities that studio recordings and logistics previously precluded: the chance for content-creators to recruit musicians on an ad hoc basis across the ether; musicians they'd have scant hope of playing with face-to-face.

I have interviewed him before, but now I am far more *au fait* with what he is doing personally, and with the whole 21st Century musical *modus operandi*. Listen to our conversation

http://www.gonzomultimedia.co.uk/radioplayer.php?id=207&play=don%20faLCONE.mp3

The Gonzo Annual 2015

Orrin Hare

KRAUTFOLK!: THE ACID FOLK OF AN AXIS POWER

What happens to a people when they lose a war? There were an awful lot of Germanese & Japanians pondering precisely this about seventy years ago. And, of course, they did what all sensible people forced to scurry together some semblance of meaning from the rubble of previous certainties and the ashes of collapsed arrogances would do: an absolute shit-ton of drugs.

Everyone knows that a tab of acid is a perfect way to start the day, but it IS possible to do it to excess. Luckily, Germany's brave musical pioneers did exactly this, and thus empowered, set about putting their own distinctive spin on the psychedelic folk music that had come wafting over the North Sea in a dope- and armpit-scented miasma during England's summer, autumn and winter of love. Let's call it Krautfolk, for want of a better word.

Psychedelic or acid folk emerged in Britain when musicians hooked on powerful hallucinogenic drugs and American popular music also found themselves hooking unexpectedly into the golden chain of traditional British folk music (which had survived near obliteration at the end of the previous century through the efforts of cultural archivists and had already undergone at least two national revivals before the end of the Sixties), discovering an almost eerie fit with their existing psychedelic sound and ideals.

Out sprang Britain's folk rock scene, with its Fairport Conventions and Pentangles, all leafy and pastoral, steeped in dreams of the benign British countryside and its almost vanished traditions, the debatable charms of childhood, and that queasy Albion quaintness that only foreigners and people with eyes sandpapered to innocence by acid can express without wincing. By the end of the decade, however, if you dug around in the

The Gonzo Annual 2015

undergrowth, you would have found something a little different (might we even say, a little more interesting?), trickling a strange little current all of its own alongside the mainstream river of folk rock. This was acid folk: a place where groups like The Incredible String Band and Comus did infinitely sophisticated and wonderful things, and were ignored. Although not, as we shall discover, by everyone.

While Britain's hippies were rediscovering the pleasures of their regional folk music, the situation was a little different in Europe. In Germany, the nation's folk tradition had been carefully tended and encouraged by the state alongside other "authentic expressions of the German people", as part of the Third Reich's *Blut und Boden* romanticism, so as the defeated and occupied country fumbled around in the post-war years for things it could safely feel German about, the folk music tradition remained in the shadow of the *verboten* agent behind the flourishing of these and similar Germanic cultural properties: the now more than a little embarrassing eccentricities of National Socialism.

It was only to be expected then that the post-war generation of Germans would have a problematic relationship with their nation's traditional music, recognising that below its surface appeal lay a narcotic mix of emotions coiling around ideas of place and nation, which bitter experience had taught them not to indulge. What German would now want to flirt with reactionary practices like the expression of a primal national German identity in the form of traditional culture? Folk music should have been tainted for a generation of young Germans, Austrians and Bavarians.

Still, at the beginning of the '70s, Krautfolk happened. Why was it that musicians from the radical student underground of left-wing communes and involved in the birth of Kosmische music/Krautrock at the end of the '60s would be moonlighting in the creation of psychedelic folk music, when their compatriots were explicitly working towards the creation of new and untarnished German aesthetics and identities to help fill the cultural vacuum left after the wreckage left by the previous generation had been swept away?

The boundaries of the acid folk scene were never fully drawn and it can be difficult to fully separate the barely-there psychedelic tinge of some acid folk groups from the more psychedelic moments of the decade's more conventional folk rock scene, but I think the reason why such a radical culture could embrace such an ostensibly reactionary – and even dangerously nationalistic – musical form, could have something to do with one of the key differences between conventional folk rock and acid folk: it's much deeper connection to psychedelic culture, which saturated its sound and imagery.

Crucially, and of particular importance to German musicians, acid folk's universalist psychedelic ideals helped it transcend any pure exploration of national folk tradition and myth in favour of a multicultural, polyglot approach, with musical ideas and instrumentation sourced from many different regions and traditions. To give one example, the importance of India in hippy culture was a crucial building block in the development of psychedelia's sonic landscape, and this and other eastern elements help expand acid folk's sound away from any narrow regionalism, with the continent's trancelike repetitions and use of drone having at least as much impact as surface exoticisms like the tabla and sitar.

I would argue that acid folk "felt" safe because it

wasn't trying to reconstruct something authentic or pure, and it didn't attempt to connect its audience emotionally, dangerously, back to any single heritage of land and race.

Ironically, it took English underground musicians in the 1980s to self-consciously row folk music all the way back to *Blut und Boden*, as in a strange recapitulation of the way avant-garde Krautrock had birthed a parallel track of German folk, often using the same personnel, musicians involved in the experimental Industrial music scene, itself inspired by the pioneering work of electronic Krautrock bands, also found themselves drawn to the transgressive possibilities offered by folk music's homeland heart-tug.

Stopping off for musical inspiration in the weirder fringes of 1960s acid folk and the relentless psycho-pastoral attack of bands like Comus, and less than a decade after the 1976 stage debut of Industrial music pioneers Throbbing Gristle, Neofolk groups like Sol Invictus and Death In June flung themselves back in time like an antagonistic custard pie, combining an introverted and deliberate esotericism with a garish manifesting of the shivery implications of race, ritual and nationalism that European folkies had spent more than forty years trying to forget. Here was folk music, unmuzzled, and it's unlikely that its Krautfolk forebears would have been too surprised when these latest ambassadors of a less culturally careful movement, quickly found their whole scene tainted, as a significant number of core bands turned from calculated ambiguity and the hints of darker purpose common in underground scenes acting against popular culture (Eric Hoffer's "When the weak want to give an impression of strength they hint menacingly at their capacity for evil"; still the only possible explanation for both teenage boys and Nazism) to a fully-hatched and brazen fascism ("It is by its promise of a sense of power that evil often attracts the weak" – thanks again, Eric!). Disaster!

Luckily, psychedelia came to folk's rescue once again, when the New Weird America and Freak Folk movements sailed across the Atlantic in the late '90s on a floating armada of Vashti Bunyan records, reviving a more optimistic, '60s-influenced strain of acid folk for a generation that might have lacked the political engagement of its forebears, but was at least doing its best to offset any whiffs of privileged and splashy shallowness, with a D.I.Y. bedroom aesthetic and lots of drugs.

KRAUTFOLK: A PRIMER:

In chronological order, here are thirteen albums released between 1971 and 1978 that include most of the major statements of the West German acid folk scene and should give some sense of the breadth of flavour it contained.

- **Siloah,**
"Siloah" [1970]:

Emerging from the same commune culture as Amon Düül, with which it had some connection, the short-lived Siloah produced maybe Germany's first

wholehearted acid folk album in 1970 with this self-titled debut, released a full year before the first incarnation of Amon Düül made its brief swerve in that direction with "Paradieswärts Düül" [1971]. How acid folk is Siloah? There's a song called "Krishna's Golden Dope Shop", which should answer that question.

- **Bröselmaschine**,
"Bröselmaschine" [1971]:
From its Emerald City cover to what sounds like Nico's baby sister breathing German language vocals through a megaphone (on "Schmetterling"), this is a lazy summer day of terrific prog folk psychedelia. Drone-drenched sitar, tabla and flute add psychedelic colour to the band's baseline acoustic strum, while the monomolecular concentration for which

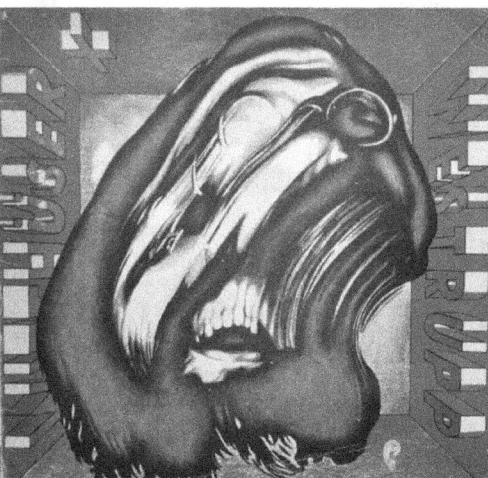

potheads are so widely acclaimed finds expression in songs whose straighter folk moments and tricksier prog adventures alike are embarked upon determinedly only to blur apart like ecstasy eye wiggles, dissolving into Indian-inflected trancey drift. Album opener "Gedanken" and closing song "Nossa Bova" are both authentic Krautfolk classics, providing a suitably beautiful whiskers and tail for one of the best collections of acid folk to come out of Germany.

- **Witthüser & Westrupp,**
"Trips und Träume" [1971]:

Literally "Trips and Dreams" – and you can't get much more acid folk than that! – this second album by songwriting duo Bernd Witthüser and Walter Westrupp rather belies the grotesque face-melting purple and red bad trip of its cover with a delicate line in fingerpicked acid folk, sung with real character and with a nice sense of space and air. Low-key vocal/violin drones and other acid elements are present throughout, helping supply the "trips" of the title, but the band also summons up dream-pop ghosts with the muffled piano and scratchy violin of half-remembered childhood music lessons. And what more can you say about the psychedelic credentials of an otherwise German language album that ends with its principal musicians both singing the words "give me the joint", in English?

- **Emtidi,**
"Saat" [1972]:

"Don't sit on the grass, it's too cold for your ass", warn the two-piece+percussion group Emtidi, helpfully. Dolly Holmes' ethereal vocals are often earthed by Maik Hirschfeldt's lustily sung harmony to help keep everything from floating away – no mean trick with Kosmische synths being out in full force – although songs like "Träume" (again) and "Touch The Sun" remain aloft throughout, with the latter building over minutes of barely-there swelling synth tones. Saving the strangest for last, closer "Die Reise" backs Hirschfeldt's emphatic semi-shouted German vocal with an organ drone, a strange jazzified electric piano and an acoustic guitar happily strumming along on a single-chord for a third of its length, before dissolving unexpectedly into In-A-Gadda-Da-Vida ... with jazz flute. Hey, I said it was acid folk.

- **Hölderlin**,
  "Träume" [1972]:

With a band named after a 19thC German Romantic poet and high-school roommate of the philosopher Hegel, Hölderlin's first release is one of the key albums of German acid folk, although the nine-piece group would likely have denied any connection to the drug culture. It opens like a weird folk Portishead with the voice of singer Nanny DeRuig floating over a violin drone, before fading quickly into nervous pattering drums and a string-drenched flute and organ jam, salted with a creepy German-language recitation by violinist and second lead vocalist Christoph Noppeney. The rest of the album alternates between intricate fingerpicked acoustic folk and the looser energies of songs like "Requiem Fur einen Wicht" and "Traum", whose multi-part prog structures stretch things out with drums, mellotron and violin drones, and delicately scored orchestral moments.

- **Kalacakra**,
  "Crawling To Lhasa" [1972]:

These German psychedelicists only recorded a single album, but the raga-inflected mantras and pulsing bowed cello drones of "Crawling To Lhasa" often give it the feel of a piece of crossover New York minimalism (maybe a mellow version of the following year's "Outside the Dream Syndicate" sneezed in from a parallel

universe), while the deranged vocals,, either gibbers, mutters and shrieks or sinister spoken word, bring to mind nothing less than legendary near contemporary Comus, although without that group's taut structure and dizzying folk musicianship. Still, this is a bizarre and highly listenable exercise in the single-chord drone, refracted through Indian raga, ultra-early sequenced drums and synths, Krautrockesque makudi and tabla workouts, and rudimentary blues. And all without changing key once! Is it Krautfolk? C'mon now ... flutes!

- **Sündenfall II**,
  "Sündenfall II" [1972]:

Following Amon Düül II's lead with its numerical band name, this is in part

relatively straightforward quavery-voiced and flutey psych-folk, almost country rock in places, complete with wailing hobo harp. Bongos and an occasional organ drone generate acid moments, although the ugly snout of light jazz is conjured unapologetically from a hellish trinity of trumpet, sax and noodling piano in "Duftes Ding", and it's not unlikely that your body may respond to the dubious poetry of its English-language lyrics with winces rather than goosebumps.

- **Gila**,
"Bury my heart at wounded knee" [1974]:

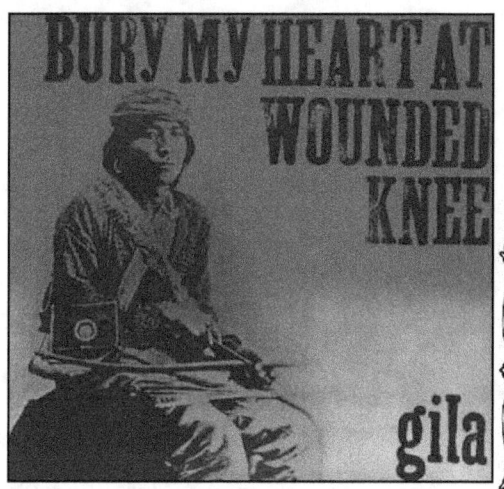

Its personnel alone should teeter it near the top of any ladder of quintessential Krautfolk, but this piece of unimpeachable pure acid folk, bubbling from a former radical commune and stirred through with dreamy analogue synths, is even better than it sounds.

Featuring Popul Vuh's guitarist Conny Veidt and leader Florian Fricke on short-loop trance piano, mellotron and Moog, everything is easy as breathing until closer "Little Smoke" hits a wall after three minutes and transforms from mournful synth 'n' strum to a sizzling halfway-to-Krautrock workout, setting the single-bar riff of Fricke's striking raga piano against an equally striking syncopated drum loop, while an echo-drenched electric lead commentates on the proceedings. Essential.

- **Merlin, Swara, Ilor & Friends**,
"Cosmic Kraut Experience" [1974]:

Opening as a very splashy tabla-driven psychedelic drone rock of real charm and Krautrockian primitiveness, the album's groaning hippy bandstand of bassoons, harps, bouzouki, flute and distorted electric mandolin solos, plus the woozy disregard paid by the musicians to hitting the notes they were probably stabbing at, all make a good case for Krautfolk. More? How about the back cover of the LP celebrating the label's

status as the home of "THE NEW WAVE OF PSYCHOSIVE & PROGREDELIC MUSIC" in large red capital letters?

- **Langsyne**,
"Langsyne" [1976]:

In part, nice folk-rock with English-language male harmony vocals, psychedelicised with natural sound effects, thin organ and buzzy synths, although it suffers a bit from a textbook version of that classic prog Achilles heel: poetry of unconvincing deepness ("There's a voice inside your mind!") presented over-reverently in incredibly elaborate settings. But the album is also capable of lifting off to explore a delicate raga-like acoustic trance, while in "Cynghanedd" you are suddenly face-to-face with the measured & stealthy dirge of a mid-'70s Godspeed You! Black Emperor.)

- **Gurnemanz**,
  "No Ray Of Noise" [1977]:

A more progressive follow-up to their debut, this is well-produced progressive

folk from the Rhineland, with a golem of Grace Slick crooning over acoustic arrangements that meander prettily while still retaining more than a pinch of acid. The twin fingerpicked guitars and double bass are capable of knuckling down into locked trance rhythms of impressive power and complexity, while the jazz comb-and-papers that pop up like duelling banjos in song after song must have sounded like a fantastic idea when the band's members were navigating the kind of spotlit wriggleworld you get by licking funny stamps.

- **Carol of Harvest**,
  "Carol of Harvest" [1978]:

Oestrogen-drenched psychedelic folk rock with a name lifted from Walt Whitman, a

16-minute opening song and a dreamy prog acid feel that invites us to "look madly into her eyes/& hear the screams of butterflies" (yuk!), this is little sweet & straightforward for my palate. Still, "Somewhere At The End Of The Rainbow" has a real hook, although the six minutes of scat singing that ends the album is more of a punch on the nose than a pat on the head as a parting gift.

- **Emma Myldenberger**,
  "Emma Myldenberger" [1978]:

Absolutely deranged folky Krautrock combining psychedelic rock elements with oompah-oompah Germanic pub folk and Benny Hill pennywhistle solos, while harmony vocals vary from drunken singalong in the Hofbräuhaus to Ataraxia-

I am as guilty as anyone of perpetuating it all, but I have to wonder how long the publishing industry based around *The Beatles* and *The Rolling Stones* is going to continue. About a year ago, after I received a copy of Philip Norman's fantastic biography of Mick Jagger, I went on a complete jag of buying and reading books about The Rolling Stones. I haven't counted but I suspect I have over 40 books on them, and probably over a hundred about The Beatles.

Why - all these years later - are they still a basis for such fascination? As many readers already know my day job is the Director if the Centre for Fortean Zoology, and one of the things that I have written widely about during my career as ringmaster of the world's largest cryptozoological circus is something I have dubbed 'The Mythologisation Process'. This is the socio-cultural process by which myths are made. One classic example can be found in the way that the media deals with the predations of a small population of naturalised big cats which appear to live on the moorlands of southwestern England.

If there was a learned article entitled something like **Feeding Patterns of a group of naturalised *P.concolor* on Westcountry moorlands** no-one would take any notice, but when *The Daily Mirror* proclaims **The Beast of Bodmin Strikes Again** then it sells a lot of newspapers.

The Great Rolling Stones Mystery (or at least one of them)

Over the years I have realised that this is a paradigm which one can also see in rock music. Take *The Rolling Stones* for example.

Let's look at one great *Rolling Stones* event: The 1969 free concert in Hyde Park.

The first thing I read about it was in a compendium of writings about *The Rolling Stones* by David Dalton. He made the gig sound so much better than it actually was. In fact, even a cursory look at the film of the event shows they were shambolic, under-rehearsed and Mick Taylor looks scared stiff.

But the aspect that I want to look at here has nothing to do with the band, the tragedy/inevitability of Brian Jones' demise, or even the fact that the British Hells Angels did a pretty good job of security which opened the doors for the incredible cock up that was Altamont six months later.

No. What I want to talk about is the butterflies. ABKCO had ordered cases of live cabbage white (*P. rapae* and *P.brassicae*) butterflies from L.Hugh Newman's butterfly farm in Kent to be released during the event, and according to Newman himself the event went smoothly.

But, determined to wring some element of chaos from the story various commentators from the music industry have alleged either that Their Satanic Majesties either forgot to put air holes in the carrying cases so that they all died, or released them successfully - so successfully that the butterflies ate all the vegetables in every allotment for miles (totally ignoring the fact that adult butterflies don't eat cabbages). All three descriptions of events cannot be true. Which one was it? Of things like this, myths are made.

PS. Look at the film about 28 minutes in. It looks like L. Hugh Newman, who is a bigger hero to me than any of the Stones was probably telling the truth. The insects look pretty healthy to me.

Merrell Fankhauser Interview

The other week I was interviewing the ever fascinating Merrell Fankhauser about his forthcoming archive project, when our conversation wandered off onto more arcane subjects...

Merrell: Yeah, the thing is, you know, the Captain, Don [van] Vliet, he's passed away now, and the bass player from MU that was also in the Exiles - Larry Willey - he's passed away so a lot of these guys aren't even around anymore and I know they would just get the biggest kick out of hearing this stuff that we all just forgot about. I'd write three or four songs a week back then in the early sixties so we were recording them just one after another, you know, so I totally forgot about them. If I didn't recognise my voice, you know, I wouldn't even know that I'd written the song!

Jon: Do you have any of them that actually have got the Captain on?

Merrell: No. He and I jammed a lot together and we jammed in his house and jammed in Woodland Hills. See, the Exiles was formed before he formed Captain Beefheart. Frank Zappa and he went to high school together in Lancaster and then Frank moved down south, down to – ooh gosh, I can't remember the name – it was southern California. And they still, you know, communicated and he helped him produce that Trout Mask Replica album and that was the last time I saw Frank, when we were all living in Woodland Hills and they recorded some of that in his house. Don Vliet would drive over and sit in his Jaguar outside of my garage and listen to the different musicians I had playing in the band as we were rehearsing and he'd have these guys go over and say "Who's playing that guitar?" "Is Merrell singing on this?"

[Jon laughs]

Merrell: So he would go try to recruit my musicians and he got John French first and then much later on he got Jeff Cotton. And then I don't know if you read the story that Nigel Cross wrote – it was in Bucketfull of Brains and some other UK fanzine thing – about how when we formed MU and we were living one canyon over in Woodland Hills and Jeff left the band and they were all very angry about it and they kidnapped him one day and held him in the Beefheart house, and I had to go over there and have like a four-and-a-half-hour battle of the brains with Don to get Jeff back and take him back home with me.

[Jon laughs]

Merrell: And it was really a strange scene, Jon. This has all been written about. I think it's in the book too, you know. You'd go over there and Don and I were friends and we'd jam and stuff together. And some of it got recorded, to answer your question, on little tape recorders and stuff but who knows where any of that went? But I'd go over there once in a while to visit them – and this was before Jeff joined me – and John French would have a splint on his finger – a broken finger. And then the bass player, Mark Boston, would walk out and he had a bloody lip. [laughs] So the Captain would decide who's fucking up the band and he'd have the rest of the members go beat that guy up!

[Jon laughs]

Merrell: Yeah.

Jon: Jesus!

Merrell: Yeah, and he painted the whole living room red because he said "That's the only way I can keep these guys awake and alert, Merrell." And so you never knew who was gonna be the bad guy. And what happened at one point, Jeff Cotton turned out to be the bad guy – this was when he left the band – and they beat him up so bad they broke a couple of ribs, and he had to go to the hospital so his parents got him and took him back up to Lancaster, and he was up there for a while recuperating. And Jeff wanted to join me and his parents were afraid to let him go back down there because they were afraid the Beefheart guys would get him. And so everything was fine, you know, for about five or six months and then they found him down at a music store. He had walked down the street from my house, and it was Bill Harkleroad and Mark Boston and John French, and they kidnapped him – literally grabbed him off the street and took him up to Beefheart's house. And I found out where he went from the music store owner so I went up there to retrieve him, and the poor guy was slumped in this bathroom, in the bath tub, whimpering and crying. Don would have a way of psychoanalysing people, you know, and really make them feel worthless and at one point Jeff was saying "Don's right, Merrell: I gotta re-join his band." And it took me a while to talk this out. I was in very good shape back then, Jon, and I'd been used to fighting [laughs] Mexicans in high school and those guys knew they couldn't mess with me, you know, so I just grabbed Jeff and took him out of there. It reminded me of a book, The Devil and Daniel Webster, and several of the guys in the band, if you've read any of those books, they still harbour ill feelings against Don Vliet, you know. And a lot of them believed he was the devil. [Laughs] And Jeff Cotton still believes that Don was the devil.

Jon: Good God.

Merrell: And the girlfriend – I know I'm rambling on – the girlfriend –

Jon: Carry on rambling; I'm enjoying this immensely.

Merrell: The girlfriend, Lori – she would dose them with LSD in their hamburgers at night and so they would start coming onto this drug and not known that they'd been dosed, and they thought it was Don's power; that he had some power, that he was doing this to them. And then he had Zappa put all of this portable recording equipment in the house and he had his cousin Victor, who ran it, and when these guys would get all high he would go "OK, tonight we're going to play a strawberry," and so you were supposed to imagine whatever a strawberry would sound like. [Laughs] And they'd all start playing and he'd say "it goes like this," and he'd play these abstract notes on the piano. I'd been there when he was doing that. And he'd try to get the guitar players to play this melody that he was making up. That's how some of that stuff was recorded: they were high on acid and they didn't even know it.

Jon: Good Lord!

Merrell: [Laughs] It was sick. A lot of people said it reminded them of the Charles Manson deal but at least nobody was getting killed! [Laughs] People were getting beat up and severely psychologically damaged. And I think it still damaged Jeff because he won't play music anymore. After MU moved to Maui he met this beautiful Hawaiian/Chinese girl who was a Christian, he then all of a sudden believed that the music, and the music business in particular, was the devil's work.

Jon: Good God!

Merrell: Yeah. It's a shame because he's a talented guy and you know, he was my guitar student at age fourteen when I met him.

Jon: It's interesting you said that people – 'cause I thought that what you were saying about the way that Don did this sort of psychic mind control of his

Merrell: Yeah.

Jon: I was thinking that sounded very Charles Manson.

Merrell: Yeah. Very much so.

Jon: And of course they were both in the desert at roughly the same sort of time, weren't they?

Merrell: Well, let's see. No, Manson went up in the desert later. The odd thing about that, if you read my book, when we formed MU Randy had a house on the outskirts of Los Angeles that went into this like deserty area, where there was this Spahn movie ranch, where the Mason gang was living and you can see this ranch, Jon. It's in old late-1940s and early-fifties movies. A cowboy'll ride by this rock with some Indians chasing him and that's right on the outskirts of L.A. Well, Randy ran into two of the Mason girls once when he was hiking in this stream, and that's in my book. Manson then fled out to the desert when he did those murders so that was later that Manson lived in the desert but yeah, they did both end up out in the desert. Don Vliet later moved way up to northern California and bought an old boy-scout camp, and that's where he tried to keep the band going and then he ended up getting M.S. and died. He was a creative guy but he was just, I would say, the ultimate control freak. He could definitely captivate an audience just by talking and he had this scary air about him that reminded me of Lon Chaney Jr that played the wolf man in the werewolf movie.

Jon: Oh, yeah, I know him.

Merrell: In a way. People were – they were afraid of him. I could see how they would be afraid of him. When I had this battle of the brains with him, with Jeff Cotton stuck in the bath tub, he had a screen cage and he would catch these various spiders in the house, and sometimes a black widow and he would put them in this cage and watch them fight. And one time he said to me, Jon, when we were talking and he goes "Isnt' that heavy? What would you think if I could make one of those spiders smoke a cigarette?" I said, "Well, that'd be a good trick, Don." But, yeah, he was really something. He could've been a great actor, I think. He really had that way of commanding an audience.

Jon: I so wish that the tape recordings of you two jamming hadn't got lost.

Merrell: Yeah. You know there was just so much bizarre stuff going on and bizarre behaviour. I am playing bottleneck slide on 'China Pig',– if it's the same take ?– I think they gave the credit to Doug Moon on that because they didn't know who had played that. But I listened to all of those recordings to see if I was on anything and several people thought it was me playing slide on this song called 'China pig.'

Jon: Oh, that's fantastic.

Merrell: Yeah. I'm on a few Spirit songs too that Mick Skidmore had something to do with putting out and they didn't give me credit for playing on that either. I played slide and bass and acoustic twelve-string on a couple of songs that were on that. I think Evangeline label; California Blues; one of the last Spirit albums that came out.

Jon: Good Lord.

Merrell: Yeah.

Jon: I'll tell you one thing that surprised me as well, when you were just talking about Manson, I didn't realise that Spahn ranch was right on the outskirts of Los Angeles; I'd always assumed it was right back, deep in the desert somewhere.

Merrell: No, it wasn't, Jon. It was out, actually just past Woodland Hills in Chatsworth. Woodland Hills is where I lived and I'd moved there with HMS Bounty, and Beefheart had moved down from the desert and he lived just one canyon over. And we bumped into each other at the music store, and he'd say "Oh, come on up and jam," and he'd come over to my house and jam once in a while. Chatsworth was going just sort of towards the desert foothills and it was just out of the San Fernando Valley, actually. They used those areas a lot for cowboy movies and stuff because it looked very rugged. There was a lot of interesting rock formations, things like that.

Jon: Oh, that changes my whole sort of mental picture.

Merrell: Yeah.

Jon: Because I'd assumed it was miles away.

Merrell: No, he ran off to the desert after he had murdered all those people and he was afraid that they were gonna find him there. Dennis Wilson, the drummer of the Beach Boys, met him, and went up there and hung out with him, and was even trying to help record some of Charles Manson's songs. They weren't very good but somehow he got interested in them.

Jon: I'm glad you say that because I've heard them and I didn't think they were any good either.

Merrell: Yeah.

Jon: But you know, I don't know what it was about them that people – 'cause Neil Young thought he was a very good song writer but I always thought they were terrible.

Merrell: Yeah, yeah. Most of the people I knew too didn't think they were very good. I mean, I think Dennis Wilson is probably lucky he didn't get murdered because Charles Manson got mad and upset because he couldn't get a record deal.

Jon: Golly!

Merrell: Yeah!

Jon: Was he a sort of fixture on the outskirts of the music scene, then?

Merrell: Well, I guess he was trying to break in any way he could and Terry Melcher, I know, had met him and he was trying to get Terry Melcher to get him a deal, and when he couldn't do that, and Terry Melcher and lived in that house where he had –

Jon: Cielo drive

Merrell: Yeah, and so I think he thought he was getting back at Terry Melcher when he killed all of those people and Sharon Tate.

Jon: Wow.

Merrell: Yeah. Yeah, that was a very strange time and the odd thing was we were watching TV, Randy Weimer the drummer from MU, and I, and they announced this thing: that they'd zeroed in on these people from Spahn Ranch, that they thought had something to do with the murders, and they mentioned Charles Manson because he was on probation or something, and Randy went "Oh, my God! Those two girls I met up the creek when I was hiking were two of Charles Manson's girls!" And he just realised that and figured it out when we got this news over the television.

THE BITCH IS BACK

Grab yourself a fashionable wall clock to enhance your fashionable sitting room. Pop over to Ebay today to get a: Vintage Light Up Clock - 1960's Elvis Presley Flashing Clock for £11.99. It lights up! It is officially licensed! And feels like your back in the swinging 60's apparently. I am not too sure how a clock can feel like my back did in the 60's, so I am going to assume the seller means 'you're'.

But – wait for it - most impressive of all: "…… with this great flashing Elvis wall clock".

Elvis Presley flashing? When? Quarterly or on the hour? Goodness gracious, great … oops wrong singer.
(Corinna Downes)

Late Last Winter, why was legendary guitarist Andy Colquhoun grinning at Le Grande Fromage?

The Gonzo Annual 2015

Well, therein lies a tale. Back at the time I wrote:

The legendary Andy Colquhoun has just found something rather groovy in his archives; songs from the legendary Warsaw Pakt.

Just to fill you in. Wikipedia says: Warsaw Pakt was a short-lived punk group which were active in the years of 1977-78, though some of its members had heritages linking them to the 1960s underground. This was apparent in their sound, which was a sophisticated punk thrash with plenty of energy but also more structure than some contemporaries.

The Warsaw Pakt

...and they continue, a few paragraphs later:

Their claim to fame is to have recorded an album (Needle Time) that was in the shops 24 hours after the first note was recorded (viz the session ended at 10 p.m. on Saturday 26 November 1977 and the album was ready to be sold by 7a.m. on Sunday 27 November 1977.). The band was trying to make a point about technology in doing this, and the album sleeve was a 12" square brown bag with stickers and rubber stamping to display the band name and album title.

He recently did an interview about them..

Real high-energy rock'n'roll in its most potent form is best captured live and in the moment. Maximum thrills, minimum frills. In 1977, London's Warsaw Pakt took that premise one step further, recording their album live, straight through, direct to the cutting lathe – no tape master, no overdubs, no mixing. The record was pressed, packed and shipped overnight and was in the record stores the following day. No procrastination. Instant gratification.

"The idea was to bypass tape and gain a very accurate recording that would be louder and clearer than any other method then available," remembers guitarist Andy Colquhoun.

The actual process was simple. "It was play Side One, break, tune up, play Side Two," he explains. "This was done three times. The engineers were very concerned about us destroying the cutting lathe heads, which ran about five grand each. At first the sound in their control room at the top of the building was very restrained.
Read on…

Andy has also found some live video from The Deviants, and - as you can see from the picture at the top of this piece - he has recently met with Gonzo Grande Fromage Rob Ayling and passed the tapes over to him.

So what happens next?

Wait and see kiddies, wait and see. Andy also has a solo album coming out via Gonzo in a few months time, and - of course - has the record he made with the late Mick Farren out now...

Peter "Pete" Seeger (May 3, 1919 – January 27, 2014)

Pete Seeger was an American folk singer and activist. A fixture on nationwide radio in the 1940s, he also had a string of hit records during the early 1950s as a member of the Weavers, most notably their recording of Lead Belly's "Goodnight, Irene", which topped the charts for 13 weeks in 1950. Members of the Weavers were blacklisted during the McCarthy Era. In the 1960s, he re-emerged on the public scene as a prominent singer of protest music in support of international disarmament, civil rights, counter-culture and environmental causes.

A prolific songwriter, his best-known songs include "Where Have All the Flowers Gone?" (with Joe Hickerson), "If I Had a Hammer (The Hammer Song)" (with Lee Hays of the Weavers), and "Turn! Turn! Turn!" (lyrics adapted from Ecclesiastes), which have been recorded by many artists both in and outside the folk revival movement and are sung throughout the world. "Flowers" was a hit recording for the Kingston Trio (1962); Marlene Dietrich, who recorded it in English, German and French (1962); and Johnny Rivers (1965). "If I Had a Hammer" was a hit for Peter, Paul & Mary (1962) and Trini Lopez (1963), while the Byrds had a number one hit with "Turn! Turn! Turn!" in 1965.

Seeger was one of the folksingers most responsible for popularizing the spiritual "We Shall Overcome" (also recorded by Joan Baez and many other singer-activists) that became the acknowledged anthem of the 1960s American Civil Rights Movement, soon after folk singer and activist Guy Carawan introduced it at the founding meeting of the Student Nonviolent Coordinating Committee (SNCC) in 1960. In the PBS American Masters episode "Pete Seeger: The Power of Song", Seeger stated it was he who changed the lyric from the traditional "We will overcome" to the more singable "We shall overcome".

http://en.wikipedia.org/wiki/Pete_seeger

SOUND & FOLK

HEARING COMES FIRST-sound from a distance
then close up-Doppler Effect
One person with one or more instruments
Ringing true to you/timbre singing with you
Then your voice activates-fills lungs-sings on
Church choir/folk song chorus/sing a long jamboree
You see how easy it sounds to sing freely
And WE has a stronger voice than I
Even if (at times) it sounds like you are the only one
singing
He has gone.
He left us the Hudson River,
Newport Folk Festival
Songs on our lips for when the going gets hard -
SING OUT!
Spirituals, Gospel, Slave Songs or Free-FOLK
means
WE over I
but it always takes one to start ..art..

(for what Pete Seeger gave to us-voice/trust..

Pete Seeger Dies--But His Spirit and Music Will Never Die

"THE KEY TO THE FUTURE OF THIS WORLD
Is to find the optimistic stories-and to sing them on".
And Pete Seeger did!
In all his 94 years he took folk songs
and shared them so well
they are now part of our cultural heritage—what
would peace rallies do without
WE SHALL OVERCOME?/
]IF I HAD A HAMMER/TURN,TURN,TURN
WHERE HAVE ALL THE FLOWERS GONE?
He sang people's songs
Founded the Newport Folk Festival,
organized to clear the Hudson River
and turned the banjo into
an instrument of folk freedom.
Awards?
He received many but did not care for them. Royalties went to causes-
he was anti--war, pro-peace, singing his way with Woody Guthrie
then with the Almanac Singers, then the Weavers. Folk lives!
largely because he would not stop
singing for and with people
When his wife Toshi died in 2013,
he was deeply affected
His songs live within us now -
he gave us our voice back
Thank you Pete Seeger!
Thank you-for our folk music!

PETE SEEGER SURROUNDED HATE AND FORCED IT TO SURRENDER

HISTORY IS A LESSON-THAT IF YOU SING
some will want you silent.
If you sing true,
others may sing with you
but they are few,
and subject to pillory, too.
So this must mean more than words
You can organize—a group of fellow travelers-
call them - "THE WEAVERS"
They can take forgotten slave songs,
freedom songs,
and sing them for the ears of Nations.
You can gather other singers—for a Festival
Call it Newport Folk Festival
and encourage the bards of future truths -
by providing a stage and audience
You can join in other people's activisms -
from Civil Rights (providing anthems)
to OCCUPY. (providing positive presence).
You start where you are -
say you are living by the mighty polluted
Hudson River.
Over years and songs ,
benefits and lawsuits,
you can have your deep river cleaned.
All is possible
It means more than words.
Words are the suit you dress up in for others
You sing in different suits on different occasions.
Words may be the same-
effect and context changes.
"Actions are the thing,wherein we capture
the conscience of the King"

Thom the World Poet

Mark Murdock Interview

Drummer, keyboardist and vocalist Mark Murdock's 'Cymbalic Encounters' features eminent progressive-rock unit Brand X alumni, guitarist John Goodsall, bassist Percy Jones, and drummer Kenwood Dennard along with legendary jazz-fusion keyboardist David Sancious and other guests. Murdock shines as a renaissance man and offers a diversified set, highlighted by the largely memorable compositions and aided by a crystal clear studio production.

1. **How did *Cymbalic Encounters* come about?**

Firstly, I am pleased that *Cymbalic Encounters* has found a home with the Gonzo family. *Cymbalic Encounters* actually started with some demo recordings that I initiated some years back with Percy Jones. Percy contributed not only bass tracks, but to some of the songwriting, including some keyboard parts. As the recordings evolved, John Goodsall agreed to partake, which was a dream come true- to have what was once *Brand X* on my tracks. David Sancious, Ryo Okumoto, Kenwood Dennard and engineer/guitarist, Joe Berger and others were also instrumental in adding to the CD.

2. How did you first get involved with Percy and John?

Well, it goes back to the remote past as a teenager when I met Phil Collins on an early *Genesis* tour in the states. Jump ahead a few years and I made it over to the UK. Phil had me over to the *Brand X* rehearsals in Hammersmith, London where I met everyone while they were rehearsing for their first record, 'Unorthodox Behaviour,' and rehearsing for their first live debut gigs. They had a percussion rig in the rehearsal studio that I would jump on and play along. I went to *Brand X's* first gig at LSE and Bill Bruford was actually playing percussion. So, years later I had relocated to New York from Phoenix only to find that Percy had moved to NYC as well. I was working in a music studio loft on 30th street where Kenwood Dennard, who plays on one of the songs on the CD, was rehearsing and recon-

nected me with Percy. I had several projects in the years I lived in NY and Percy supported a few recording projects and a few live gigs. One project was called 'Eyes Down' which is available as a digital download. It featured Shakar's recording on electric violin and others guest artists.

3. Where was it recorded?

I recorded my drums at Revole Studios here in Tokyo. And my other tracks at Offshore Mobile Recording. Apart from the 21st Century method of recording, as you mentioned in your John Goodsall interview, where we share our tracks over the internet. Some of the tracks were actually recorded in NYC at Unique Studios, at least the ones with David Sancious. Percy also went into the studio later and did some tracks. The others were intercontinental. John recorded his tracks at RedStar Studios in Minnesota and Percy did additional tracks at home. All tracks were shuttled across the globe.

4. Were the songs prewritten or composed in the studio?

I actually camped out at David Sancious' house in Woodstock where we wrote and expanded on my initial ideas. It was such an honor to be acknowledged by David. The song 'Waters Of Marsh Harbour' ended up on the CD. There are a few more songs that may or may not go onto future works.

Most of the songs that Percy and I wrote were a kind of 'Fill in the blanks' where I would write a section and then ask Percy to write the next section. The amazing element was when John came into picture as he complimented the music in a way that brought everything to life. It was obvious that John and Percy have an incredible musical chemistry. There are a few tracks that someone commented that sound like early *Brand X,* which was never my intention for that to happen. It must have been the chemistry at play.

5. How long did the recording process take?

Some tracks went through a kind of evolution spanning numerous years and others were recorded literally right before the CD was released. I ended up using some of the demo takes rather than the studio recorded takes of Percy. I think it's true that working from a home environment is more favorable for creativity. You are not looking at the clock but there are other distractions. Sound wise, my engineer, Joe Berger at BEAM Audio NYC brought the whole thing to life with his excellent mixing and mastering skills. Joe also played several or more mean guitar solos on the CD. He and I go way back to high school in Arizona.

6. What is your next project?

Currently, I am still working tracks for the new CD, which again feature Percy and John and Japanese progressive rock keyboardist, Hiroyuki Namba, also Paul D' Adamo and Dave Juteau will be doing some vocals.

There are a number of elements that were not featured on my first CD that will be on the new 2014 release. I can't reveal too much, but there are a lot of different grooves and sound textures. I'm both a prog-rocker and a jazz-rocker at heart, so the best of both worlds.

Oh, forgot to mention that I am involved in *The Dave Juteau Band* which I played drums and produced his new pop/rock/funk CD, 'Seeking Higher Ground' which will be released here in Japan and soon overseas. Also. a Japanese progressive- rock band 'Machine Messiah' which I have started recording drum tracks for their upcoming CD.

7. Has there been any attempt to play live?

Yes, *Cymbalic Encounters* the live band is comprised of local Tokyo musicians. We recently played a live debut concert here in Tokyo. To line up is: Tetsuya Ueda on fretless bass, Daniel Kubota from Chile on guitar, my son, Preston, 16, plays electric sitar on a few songs and previously mentioned, Dave Juteau from Nova Scotia on lead vocal and various instruments. Speaking of Dave, he actually played bass on the bridge on the song 'Illusion Nation.' The Tokyo band members are also featured on some of the tracks of the upcoming CD. as I want to feature

this current line-up on the new CD so it will help represent the CD a little better.

There was actually an attempt to bring Percy and John over to Japan after my CD was released. There are still a lot of *Brand X* fans here in Japan. To make along story short, one of guys wasn't up to reliving the past, which I can respect that decision. Actually, I had everyone from the old camp willing to come over, Robin Lumley, Kenwood Dennard, Mike Clark, but without one key element I couldn't convince the promoter. It was a nice attempt, nonetheless. Not giving up the ship though. Hopefully, *Cymbalic Encounters* can build its own fan base

An Interview with Stu from Galahad

Galahad are an English Progressive rock band formed in 1985. They have released 8 studio albums, 4 live albums and 3 rarities collections.

Over the last 25 years they have played with the likes of Pendragon, IQ andTwelfth Night. Galahad have performed their own shows and at festivals in Europe and North America, and have sold tens of thousands of albums despite never having had a major record deal. All releases are on their own 'Avalon Records' imprint other than some re-issues which are released in association with Polish label 'Oskar Productions'. In 2012 and after 27 years of existence Galahad released their first ever LP 'Battle Scars' in conjunction with Ritual Echo Records, on high quality 180 gram vinyl, in a gatefold sleeve, as a limited edition pressing of 300 which is already fast becoming a collectors item.

Stuart Nicholson talked about Galahad's early days: "...the band was formed just after the so called second wave of 'Prog' bands such as Marillion, Pallas, IQ, Twelfth Night, Pendragon etc. of Prog bands came to the fore in the early Eighties. They all started around 1978 – 1981 and we started in 1985 after the bubble had effectively burst, but didn't really get going seriously until 1990 onwards.

To be honest we really did play just for fun in the early days and weren't really that concerned about record deals etc. It was only after playing with some of the bigger bands when we thought. Actually, we are just as good as these guys so why not give it a go..."

http://www.gonzomultimedia.co.uk/radioplayer.php?

MORE LIKE A MAGAZINE: Converting the potato shed

The other day I had one of those debilitating 24 hour colds (touch wood) and for the afternoon I disappeared off to bed with little Archie and a clear conscience. Archie is, by the way, a small dog, just in case you think I am being even more decadent than usual

While I was asleep my new mixing desk arrived. As some of you may know I am upgrading my recording studio set up because I have a whole slew of exciting new projects in the pipeline. However, (as some of you may also know) I have a bad habit of not reading the adverts on eBay properly, and on this occasion it has turned round and bitten me on the bum. Because said mixing desk is enormous - nearly three times the size I thought it was, so the converted potato shed which doubled (triples?) as my study, office, editing suite and recording studio, as well as being home to two

colonies of tropical cockroaches and various tropical fish, now needs a major overhaul just to fit the blasted thing in. Graham, Mark Raines and I (mostly Graham) manhandled the new mixing desk into the office, and much to my surprise it fits perfectly. We decided not to try and use it until we had sussed it out a bit, but then - to my great pleasure - we found an operating manual for free online.

I haven't broken the news to young David (my nephew the electrician) yet that he will have to plumb it in, but I am sure he will roll his eyes in horror. Then mutter something about the fact that I should have consulted him before buying it, and then do a magnificent job. (I know that 'plumbing in' is the right word for washing machines, but as no plumbing is actually involved I don't know whether it applies to mixing desks, but I cannot think of a better term, and cannot be bothered to try).

What are my exciting new projects that rely on me filling the potato shed with second-hand hardware? Well, I am not quite ready to divulge them just yet, so I am afraid that you will just have to wait and see...

The Gonzo Annual 2015

back in the early spring i wrote........

There is now Gonzo Beer. It is nothing to do with us, but the blurb reads: *Like Hunter S. Thompson...Gonzo Imperial Porter is deep and complex. This turbo charged version of the Road Dog Porter is mysteriously dark with a rich malty body, intense roasted flavors, and a surprisingly unique hop kick. With Gonzo weighing in at 9.2% ABV, it will bite you in the ass if you don't show it the proper respect. IBU's: 85.* As I said, it is nothing to do with us, and I very much hope that I don't come across as the sort of person who will try and blag a few cases in return for some spurious product placement! Don't answer that question!

Leaves from Liz Lenten's mythical scrapbook

Back in February my best laid plans went pear shaped. I had been planning to have the world exclusive of some of the footage that I shot of both Auburn and Jefferson Starship in Wolverhampton, but, probably because of the ongoing buggerings around in my office, the firewire card on my computer (which for the uninitiated is the doobrie that I use to take film and sound off my broadcast quality video camera and onto the computer) packed up. As a result my plans to have anything using the Sony PD150 were scuppered. Now I don't know whether Liz Lenten of Auburn actually keeps a scrapbook, but she jolly well should! And for the purposes of this feature she jolly well does. Totally ignorant of the fact that my feature on them had disappeared up the proverbial creek without the benefit of a paddle, Liz sent me a bunch of her pictures from the last tour, and I decided, that they should be presented as her hypothetical scrapbook. So there!

Auburn on stage in Manchester

Liz with Jefferson Starship manager Michael (left) and guitarist Jude and with Chris the keyboard player (below)

Liz with Cathy Richardson

Liz with David

Liz (right) on stage with JS

Bridget Wishart interview

Bridget Wishart sang with Hawkwind during what some people (including yours truly) think was one of their most interesting periods. But what happened next?

1. How did you first get involved with Spirits Burning

Good question!...I like telling this staory. :-)

My daughter Hannah was a baby, so this must have been around 2003, and while she was napping one day I thought I'd google what Hawkwind were up to...I came across the Hawkwind Museum, I hadn't done much surfing and found the site really interesting

I hadn't realised how much interest there was in past and present band members so I posted on their guest page to let everyone know that I was still alive, married with a young daughter. Shortly after posting Dave Law got in touch arranged for me to do an interview for the website. He also kindly let me know that my posting left me open to being emailed by anyone who read the post...he kindly removed the post but not before Ian Abrahams, the writer had found the post and been in touch, that was how he found me and got an interview and some photos for his Hawkwind book, Sonic Assassins'.

We got on well and went on to write Festivalized, a book about the free festivals. Sadly our publishers went bust at the crucial moment...anyways, I got off track a bit there...back to the question. Don, Spirits Burning's trusty multi limbed leader read the interview and asked Dave if he could pass on a message to

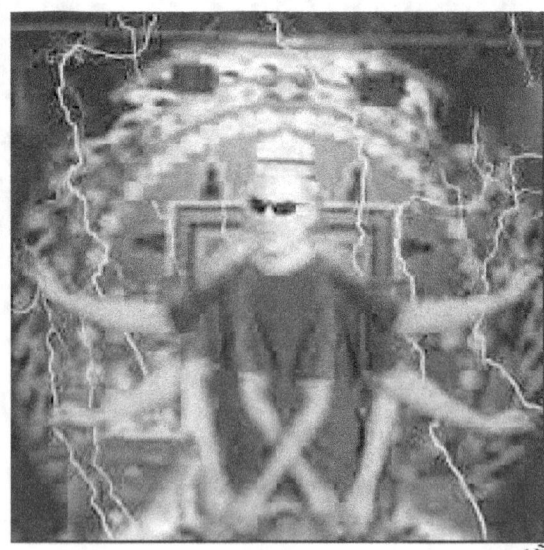

me, inviting me to contribute to a track. At that time in my life I was adamant to stay 'retired' but had a few unused vocal tracks kicking around from a previous band that hadn't made it out out of the living room. I sent Don one of these...It was the vocals for Salome. A month or so later he asked if I wanted to add another track...I had one more good recording; Another World, so I sent that. I didn't hear what became of the tracks until Don sent me a cd and vinyl copy of Alien Injection. I loved Salome but was less sure about Another World. That was the start of a long distance partnership that has been the most creative of my career.

2. What did you do in the intervening years between Hawkwind and Spirits Burning?

Ahhh, this question covers a fair amount of ground. Some rather rocky...

After I left Hawkwind, I formed a duo called Daze with 2000DS guitarrist Danny Smith. We wrote some great songs, did a few gigs and had a song or two played on local radio but Dan had some life issues to address so we folded the band. I got quite depressed. I'd given up my teaching job to tour and record with the Hawkwind and it wasn't easy to find another one. I had a few interviews at schools and colleges in the area but remained unsuccessful in finding work.

My folks were really supportive and helped out financially so I could retrain. I did an intensive TEFL course. Got work teaching a student one to one and a few days at the local college but I knew to get proper work I'd have to go abroad. It was at this point that Klive (Farhead) approached me about his Techno Pagan project. He'd been Alan's roadie on the European Tour 90 and knew my interest and abilities with costume, performance and dance. He was interesting in forming a UV theatrical dance troupe who would perform while he played. I was captivated by the idea and loved the music.

TEFL went out the window and in thru the outdoor came stripey costumes, metal trees, giant UV jellyfish and a troupe of crazy young people to choreograph. The gig I remember best was in Larkhall Square, Bath. Klive organised their local mardis gras on condition his band got the headline slot. We had a huge rig, Anarc Lights (Hawkwind's light show) and a massive crowd.

All the tree protesters came down from their

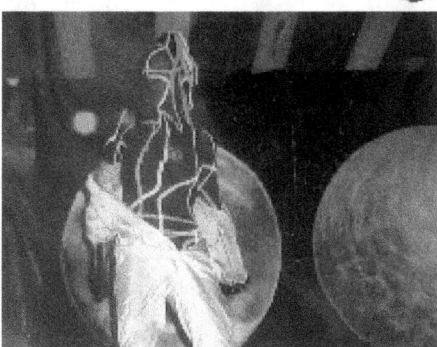

Techno Pagan, Larkhall Square

Siam Tent WOMAD

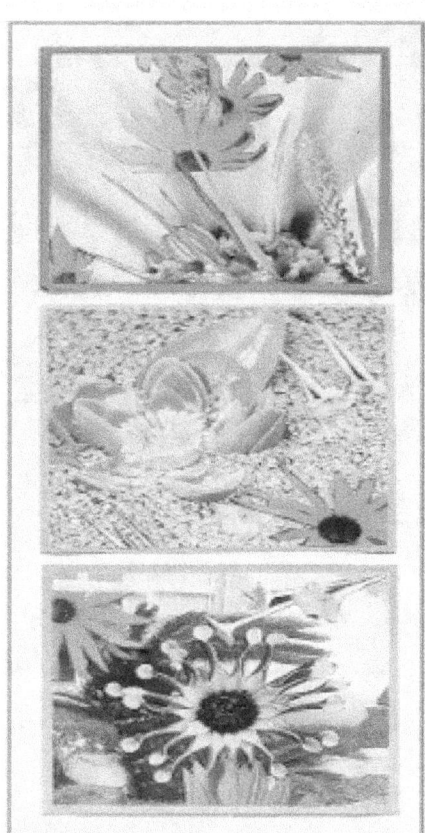

A popular design and a fun shape...very tall :)

Ooops...Can't remember what the title of this collage is...it was sold from an Art Gallery in 2003

trees and joined the crowds. Local kids sat on the stage and screamed in semi fear whenever a new costumed character came on stage. Chris Pink cranked the volume up and the neighbourhood quaked. Jeremy Guscott's wife came out of her cottage which was a few scant yards from the stage and screamed at the local butcher to pull the plug...the butcher looked at the shouting, dancing crowd and rightly decided to leave well alone...ahhh them were the days :-)

We did a Temple Ball gig in Reading at the Leisure Centre...there was a chap (Tim Carroll RIP) there who I met who was putting up some UV decor. I was struck by the idea of covering large areas of mundaneity (is that a word?) to create a condusive environment for gigs. When I was at Art College I worked with Installations and loved creating them. So when Klive and I had a falling out (I can be very stubborn and pigheaded!) I knew exactly where to go and what to do. Within a few weeks Tim and I had formed a company called Temple Decor we worked with the Temple Ball crew; Electric Groove Temple (host band) and Pogle (Anarc lights). I designed and we painted, sewed and created a sympathetic, psychedelic UV drapes in order to create Temple like environment for raves and gigs.

We got a lot of work with WOMAD who loved our environments. By WOMAD 96 I was overworked, underpaid and highly stressed. I resigned but the damage to me wasn't so easily resolved. I became unstable and suffered a complete breakdown.

I was hospitalised after stowing away on an aeroplane at Heathrow. (Thought I was catching a flight to Mars) I spent four months in hospital, was sectioned twice, ran away twice, got as far as Gatwick, saw the inside of a few police stations and through out all of it, everyone, the police, my friends, family and the hospital staff, they were all brilliant. As I gradually recovered my health and stamina the thought of being creative through art or music was just unapproachable. I felt like I'd never draw another picture or write another song, ever! I wanted to find work where I could make a positive input into people's lives.

I worked for four years in the care sector looking after children and young adults with special needs. Now there's a challenging and rewarding and low paid job for you! The job played havoc with my back and after leaving to have Hannah I decided not to go back. I got a cleaning job which was the same money, not as fulfilling but totally less stressful. Gradually my creativity was seeping back. I became interested in designing cards, I did individual cards for friends and their children and was slowly setting up a business selling cards and collages.

The local art gallery took my collages and cards.

I was on the verge of expansion when I found that I had my music mojo back thanks to Don and to Steve Palmer from Mooch who played guitar on Another World, but only on condition that Don passed on my email address so he

Jasper recording for Spirits Burning & Bridget Wishart

could invite me to contribute to his best CD ever; Dr Silbury's Liquid Brainstem band. The songs on this CD; Cycad, Sandman and Silver Violet Flame and were my first song writing ventures in many years and then once started, writing the first SB/BW CD; Earthborn, became a passion that overtook everything.

I still do collage and make cards for friends and family and also gain an immense amount of pleasure designing our CD covers. Karen Anderson does a fantastic job taking the artwork into the graphics world and creates a whole package that is always beautiful and carefully thought out.

3. Where were your parts recorded?

I record all my parts at home. We have Ntrack recording software on the computer(designed by Flavio, an Italian programmer) and though Martin has since moved on to Reaper I'm a stubborn old dog and stick with what I know. Martin records all his parts in Reaper :-)
We have a good recording mic, a Rhode I think, and a recording shield which is ace, plus the usual sound cards and a diddy mixing desk and a tone port that the mic's and guitars use.

When recording with the EWI my preferred option is to use it as a midi controller and use the Garritan software... a fab sampled orchestra...so I can be playing oboe or violin, cello whatever, but not sax, orchestras don't have a sax in them...too recent an invention I hear. Musicians local to us use our house to record their parts too...eg Richard Chadwick, (Hawkwind) and Jasper Pattison (Citizen Fish)

I have been in a professional studio to record; Rockfield, in Monmouth, with sound engineer Paul Cobbold, fab bloke! when we recorded Space Bandits. It was an unforgetable experience but I have to say I prefer no one around when I record, I quite often don't know where the song is going to go, what harmonies I'll find and quite often the lyrics need some rewriting as I go along. I need an empty house for the creative process to take place.I also like to make my experiments and mistakes in private :-). Once my parts are done to my satisfaction (tho' I have been known to later change my mind and do them again) I clean them up, bounce them down and upload the wavs to Don.

Then, once there has been more work done to the track by him/others he uploads the results and we give each other feedback on the track, the process of addition and subtraction continues until we say yep that's it that's our song! Sometimes they takes years to finish, sometimes just days.

4. How long did the recording process take?

I guess you're talking about our third CD, Make Believe It Real? I checked with Don the other week as it seems to have been going on forever, we reckon this album has taken about three years start to finish.

Some musicians do take their time when contributing parts. It's understandable; they have other agendas and priorities and it's important they record when they feel ready to...though it can be hard to be patient. :-)

We sent one of the songs, Skyline Signal to Keith Tha Bass (Here & Now) he said he wasn't too keen on it, so I sent a different one and passed the 1st song to Jasper (Pattison) who loved it.

Then around six months later when Keith sent his bass for Journey Past The Stars, it turned out he'd also decided to record a line for Skyline Signal too! Hah! :-) Don and I decided, as both performances were really good, to have both basses play on the track and, unusual though it is, they complement each other perfectly! Luckily, one is high and the other low.

5. How does the compositional process work?

There are no hard and fast rules. Don or I usually start a track. If it's Don it usually has synths and a beat, if it's me it usually has just a BPM and the sung lyrics and lots of space. On the odd occasion we'll invite someone else to start a track. Don sometimes invites musicians to play on a track before it comes to me and sometimes I do the same. Martin might put some guitar on a song.

If I have a fixed idea of who I think would sound great on the track I might mention it to Don. Usually we go with the flow and send pieces out to musicians and see if they like the track and want to work on it. Some people find it challenging to be presented with a track that has nothing but a vocal line on it and prefer to play their part once others have filled in the gaps and others are inspired by the freedoms offered.

Quite often a piece will come back from different directions at the same time and the guitar will have been recorded at the same time as the bass but neither will have heard what the other musician did and it will be up to Don and I to 'marry' the two tracks.

Sometimes the songs seem to have been already written with just vocals and a guitar there and the rest of the music is kind of filling out and adding to the song. At other times a song isn't written til the very last musician records their part and all of a sudden it all hangs together perfectly. There aren't many songs that fail to work. I think we left one off the first CD, one off the second and none off this one.

The last CD we did together, Bloodlines, had a historical theme running through it and many of the songs I felt needed a tight rein on them to ensure they stayed true to themselves...it is hard to argue for edits via email but I did! Lots and lots! This time round I vowed to let the songs flow more and that has been much easier for us both and our servers. Also with a Sci Fi/Fantasy theme running through the album space rock should always have galaxies far and wide to explore. So, although there are odd corners in the tracks where my fussy hat perks up, mostly, I am totally pleased and very proud with what we have created. The best yet! Oh yes :-)

6. What is your next project?

Uhhh, lets see... I'm in the middle of recording tracks on an album called Moments with Hola One. Once finished the music will be available for free download. You can find Hola One on FaceBook and his music on Sound Cloud, a breath of fresh air :-) ...check out Mandragora's vocals they are exquisite.

With Don, I have some EWI parts to record for his SB/Starhawk project and we'll be starting work on our second Astralfish CD in the near future. Myself and Martin are still recording our Chumley Warner Bros CD, we are doing less live work this year with the plan that we will record more. Watch this space!

...I'll probably also do the odd track with Mooch, Steve is fairly regular at kicking something my way. Late last year I recorded a track for his latest project...love his stuff :-) Recently I recorded four tracks with Spaceseed for their next CD which is due to see the light of day this year. They're even going to be playing in Britain this year (Sonic Rock Solstice) Yay!

That's enough to be getting on with methinks :-)

The Gonzo Annual 2015

ROY WEARD: Music and why we do it

Roy (that's him singing above) was the founder member of Wooden Lion - a band that played the Windsor and Watchfield free festivals in the 70s. He later went went on to sing, write and record with both Dogwatch' and ' Roy Weard and Last Post'. In 2006, Roy, together with The Cardinal Biggles, synth wizard from the original Wooden Lion, and Steve Bensusan, guitar virtuoso from the Last Post began to put That Legendary Wooden Lion together. This band gigged through to the end of 2011 but broke up the following year. A new line up of the band is now gigging. I have known Roy for many years, and was very pleased and touched when he contributed the following essay to the Gonzo Weekly.

A conversation that I had earlier on today neatly coalesced some thoughts that have been going through my mind over the last few weeks. Music has travelled a strange and tortuous path over its long history, and for many of us, certainly for me, and possibly for many of the readers of this magazine, it has a very special place in our hearts. It was not always an object of veneration in its own right and has slipped neatly between being an art form and a commodity many times – especially in the last few decades.

It has existed in every civilisation way back into history and probably beyond. There were no doubt cavemen indulging in, what Douglas Adams called, 'banging the rocks together'. It probably had some origins in making sounds to lure animals to be hunted and then in repeating those sounds as said animals were being cooked and eaten. No one really knows. Hollow bones with holes in their length were found by archaeologists in ancient settlements and believed to be musical instruments. Whatever its origins music evolved and went from a primitive form to becoming standardised, written down and accepted as 'art'. Of course, once you paste that self adhesive, ego boosting, epithet to something it magnetically attracts all sorts of other concepts and with them, a whole gamut of poses. People become inflated with the idea that they are 'an artist' and therefore need to be respected, paid, or showered with gifts and the favours of the opposite (or in some cases the same) sex.

My concern here is really with what we regard as modern music and the reasons for making it. If we take a bandsaw and hack off everything prior to the fifties we can examine the concept of popular music in more detail. I have had no real contact with people who were part of the 'swing' era but anecdotally it would seem that many musicians of that time saw it as a paid job. Making music for dances and other events - and having a good time in the process. Things began to change radically when recorded music began to be bought in larger quantities and played on radio stations. Payment, in those days, was made through many middle men. If you were a writer you would have a publisher and they would print sheet music to be sold in music shops so that other musicians could play your work. The writer would get royalties on that. If you went out and played for an event you would either get paid, either directly by the organiser, or, if you had an agent, through them. Publishers and Agents would take their 'cut' but, in many cases, would work for this by distributing your compositions or by trying to find you work.

By the time the pop phenomenon has rolled around in the 50s publishers would hawk their clients songs around to the various recording stars of the time. Scores of dodgy deals were done back then with publishers and managers colluding to get artists to take a song and record it and then pocketing a backhander. The actual performers very often had little say in what they recorded and there was no way of knowing if the sales of records or sheet music were accurate. Publishers and agents often got rich while artists and composers received very little. At its height in the early to mid 60s this was a lucrative business and, as the west's disposable income rose, radios flourished, record sales soared and more and more money was earned by the pop industry. All of this worked in favour of the agents and publishers because they were the ones writing the contracts, controlling the percentages and reporting the sales.

Everything changed when the Beatles and some of the other bands of that time decided to do their own songs. It changed again when they began to run their own business affairs. Record companies set up publishing arms because they wanted to claw back that part of the money for themselves and not give it to the traditional publishers but bands began to form their own publishing as well as trying to take more control of their output. There followed a struggle between the big labels and the bands and a period in which some of the bigger bands got paid very well and the era of the superstar came into being.

All of this worked because, if you wanted the latest Stones album, you had no choice but to go and buy a copy. Tours were basically promotional vehicles, often making a loss but racking up more album sales and a nice loss making tour could offset tax as well. Ticket prices were, on the whole, relatively low. Into this mix we introduce the cassette. Suddenly one person could buy an LP and, if one of his friends had a cassette tape recorder, ten of his mates can have a copy – for the price of a tape, and with no money going to the artist. Technology was crude in those days so it was an inferior, hissy thing which often wound up as a string of tangled spaghetti looping out of a tape player but it put the first dent in the business. One other thing that had worked in the bands' favour in the 1970s was that the established music business of the time did not know how to handle or market them. The most dangerous acts that they had handled in the 60s were people like Elvis, Bill Haley, Tom Jones and the like. Tame little pussycats compared to the drug taking, swearing, and free sex endorsing hippies. By the time that punk had emerged a new, leaner and more streetwise bunch of people had risen and they were onto it straight away. Clip on safety pins, tartan skirts and bondage trousers could be bought on the high street but technology had advanced as well and cassette recorders were cheaper and more widely available. Not only that but they sounded better too. A few bands managed big advances from the music industry but, on the whole, the punk scene was mostly run on small labels and small budgets.

Bigger blows were to follow though. CDs seemed to be an ideal successor to vinyl with the added advantage that the companies could sell the fans new copies of their old, worn out LPs. That is until cheap CD burners came on the market. Now you could have a copy of a CD your friend bought that sounded every bit as good as the original. MP3s made it even easier to steal stuff. Computer technology and the Internet were the final nails in the coffin of paid for music. A whole generation arose who could not see why they should buy something they could get for free and that leads us to the state we are in today. Back in the 70s labels like EMI would take a chance on a few unknown and unusual acts in case they became the 'next big thing', partly because they did not expect bands like Genesis, Yes, ELP, or The Pink Floyd to sell many records when they started out, and partly because they were awash with money and needed to spend it. These days they will put a bit of money into One Direction or the X Factor winners because they will sell enough mainstream stuff to make a profit. Ticket prices are huge because artists are not rolling in cash and cannot afford to make a loss on a tour – in fact they have to make a profit. This is now their bread and butter.

When I started touring in the 70s the crew would stay in the Hilton or the Intercontinental or one of those big chains. Money was more abundant than the Evian in the dressing room. On the last few tours I did in the 90s we were on a sleeper bus and did not see a hotel unless it was a day off. The conversation I had today was with someone who was going to tour manage a 70s star's next tour. He had worked with the guy many times but this time the crew was down from 8 people to three with the drummer setting up the keyboards and the drum tech doing follow spot! He had to make a profit.

If things are bad at that level look at how it is in the grassroots. I live in Brighton which has a very good music scene and a lot of venues but bands don't often get paid much and many do gigs for free – especially if they are playing their own music and not doing carbon copy covers. In some ways this is understandable because a tight covers band will often fill a pub whereas a band playing their own stuff is a more risky bet for an evening's entertainment. If a pub has a poster for a band called 'Slim Tizzy' you can be pretty sure it is some guys playing 'Thin Lizzy' songs and if that is what you like you can go along. If the band is called 'Partial Regeneration Helix' or 'Mr Thompson's Cat' or something like that you don't know what you will get and may not want to risk going to check them out. I know where I will be and that is checking out the bands with the obscure names because if they put that much effort into making up a name and not doing a banal pun the chance is that they might just be interesting. The final part of this is the thorny subject of getting paid. I recently had a conversation about bands being paid for gigs. Facebook, the forum well known for its balanced viewpoints and considered opinions, often sprouts status announcement like 'I asked a promoter to pay us $2000 for a gig and he said it was too much so I asked him to get six plumbers to work for him from 6 in the evening until midnight and we will work for half of that' or variants on that theme. This is somewhat insulting. I am not denigrating plumbers as such but all the people of that profession I have ever met have only been in the job to put bread on the table. It was not a calling, an inner urge or a creative tendency that drove them to lay under a sink and unblock pipes or install toilets. I don't know any of them that wake up in the morning and think 'Great, I will get to bend a pipe today and install a shower'. If I have a gig I always wake up excited about it – even after 40 years of being involved in music!

For my part I am a songwriter and I put my band together to play my songs. I enjoy it. It is better exercise than playing squash, it gives me pleasure and I hope it gives my audience pleasure. If someone wants to pay me for doing that I will gratefully accept the money but it is not a prerequisite of being on a stage. I don't mind doing free gigs if the audience gets in for free and the rest of my band are OK with it. I feel that, if a band can get 100+ people to come along and see them every time they play then they can start thinking about asking for a fee. If you make getting paid one of the criteria for doing the gig you will find that no one is going to promote a gig and pay a band if they don't think they will pull and audience to pay the fees. If you are playing free in a pub then there is no loss to the person who runs the gig. It is 100% down to the band to inspire people to want to go and see them again. Once they can do that they can think about getting paid to play.

The other side of this is the audience themselves. Many people don't want to go out and see a band. They may look at a video on YouTube but getting out of the armchair and paying to go to a venue seems to be a step too far. I am completely in favour of original music. The process of creation is what interests me. I don't want to go and see a band recreate 'The Dark Side of The Moon', 'The

Lamb Lies Down On Broadway' or any other famous show. I don't want to hear Rolling Stones covers, or any covers really, and I try to persuade everyone I talk to about this that they shouldn't either. We only have the classic songs by those famous bands because at one point they played in small clubs in somewhere-ville, blew the audience away, got famous, and wrote them. If we consign original music to the dustbin we will be condemned to live a life of repeats and re-runs and life is only really interesting when it is fresh, vibrant and in-your-face new.

Every time you copy a CD, or download an illegal MP3 you are, in effect stealing something from the people who made it and you are cheapening your musical experience. Every time you eschew buying the CD just put it on your Spotify playlist you are spooning a sum of money into a business that pays the artists very little for their product. The circle has almost been completed and the companies have found new ways of making money out of music and not passing much of that cash back to the artists. The one glimmer left is that it is now easier to make a decent recording on equipment that is within the reach of many people. You no longer need the big studios or labels. Artists can, and do, record, mix and produce their own product and the cottage industry ethos that put many punk records out is still there. If you like a band, buy the CD don't download an MP3 or put it on a streaming service playlist. Buy the CD from the band too if you can. Not from Amazon. At the very least find an independent record shop and get it there. Put the money back into the hands of the people who make the music

.I don't want to see a return to stadium tours and bloated superstars but I do want to see a music scene that is blossoming and not festering. Many people say that all the good music was in the 70s but that is because they have stopped trying to listen for it. Take the phone's headphones off and go to a gig. Recall how it is to feel the music and not just listen to it while reading a paper on a bus

.

Right now the music scene is on life support and looking very sick. Let's nurse it back to health.

https://www.facebook.com/
Thatlegendarywoodenlion

The Bitch is Back

BEATLES HAIR POMADE PACKET MADE IN THE PHILIPPINES IN THE 1960S
As the seller writes: "*Another wacky item of early Beatles Memorabilia.*"

And what, you may ask, is pomade? I admit that I had to look it up. Hitherto, for £2.99 you can receive a packet of a greasy, waxy substance to style your hair. You can be the envy of your family, neighbours, friends and colleagues when you reveal your hair looking slick, neat and shiny. But beware buyers, pomade doesn't dry and may well take several sessions under the shower to be removed. Or you can try the shorter route of washing your locks in washing-up liquid.

However, considering the age of this particular item I would probably err on the cautious side and not actually attempt to use it. It may well cause a premature and unwanted Yul Brynner look. Although, I must say, he was rather dishy.

The Gonzo Annual 2015

I have been in a peculiar situation here, because I have known some of the details of The Pink Fairies reunion for several months. Or, to be more honest, I knew that there was going to be one, and I knew who two of the members of the reunion lineup were going to be.

But I didn't know anything else for sure. When extraordinary rumours started being posted on the internet, when one of the people I KNEW was going to be in the band denied it publically, and - above all - when the other one asked me to keep schtum about it, I realised that discretion was the better part of valour...

FOR THOSE OF YOU NOT IN THE KNOW

Pink Fairies were an English rock band active in the London (Ladbroke Grove) underground and psychedelic scene of the early 1970s. They promoted free music, drug taking and anarchy and often performed impromptu gigs and other agitprop stunts, such as playing for free outside the gates at the Bath and Isle of Wight pop festivals in 1970, as well as appearing at Phun City, the second Glastonbury and many other free festivals including Windsor and Trentishoe.

The group was formed after the three musicians from The Deviants (Paul Rudolph, guitar and vocals, Duncan Sanderson, bass and Russell Hunter, born Barry Russell Hunter, drums), sacked their singer and leader Mick Farren during a disastrous tour of the West Coast of the United States. Prior to the tour these musicians had collaborated on the Think Pink solo album by Twink, former drummer of The Pretty Things, using the name Pink Fairies Motorcycle Club and All-Star Rock and Roll Band, taken from a story written by Deviants' manager Jamie Mandelkau. Twink (drums), Farren (vocals), Steve Peregrin Took (guitar) and Twink's girlfriend Sally 'Silver Darling' Meltzer (keyboards) hooked up in October 1969 for one sham-

The Gonzo Annual 2015

bolic gig at Manchester University, billed as The Pink Fairies, and went on to record Farren's solo album, Mona – The Carnivorous Circus.

Within a few months Twink had left, followed by Farren, by which point Took had renamed the embryonic band Shagrat. In 1970 Twink recruited the remaining Deviants to a new Pink Fairies line-up.

Took meanwhile continued with Shagrat as a vehicle for his own songs, and the two bands would appear as separate acts at the Phun City festival that summer.

Their music was upbeat good-time rock and roll, often jamming on The Beatles' "Tomorrow Never Knows", The Ventures' "Walk Don't Run", "Ghost Riders in the Sky" and other standards. Their sets climaxed with the lengthy "Uncle Harry's Last Freakout", essentially an amalgam of old Deviants riffs that included extended guitar and double drum solos.

They were closely associated with the UK underground, being based in the Ladbroke Grove scene and playing festivals, benefits and free concerts. The band had strong connections with Farren's home town Worthing, playing gigs for the Worthing Workshop. These included an appearance on a float in the Worthing Rotary Club Carnival Procession and a free open-air concert in Beach House Park.

Playing for in June 1970 free outside the Bath Festival, they encountered another Ladbroke Grove based band Hawkwind, who shared similar interests in music and recreational activities, a friendship developed which would lead to the two bands becoming running partners and performing as Pinkwind. Sensationalist coverage in the (Mick Farren edited) International Times solidified their rebel reputation

Last Saturday, whilst putting the finishing touches to #64 of this august periodical, I was both hungover, and suffering from a horrible cold (which affected my performance far more than the hangover). But this didn't stop me from telephoning a secret number to speak rather croakily to Andy, Russell and Jaki from the band.

http:// www.gonzomultimedia.co.uk/ radio/player.php?id=219

SANDOR KWIATKOWSKI INTERVIEW

As regular readers will be aware, even as people who have read this issue so far will know, I am getting increasingly fond of the music of Clepsydra, and never pass up an opportunity to plug them unmercifully. But as well as the musicians, from the beginning they have had the exquisite visuals of Sandor Kwiatkowski. Just after Christmas I got hold of him for a chat…

How did you first meet Clepsydra?

Andy Thommen, Phil Hubert, Lele Hofmann (the first guitar player) and me were school friends years before Clepsydra even was born. When in 1989 the project started, first as an instrumental band in search of a singer, I just had graduated at the art school as graphic illustrator and so it was somehow obvious that I would have designed their first record artwork. Together with Lele I also wrote the lyrics for the song "Hologram".

As Aluisio Maggini joined the band, things were getting serious!

The "computer"-era was at its beginning and today it's funny to remember that the "Hologram" artwork was entirely hand-designed by me over months working closely together with the band. We still have a lot of sketches of that period in our archive! In that time I had known the world famous Swiss' artist HR Giger (Academy Award winner for "Alien") and so we had the chance to use one of his creations for our hologram on the cover!

Tell me about the artwork for the box set

For the "3654 DAYS"-box I have a "supporting role" for Mark Wilkinson, who is designing the artwork, providing him as much archive material as possible (photographies, original cover material, etc.).

I also redesigned the complete band website for the box release (and the 2014 tour…!) and I do all the graphics of the Clepsydra-Facebook-Page.

Tell me about the animations you are doing for next year's tour

After having created the four teasers for the release of "3654 DAYS", Andy did send me a few weeks ago the scheduled playlist of their concert, asking me to do some short animations inspired by the lyrics of the songs to be used during the show.

The first idea I got it for "4107" and in the end I designed a complete "video" for that song, which can be seen on Clepsydra's Youtube channel.

Right now I'm working on other animations… Come to their shows to discover them…!

What else are you working on?

Right now I am designing the poster for the 2014 edition of "RoSfest"-Festival in Gettysburg, where Clepsydra will perform im May and I am working on the artwork for the new record of Swiss' rock band "May Day" to be released soon.

Then I go on creating my surreal images. If anyone of you is interested in having an outstanding artwork for your next record, visit my website (which I have just completely redesigned) and don't hesitate to contact me…!

Contacts:
www.kwiatkowski.ch
www.facebook.com/SKDesign.SandorKwiatkowski
www.clepsydra.ch

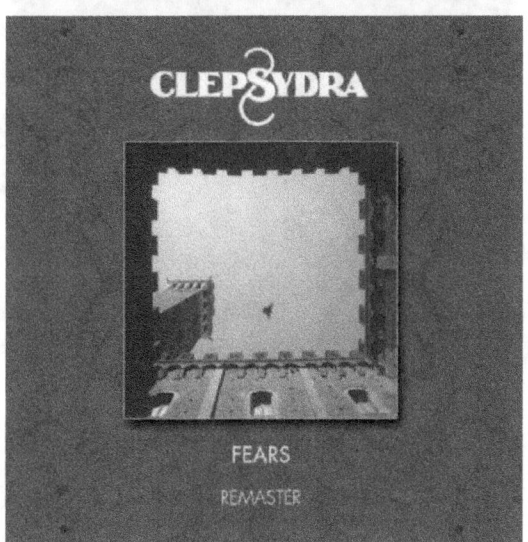

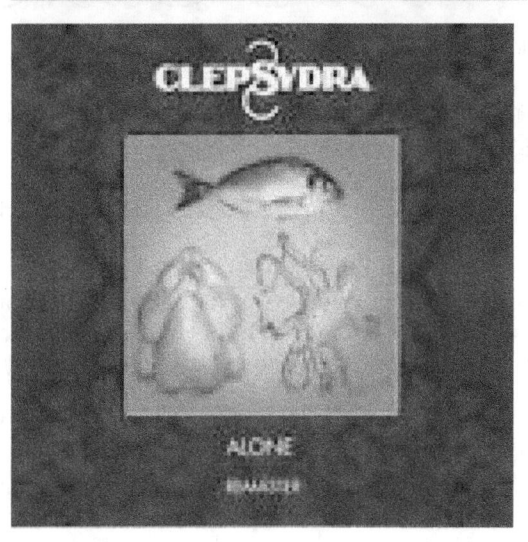

The Gonzo Annual 2015

THE BITCH IS BACK

NEW Iron on / sew on patch - Guns n Roses- 13 cm wide

I only added this because the figure reminded me of the Lincoln Imp….

And if you are in any way interested here is a brief explanation of the little chap that I wrote on my blog (http://cryptochick.blogspot.co.uk/)

According to legend, way back in the 14th Century, Satan sent two imps to earth with the prime objective of doing mischief. In some versions of the story, they first went to Chesterfield where they set upon the spire of the Cathedral and twisted it – their handiwork still in evidence today. They were then sent to Lincoln Cathedral to cause mayhem there. As the story goes, they set about their work with obvious glee, smashing up tables and chairs and even tripping up the poor Bishop. However, when they started to interfere with the Angel Choir, one of the angels decided that enough was enough and told them to stop. One of the imps was brave and started throwing rocks at the angel, but the other imp cowered under the broken tables and chairs. The angel turned the first imp to stone and this gave the second imp a chance to escape.

There are a few different variations of the story, one telling that the second imp that escaped did so with the help of a witch, by jumping on to her broomstick. However, she became so fond of the imp that she turned him into a black cat. However, in another version, this escapee was said to have travelled to Grimsby where it entered St James' Church and began repeating its destructive

and began repeating its destructive behaviour. The angel then reappeared and gave the imp's backside a good thrashing before turning it to stone like its friend. The Grimsby Imp can still be seen in St James' Church, clinging to its sore bottom. Another legend has the escaped imp turned to stone just outside the cathedral, and sharp-eyed visitors can spot it on a South outside wall.

Other stories tell how only one imp was blown around the country by the wind looking for places to cause mischief, and following his efforts in Lincoln Cathedral the angel turned him to stone after he had gone to the top of the nearest pillar to admire his handywork. Hence he is found there today with his legs crossed sporting an evil grin upon his face.

A more detailed version goes into how he was sent to plague the clergy in the cathedral and how he was blown through the great west door by the west wind and blew out the candles, scattered the hymn sheets and attacked the choristers. He then flew into the angel choir and it was when he threatened to pluck out the angels' feathers, that the smallest angel turned him to stone.

Whether you believe there were two, or just the one, or - indeed - if you do not believe it at all, measuring 12" in height, he is definitely still sitting there now, grinning down, cross-legged at all who pass below. He has become the symbol of the City of Lincoln, has the local football team named after him and is used on many a company logo. He has become the symbol for good over evil. My late ex-mother-in-law had a tiny model of one in her kitchen – as, indeed, do I.

And yes I digressed badly there so I apologise with good grace. But the I find the Lincoln Imp a darn sight more interesting than Guns n Roses to be honest. Each to his own eh?

In Search of the Space Ritual

Hawkwind have been part of my life for a very long time. Back during the summer of 1972 when I first discovered pop music for myself, *Top of the Pops* had a bewildering amount of goodies on show; as well as the poppy glam stuff that I favoured there were occasional forays into the charts by more exotic artistes. Like the bunch of hippies who rather scared me, with the peculiar video featuring lots of bubbles and a statuesque girl that my best mate at school told me was called "Stacy" whom (it was whispered at school) *actually danced on stage with no clothes on.*

This was enough to make the hormonally naïve 12 year old Jonathan a massive fan overnight, and as I was also discovering the Science Fiction juvenilia of Robert Heinlein at the time, the shouted chorus of "I've got a silver machine" fitted rather well into my adolescent inter galactic fantasies.

The first *Hawkwind* album that I either bought or heard was the double live *Space Ritual* that was released in 1973. The album was recorded during the tour to promote their Doremi Fasol Latido album, which comprises the bulk of this set. In addition, there are new tracks ("Born To Go", "Upside Down" and "Orgone Accumulator") and the songs are interspersed by electronic and spoken pieces making this one continuous performance. Their recent hit single "Silver Machine" was excluded from the set, and only "Master of the Universe" remains from their first two albums.

The *Space Ritual* show attempted to create a full audio-visual experience, representing themes developed by Barney Bubbles and Robert Calvert entwining the fantasy of Starfarers in suspended animation travelling through time and space with the concept of the music of the spheres. The performance featured dancers Stacia, Miss Renee, Jonathan Carney (later of the V8 Intercepters) and Tony Carrera, stage set by Bubbles, lightshow by Liquid Len and poetry recitations by Calvert. On entering the venue, audience members were given a programme (reproduced on the 1996 remaster CD) featuring a short sci-fi story by Bubbles setting the band in a Starfarers scenario returning to Earth.

I first saw them live at a peculiar festival at Snapper outside Barnstaple in 1981. It was peculiar not just because it was my first rock festival, but for other reasons as well. In those days I was an innocent and not very streetwise fellow in my early twenties, and I still believed that world peace could be achieved by the ingestion of various noxious substances whilst sitting in muddy fields listening to musical ensembles make whooshing noises on (what seem to me now) to be very primitive synthesisers.

I was, I believe, watching *Hawkwind* playing a spectacularly odd version of *Master of the Universe,* and like most of the rest of the audience, who were cold, muddy and uncomfortable, pretending that I was enjoying myself whilst in reality I was in dire need of both a lavatory and a nice cup of tea, and totally unwilling to avail myself of the horribly rudimentary versions of either facility that had been laid on for our "comfort" by the euphemistically named "organisers" of the event. About a hundred yards to my right were the serried ranks of the local Hells Angel fraternity who were encamped en masse like an iron clad phalanx of doom. It was only twelve years after Altamont, and even in the bucolic wastelands of rural Devon, they felt that they had something to live up to. Unfortunately, for me at least, they had decided to set up camp immediately between the area where I had set up my tiny tent and parked my car, and the main exit, and several of the nastiest and meanest looking of them were patrolling the area armed with pool cues and what I think were hollowed out pickaxe handles that had been filled with molten lead. I was therefore somewhat marooned, and feeling uncomfortable, isolated, alone and more than a little frightened.

Suddenly, in the middle of what appeared to me to be a sea of greasy black leather jackets, emerged a delicate, fey looking figure, wearing an extraordinary array of satins and silks in a variety of peacock colours. It looked for all the world as if one of the gaily coloured inhabitants of one of Arthur Rackham's fairy paintings had suddenly been transported into the middle of a field of leather-clad Neanderthals. The figure tripped gaily towards me, and appeared to my addled brain to be floating like a surreal, and rainbow-hued butterfly above the sea of mud and motorbikes. As it got closer I could see that it was a youth, hardly old enough to shave with an angelic halo of light brown hair surrounding a face that was covered with intricate paintings of butterflies and lotus flowers. He came and sat next to me and my companions.

Much to my amazement everyone else who was with me seemed to take this apparition in their stride. *"`Lo Danny"*, one of them grunted cheerfully, *"`ow are y`doing?"*. Another friend asked him what the hell he had been doing wandering blithely through the middle of the taciturn, unfriendly and potentially dangerous crowd of bikers. *"Ahhhhh they`re harmless."* he said, in an Irish accent that he seemed to be able to turn on and off at will, *"and anyway they wouldn`t hurt me...I am legion, I am many"*.

I saw *Hawkwind* maybe a dozen times over the next decade, usually in the company of Danny and my other degenerate friends, culminating in the legendary Treworgey Tree Fayre in Cornwall during the long, hot and rebellious summer of 1989. Then, for some reason that I am not able to adequately explain, I didn't see them again for nearly 25 years.

In those 25 years the music business, and the counter culture that had fuelled the activities of bands like *Hawkwind* had changed beyond all recognition. Despite what people like to claim there is still a music business and there is still a counterculture, but neither of them are as high profile in society as they were when *Hawkwind* first released *Space Ritual* forty-one years ago. So it is a strange time for *Hawkwind* to have – almost out of the blue – done what people have been pressuring them to do for many years, and - for two nights only – they played the *Space Ritual* live on stage for the first time since 1973.

And Gonzo was there.

The dates were announced late last year, *Hawkwind* posting a message "Hawkwind to play the Space Ritual (yes you read that correctly)" on their website, and over the next few weeks the twin events were revealed to be even more extraordinary: "We are thinking about doing a full day dress/production rehearsal for

our Space Ritual show, which takes place at the Rock 4 Rescue event at The Shepherds Bush Empire on Feb 22nd... It would be on Friday February 21st in Seaton in Devon...We would be trying things out all day with a full run through of the show in the evening..." the message concluding with an invitation to contact them if you were interested.

I heard all about it via my friend and colleague Graham Inglis who lives in a peculiar corner of my house, and was not at all surprised to find that – being a *Hawkwind* fan of Biblical proportions – he was intending to go to both events.

Then fate, in the person of the Gonzo Multimedia *grande fromage* stepped in. At the beginning of February I had a terse email from him instructing me and Graham to keep the weekend of the 21/22 free. A few days later I had a very crackly 'phone call from Nevada in which he told me what was happening.

A few days earlier this announcement was posted on Facebook: *"We are happy to let you know that "Space Ritual Preview Day" is going ahead as planned at The Gateway in Seaton, Devon, on Fri 21st Feb 2014. Doors will open at 2pm for sound check, production rehearsals and run throughs of various parts of the set with lightshow and dancers. We plan to have a complete dress rehearsal early evening (approx 6pm – 8pm or 7pm – 9pm depending on how the day has worked out).*

As this is a rehearsal day and the unexpected can happen, all times are approximate and the programme is liable to change without notice". There will be a full bar and food available throughout the day. Filming is expected to take place throughout the afternoon and evening. Your attendance at the event will be taken and accepted as your consent and agreement for your image to be used in any media produced from the event".

Yes, it certainly was being filmed and guess who the crew filming it were?

Graham and I left home at an unfeasibly early hour and arrived in Seaton soon after our target time of 10:30. We had been led to believe that the band were due in just after mid-day, and we wanted to show our professionalism and be there before them. In the event nothing happened for several hours and whilst Graham prowled around the neighbourhood I fell asleep in the car. At around about mid-day we wandered into the hall and set up our equipment, and again, for some time, wandered about the place doing very little. By 2:00 people (both band and punters) were beginning to arrive; we introduced ourselves to various band members including the two dancers (Laura and Steff) and Mr Dibs, and Niall Hone, and interviews were duly carried out. At this point I should probably explain that we had been booked to film extras for the DVD release of the concert later in the year.

By 3:00 various musician types were vaguely wandering about on stage and the silence was rudely interrupted with beeping noises from synthesisers and aggressive guitar chords. There was no sign of Dave Brock or Tim Blake or Richard Chadwick, but then suddenly there they all were and the entire 2014 incarnation of *Hawkwind* were on the stage playing remarkably sprightly. And then suddenly they weren't again, but then again they were back again.

This is actually the first time I have seen *Hawkwind* with my central nervous system buoyed up with nothing more potent than chocolate, tea and Benson and Hedges (which considering that was supposed to have given up smoking in 2008, and that I am a diabetic who shouldn't even *look* at chocolate that was – I suppose – as harmful as anything I used to take back in my mis-spent youth. But, even without drugs, the whole event had an unreal, *Alice in Wonderland* type quality about it. It wasn't just that here was a major band rehearsing and soundchecking in front of us, doing in public what most performers do only behind locked doors, but the whole fabric of reality was pushing us into a mindset that I hadn't experienced in years.

Surprisingly there was no-one there in the audience that I knew. We were only twenty something miles away from Exeter where I had lived for twenty years and hung out for much of that time with various reputable and disreputable members of the local hippy subculture. But none of them were to be seen; either they had all died, or grown up, or been forced to get proper jobs. I couldn't believe that none of them were interested.

There was something very humbling about being able to watch the creative process in action. As I commented later to Richard Chadwick, usually when you see a band on stage there is the "us and them" syndrome – performers vs audience. But here was something completely different. Usually one sees a band on stage, doing their thing, and a song begins with a shout of "1-2-3-4" or four taps on a hi-hat or whatever. But here it was much more organic!

The various musicians intermittently doodled on their instruments, but sometimes – hesitantly at first – one or more of the players would join in with someone's playing, and almost imperceptibly the whole band was playing together in unison. It was akin to watching one of those huge murmurations of starlings, when thousands of them, following a cue that only makes sense within the flock, suddenly change direction and start doing something completely different. It was very organic and very special. In fact it was magickal in the truest sense of the word.

There has always been something magickal and invocatory about *Hawkwind* – not for nothing was the most iconic record in their canon of work entitled the Space *Ritual*. For it was a magickal working, utilising a piece of theatre, and a vague literary concept to produce something very special which spread positive vibrations through everyone who was present, (and I suspect, much further afield)

The evening show was astounding. *Astounding sounds Amazing music* if I may recoin a term. There was a warmth that I really had not been expecting from the band. I have seen them on multiple occasions, and followed their career for four decades, but warmth is a concept that I have never associated with the band. Maybe it was the fact that I was sober for the first time at a *Hawkwind* gig? Maybe it was because both the band and I had grown up? Maybe it was just because it was a beautiful, magickal event at which no-one could possibly have been arch. Who knows? Who cares? It is the synergistic result that matters.

It was the first time I had ever had anything to do with the legendary Tim Blake, and I must say that he is an extraordinary fellow. A gnomic sonic magician, he hunched over his instruments with a manic gleam in his eye, conducting rites of musical alchemy, and occasionally capering about the stage with the energy of a man half his age. I suspect that he is not entirely human, because there is something of the faerie realm about him. The rest of the band were true to the description Michael Moorcock gave when he described them right at the beginning of their musickal journey: "When I first saw them, they seemed like barbarians who'd got hold of a lot of electronic gear: instead of being self-conscious and pseudo-intellectual, they were actually of the electronic age. They weren't impressed by their own gear. They weren't anti-technology - they celebrated it.." And Blake is some sort of an emissary from another world who had been conjured into this one by their musickal (the K is intentional) rites of Spring.

All too soon it was over, and Graham and I gathered up Rob Ayling (who had arrived at about 5:00 after two days of insanely stupid travelling) and took him back to North Devon and our tumbledown cottage full of animals and music for a few hours well-deserved sleep.

The next day we drove to London. This is not a travelogue as such, and so I will not bore you all with descriptions of the journey and its alarums and excursions, but needless to say we arrived in London just about in time to see the end of the soundcheck. The whole vibe of the Saturday show was perforce far more serious and intense than the day before. Whereas Seaton had been like an afternoon picnic for the extended Hawkfamily, this was serious stuff. The band played like daemons, and the whole performance was elegantly brutal, and one of the most intense things that I have ever seen. I am seriously looking forward to the DVD.

But as an experience I preferred the gentler vibe of the day before; the small children, the pretty girls in ridiculous home made silly hats and the elderly hippies dressed like oversized garden gnomes. The Saturday show will undoubtedly be seen as one of the great cultural events of 2014, and I wouldn't have missed it for the world. I am also very proud of being part of the team that will be bringing you the DVD package. But I enjoyed the Friday more, and for me at least it was a truly life affirming experience.

Om Shanti

Gonzo Weekly #68

EXCLUSIVE: The slightly convoluted tale of Rick Wakeman, Jules Verne, *Dad's Army* and *le petit fromage*

EXCLUSIVE: Cyrille Verdeaux interviews himself

EXCLUSIVE: Doug Harr on The Musical Box

EXCLUSIVE: Extensive reissue programme for The Deviants

THE INCREDIBLE JOURNEY

UNCLE RICK, DAD'S ARMY AND A JOURNEY TO THE CENTRE OF THE EARTH

I think that it is one of those well known truisms within the music industry that Rick Wakeman is a nice bloke. In fact, although I have never met him, I have first hand experience of this. About a year ago we fostered an eight month kitten called Buttons. He never really settled in with us and roamed at will around the village, although he was perfectly friendly when he saw us. About a month after he first arrived he was hit by the garbage truck, and that was the end of Buttons. Rick Wakeman, who loves cats, sent me several kind e-mails, and ever since I have had a soft spot for him.

So, therefore, it is a great pleasure to be able to tell you (in a rather convoluted way) that there are all sorts of exciting Wakemany things on the horizon. Gonzo are doing the merchandising on Rick's forthcoming UK tour. If you are an aficionado of prog, you must have been deaf dumb and blind, or possibly living in a small hole in the Sahara Desert for the last six months or so if you don't know that our favourite grumpy old dude (I love the hat, by the way, and as an aspiring grumpy old dude myself I very much want one, maybe one of my stepdaughters could knit me one) has been revisiting one of his undowbted career highlights recently.

The story behind Journey to the Centre of the Earth is a complicated one. Rick had originally started work on a concept piece based on Jules Verne's 1864 sci fi novel, as early as 1971, but it was put on the back burner while he completed various projects with Yes, and his first solo album. It is the story of Professor Lidenbrok, his nephew Axel, and their guide Hans, who follow a passage to the Earth's centre originally discovered by Arne Saknussemm, an Icelandic alchemist. Wakeman performs with the London Symphony Orchestra, the English Chamber Choir, and a group of hand-picked musicians for his band which later became The English Rock Ensemble. Actor David Hemmings provides the narration to the story. The cost of making a studio recording of the piece would have been prohibitive, so the album was recorded live on the second of two dates at the Royal Festival Hall in January 1974

The piece was originally 55 minutes long but had to be cut so that it would fit on to two sides of an

LP record. Rick always intended to release a complete version, but life got in the way, and the scores were lost, and Rick presumed that this was a permanent state of affairs. However, a "huge cardboard packing case" arrived at his house in 2008 which stayed in his garage for "about five months" before he found the score at the bottom which was damaged by water. A year was spent digitising and forming the complete score with conductor Guy Protheroe. Wakeman re-recorded the album with an orchestra, choir, and members of his English Rock Ensemble band as a studio album, incorporating 20 minutes that was previously cut. As Hemmings died in 2003, the narration is voiced by actor Peter Egan.

Now it is time to take the show on the road for the first time in the best part of four decades. The tour dates are elsewhere in this issue, and will be plugged mercilessly over the next few months. But what has this got to do with Dad's Army? And why are Rick and Hunter Ayling pictured on the front cover? Hush, best beloved. All will become clear.

Some weeks ago, just as the final fag end of winter was beginning to splutter out, Rob Ayling, the Gonzo Grand Fromage, and his son Hunter (henceforth known as Le petit fromage, An Cáis Sóisearach or ?????? ??? - take your pick) visited Casa Wakeman to collect some merchandise and other stuff what the great man had secreted around his premises. The three of them loaded it into the van and Rick (who is very fond of Hunter) gave him an affectionate hug, which explains why they are pictured in front of what appears to be the open tailgate of a Ford Transit.

But there's more, Mr Mainwaring.

Rick Wakeman and Hunter Ayling have something in common. They are both fans of the classic UK sitcom Dad's Army, and so later that day, The two Cheeses (that sounds like a sitcom title in itself) went off to the Dad's Army Museum. What? There's a Dad's Army museum? Yup. In May 2004 a Dad`s Army Trail was launched in Thetford. It showed the locations used during the filming of Dad`s Army.Several of the cast and the producers were in the town.The leaflet was largely written by Tony Pritchard of the Dad`s Army Appreciation Society and included a map of the trail, information on the show and a quiz. Many thousands were sent all over East Anglia.Later that year in response to requests, guided tours started, these were mainly for coach companies who brought visitors to the town for the tour and later took them onto Bressingham where they have had a Dad`s Army area since 2000.

And so to mark this occasion le petit fromage decided to dress as Private Pike, and le grande fromage channeled the spirit of Captain Mainwaring from another universe somewhere on the "World as Myth" timeline, and a splendid time was guaranteed for all.

And I've just realised something uncanny. Both Dad's Army and Yes started their activities in 1968. Dads's Army finished its nine year run in the July of the year that two sevens clashed. And in the very same month Yes (featuring Rick Wakeman for the first time in years) released their magnificent 'Going for the One' album, which was completely recorded in Walmington on Sea and featured Air Raid Warden Hodges on Vibraphone. (Yes they did, no it wasn't, and no it didn't).

Uncanny eh readers?

An auto-interview from Cyrille Verdeaux

Thank you very much for taking your time and effort to answer to my questions, Cyrille. I would like to ask you first where did you grow up and what were some of the early influences on you?

Hello everybody

I was born in an interesting place: the American Hospital of Neuilly sur Seine, (a rich neighbourhood near Paris) on July 31st 1949. It was a very hot day according to my mom and without AC machines, of course. This detail is important because from this first day, I never could appreciate cold weather, only hot, and dry if possible. Right now I am in a hot, and for half of the year, dry part of Brazil and my body and mind are both very happy here.

As you can imagine, just a few years after WWII, Paris wasn't as it used to be; the most beautiful city in the world. It was poor and dirty for the main part. My father was working at the American Hospital as a doctor, and this is why I could be delivered in this safe environment by my mom. Interestingly enough, I was born in the same hospital, and even the same bed and exactly 100 days after Dominique Strauss-Kahn's birth. I guess everybody knows now who DS-K is, and not for good reasons probably! I need to say that my sexual life (and life in general actually) has been very, very different from this guy. And all things considered, I prefer mine to his!

About my first influences. It has been very open from the start, I was hearing the music that my parents were listening to (they love classical instrumental), the music that my big brother (7 years older than me) was listening to (he loves essentially jazz and later became a good trumpeter and one of the pillars of the Jazz Hot Club de France) and the music that I could get with my little transistor radio, basically the first years of rock 'n' roll, with Chubby Checker, Little Eva, Ray Charles, Bill Haley, Eddie Cochran, Buddy Holly, Chuck Berry and of course the Franco Belgium local rock star glory, Johnny Hallyday.

In 1960, at 11 years old, I received as birthday gift a little teppaz turntable. I started to buy records on my own with my pocket money when my friends were buying candy bars and screwing their teeth.

Now, it is no problem for young people like it was for me; they can free download everything they want from their home. This is why my personal humble indie online record Cie, clearlight888music.com went almost bankrupt, but this is an other story! The new story is to have my back catalogue and new album distributed by Gonzo Multimedia and this is what matters.

You studied in Paris composition, harmony, and piano. Did you record anything before starting Clearlight? Any releases perhaps?

I began my musical studies at the national Conservatoire of Paris in 1965. The only tape recorders on the market back then were sophisticated "nagra" or revox; only for professionals. I made some attempts with the cassette recorders but the sound was too horrible to my ears, so no, I had no recording of anything audible before 1974, the date of my first recording ever.

It was few months after the end of my first band, Babylone, led by Christian Boule (RIP). There is no recording of our concerts back then. It's maybe better this way. Most of the Babylone's repertoire had been recorded a few years later (1978) in good condition in a recording studio and distributed first by Polydor, and after the premature death of Christian Boule, by Musea. It is called Photo Musik and I produced it for Polydor who was also distributing my 3rd album, Clearlight Visions. Even now, this album is really good, with Gong and Hillage influences.

Back to 1974, and I recorded what became later the Clearlight Symphony with a 4 tracks TEAC one night of a full moon (in the sky with Lucy). I had only at my disposal an acoustic piano (a superb half grand Gaveau with an inspiring sound) that has always been in my mom's country house. This night I was all alone and spent most of the night playing and recording. It was a true "clear light" experience as it is described in Timothy Leary's books. This is why the title of this music wasbn't difficult to find. I had no idea that I would base all my future career on this very first recording, though. I even receive, from time to time, mail from new young fans discovering this 40 years old creation with vintage gears.

What is the story behind Clearlight? How did you manage to get musicians such as Didier Malherbe, Steve Hillage, Tim Blake, Gilbert Artman, Christian Boulé and Martin Isaacs to work with you on the album?

It was quite fast. After this full moon recording, I added some organ parts (the synthesizers still did not exist on a large scale, so I had only a Wurlitzer organ to make the faked symphonic parts above the piano track.)
I began to share this demo with some friends involved in musical reviews but they all said they couldn't help me with this tape (2 pieces of 20 minutes each non-stop, totally non-commercial, compared to the requirement of 3 to 4 minutes songs that the show biz was imposing on musicians for radio broadcasts.) But one of these guys liked it, Jean Pierre Lentin (RIP) from the underground magazine *Actuel*! Sometimes, one is enough and makes a great difference, because he is the one that suggested that I show it to Virgin. Why? Because "Tubular Bells", the first album released by Virgin, very new on the market, was beginning to become a big hit thanks to the great success of *The Exorcist* movie, where a few lines of Mike's album were used.

By coincidence, this album was also made of 2 parts of 20 minutes each; I guess this is why Jean Pierre suggested me to go to Virgin's office. He gave me the address in London of the squat of Tim Blake, Gong's synthesist (in London, a lot of artists were living in free squats in the '70s). I had met Tim twice already when Babylone was playing in the same festivals as Gong.

So I took my precious tape under the arm, bought a boat ticket for Paris to London and arrived in London with, as only the tip, Tim Blake's squat address, period.

Luckily, I found also there my future manager, a French English teacher named Jacques Reland, who was sharing the squat with Tim and his girlfriend Brigitte. My English was very bad at the time, so I was needing a guy to assist me to meet Virgin's A&R, (named Simon Draper) and I asked Jacques to be the translator, and to study the contract for me, and this is how he eventually became my manager for 4 years. Simon Draper was Richard Branson's right arm. In spite of the low quality level of this demo (nowadays, it would be totally utopic to hope to have the attention of any A&R for more than one minute with such a sound, but in this blessed time, everything was yet possible, especially at Virgin). Simon accepted and proposed a recording contract. Few weeks after, the contract was signed in Branson's office. I was really happy. Tim Blake also signed the contract as artistic producer for this project.

When I returned to France with the contract, I began to look for musicians. Virgin was a good name already and I could easily find the musicians needed. Tim helped me to convince Steve Hillage and Didier Malherbe in London, and I took care of the French crew (Christian Boule and Gilbert Artman) in Paris.

What is the main concept behind the album and what can you tell me about the recording and producing sessions?
When I listened back to the day after the fruit of my magical night, the concept was easy: it was a rock symphonic album where both my scale in classic and rock knowledge was displayed. But it was also a spiritual "clear light" experience where I had crossed the 7 bardos of consciousness according to the Tibetan book of Death) and was transmitting these feelings to the piano. For side B, more classical and drum-less, I recorded first the piano parts at the Manor and the rest was recorded at David Vorhaus' (White Noise) home studio. And for side A, more rocky, I recorded all the parts at the Manor with my French fellows one month later, which gives this difference of sound and atmosphere between the 2 sides.
According to the contract, I was my own producer, and Virgin was only advancing me a certain amount of money to pay the sessions, the musicians and the renting of the instruments and it was not enough money to record the 2 sides at the Manor with a real symphonic orchestra, as Mike Oldfield could do with his *Tubular Bells* and the London Symphonic.

What gear did you guys use?

As I said, I had a low budget, so the best I could do at this time, when numeric sound samples didn't exist, was to rent a mellotron to create all the symphonic orchestration with this imperfect tool. For instance, I couldn't use the notes for more than 5 seconds each, because the tape was making a big "clack!" after these 5 seconds. It was the first time I had the opportunity to play this mythic instrument, so I spent a couple of hours trying to find a good way to play all the parts in spite of this stupid 5 seconds of limitation. I also used a Hammond for the organ parts. Tim used his EMS synth for the spacey noises. That's it.

What can you tell me about the cover artwork?

Jean Claude Michel, the painter, was a good friend. He was working at the time on illustrations for a book of anatomy, so he used one of his works on the human head to create the cover. Since he was listening to my music while painting, he added the psychedelic elements. A real masterpiece of surrealistic art, appreciated by everybody at Virgin when I showed it.

Later on, it was selected to figure in a book collecting the best rock albums covers. And both the Clearlight Symphony and Clearlight Visions figure now in the list of the 100 best progressive rock albums of all time published by the Billboard Guide magazine. It was a good beginning, to say the least!

Apparently, I am also the only French musician present on this Billboard list, but I find it a little hard for Magma, for instance.Christian Vander's music should also figure in the list of best 100 progressive albums of all times, in my opinion.

In 1975 you released another Clearlight album called "Forever Blowing Bubbles"and then you started another project called Delired Cameleon Family. This was somehow a project for the movie called Visa de censure n°X, right? Would you like to tell me the story behind this release? I would also like to hear more about this film…

The story is quite simple. I had a friend, Yvan Coaquette, guitarist and former soundman of my first group Babylone, who was friend with Pierre Clementi, a famous French actor. Between 2 movies, he was shooting his own small budget movie, mainly with his friends of the "nouvelle vague", Jean Pierre Kalfon, Valerie Lagrange and others, and he was looking for a soundtrack, so Yvan introduced me to him, knowing that I was able to compose music for movies. So I worked a few days while watching the movie to find musical themes. When done, Philippe Constantin (RIP) and friend of Pierre's proposed to be the producer and interface with EMI France and when I was ready we could obtain a budget to rent only 3 days of recording studio. 2 days to record and 1 to make the mix with the movie. Very ridiculous but better than nothing at all! Then Yvan and I decided to invite all the good musicians' friends that we had for a free non-stop session, 16 hours a day. The 2 engineers were relaying 8 hours each. It has been a lot of improvisation in this session, with a very special atmosphere of intense work, this is why I found the title: Delired Cameleon Family. The movie itself was very special, with several fast motion pictures mixed together. It is difficult to tell the story line of this movie; very avant garde. This movie and soundtrack figures now in the permanent list of original psychedelic movies at the Musee Pompidou, in Paris. But it has been a commercial flop. The French market was not familiar with this kind of art.

Les Contes du Singe Fou is your third Clearlight album, but this time your style changed a lot. Same goes for Visions. Why do you think?

Forever Blowing Bubbles was the second and, unfortunately, the last project with Virgin. I had a contract with 3 albums but when Richard Branson asked me to move out of Paris to live permanently in London to ease the promotion of the band, I had to refuse because my wife was 7 months pregnant when he requested it and of course my wife didn't want to leave Paris and her mom at this stage of her pregnancy. So, when you say NO to a Branson request, this is it. Virgin cancelled my contract (without any compensation whatsoever) and I couldn't do my third project there with them, the almost ready Les Contes du Singe Fou. I wanted to try a new form of concept for my third project, a Space Opera type of album. I gave the theme and story synopsis to my gifted anglophone friend Francis Mandin, a great fan of Yes and Genesis.

After a few weeks, Francis brought me some wonderful lyrics in English. I had planned to have John Wetton (King Crimson) on vocal and bass, Bill Bruford (not a King Crimsoner anymore) had been approached but with the premature end of the Virgin contract, all that had been cancelled. So, I realised this album with a low budget in a Parisian studio, instead, with an obscure small label ISADORA and not very known musicians, that didn't know how to promote music, so it has been also a commercial flop.

Seeing that, I decided to produce my fourth project, Clearlight Visions, myself. I went back towards a more instrumental style, more simple to organise. That album was also my first where I was deciding everything. I paid musicians and studio myself, so that nobody could decide things for me. I asked to Didier Malherbe (sax-flute) and Didier Lockwood (electric and acoustic violin) to bring their talent, and Christian Boule on guitar and Jacky Bouladoux on drums to complete the crew. I also began to use natural sounds (ocean waves, birds, woman having a climax (in spirale d'amour) to go with the music, which was very revotionnaire at this time where new age music didn't yet exist.

During the '80s until now you have released many solo albums. Tell me something about that period of your life...

The 80's began with a very nice experience : Along with Frederic Rousseau and Jean Philippe Rikyel, I decided to produce an album by renting a mixing table and an ATARI 8 tracks for one month, creating a home studio in the living room of the country house of my parents and the same familial piano that I used to learn music and record Clearlight Symphony's demo. The result has been "Messenger of the Son". But before I was able to propose it to various music labels, the worst thing that can happen to a human being happened to me: the accidental death of my 5 year-old-son, Jonathan.

I left France right away, leaving behind all my musical projects and went to an ashram in Arizona where I could learn yoga and meditation. I met some musicians there such as Dean and Dudley Evenson, musicians and owners of the small new age label "Soundings of the Planet". I became good friends with them and began to release new age music on their label. Offrandes, Nocturnes digitales, Shamballa, Journey to Tantraland.

One year later, I moved for California. There, a US fan of Clearlight from the early days, Josh Goldstein, former manager of Happy the Man, offered me his services to represent me. He was a Vietnam vet and had lost a leg there in a helicopter crash, so he had received a good sum of money just before our meeting. He proposed to produce my new music. I completed the tracks of Messenger of the Son with some local musicians, and tried to submit this album to a Californian label. One was interested right away, Fred Catero, former chief engineer of CBS. He had recorded Bob Dylan, Blood Sweat and Tears, Chicago and many others stars during his CBS career. He was now retired and wanted to create his own label. I was very proud that he picked up Messenger of the Son to figure in his list of first releases on his label. So Messenger of the Son became my sixth and last vinyl. Unfortunately, his label Catero records went bankrupt quite fast because his spirit of independence didn't please the local show biz mafia and they made the distribution of his catalogue impossible!

I didn't lose everything because Windham Hill new age label signed one of my Messenger of the Son's song, Remember Jonathan, a kind of short requiem that I had composed just after the death of my son and had added to the Messenger album.

This very emotional piece is now for ever in the PIANO SAMPLER ALBUM 86 (but also in the CD of Messenger of the Son).

This Piano sampler album experienced huge sales, fortunately. I was sharing the royalties with 7 other pianists and yet I could finance the birth of my twin daughters in Santa Cruz, CA.

In 1986, my French wife wanted to go back to France, so we packed and went back to France, where I decided to continue alone, to record new projects and my very first CD: Rhapsody for the blue Planet, followed the next year by a new Nocturnes Digitales. I also became teacher of music during this French stay. Money, money...Most of the labels selling my music didn't pay me my royalties correctly, so...I couldn't sue them, so I dropped the idea to continue to make money with my art only.

In the '90s, I met Pascal Menetrey (RIP). He had a huge collection of natural sounds and with his sound material and E-Mu sample gears, I recorded Ethnicolours and Tribal Hybrid Concept, to honour all the human tribes facing extinction. The style was new for me, based on house and tribal rhythmics surrounding hundreds of different sound samples. It should be in the Guinness Book of Records in this category if it existed, lol! Ethniclours was the yin version, more mellow, and Tribal Hybrid Concept the yang version, more wild.

Then I met Patrick Meynier, owner of a record store in Paris, Legend Music. With his help, I could remix Clearlight Visions on CD with several bonus tracks in it. Then with his wife violonist, Genevieve, I recorded Solar Trance fusion and Aerobix, two powerful albums of progressive house music, if I may say.

All these years I was going back and forth between France and California and in 1995 I met a good singer, Leah Davis, with whom I recorded Flowers from Heaven, along with other singer friends, Frances Key, and Gunnar Amundson. I was recording where I could, song per song, the home studios were becoming more and more serious and well-equipped in numeric and small equipment. This album is the only one that has only songs in it. The lyrics created by the singers are all excellent and meaningful, making this album a very initiatic one, philosophically wise.

This brings us to the 21st Century. I met another Clearlight fan, Dan Shapiro, living in Santa Barbara. First he proposed to produce a solo piano album, Piano for the 3rd ear.

Then Dan told me about his huge fantasy, which was to produce the re-recording of the Clearlight Symphony, with all the numeric sounds that didn't exist 30 years ago. I spent 3 weeks in a home studio in Santa Barbara, alone with a Kurzweil 2600 and recorded Inner Peace Concerto, a reprise of musical themes of the Clearlight Symphony with many improvements and new themes.

After that, we decided to create an online music label together as a little start up, www.clearlight888music.com. We converted all my vinyl music into numeric and made CDs with it. Plus, the label was releasing also the Kundalini Opera, a 7 hours synthesis of 7 of my CDs, each of these CDs harmonizing a specific chakra. I was mixing here all my knowledge in yoga and music together.

- Tribal Hybrid Concept takes care of the 1st chakra
- Journey to Tantraland, the 2nd
- Solar transfusion, the 3rd
- Flowers from heaven, the 4th
- Rhapsodies for the blue planet the 5th
- Piano for the 3rd ear, the 6th
- Inner peace Concerto, the 7th

Inner Peace Concerto was sounding so great to his ears that Dan decided to pay for more sessions, with other musicians, a violinist, a sax-flute player, a drummer and an electric guitarist. I called this final result "Infinite Symphony" because it ends exactly as it begins, as a Moebius ring. Hey, I had a new band, eventually ready to go to play in US progressive rock festivals.

Just a few days before the departure for our first festival, the drummer, Shaun Guerin, decided to kill himself because of some problems with his wife and probably a bad trip with bad drogues! Unbelievable!

But true, alas. After that, the other musicians decided to quit the band idea and my last chance of restarting a public career with a Clearlight band stopped right there. And on top, I had to leave the country, having no more professional reasons to get a green card and a work visa.

I had met a charming Brazilian lady on the internet a few years ago (2002), and I decided to answer to her invitation to visit her in Brazilia. This is now where I live permanently and I am married to her. Life with its permanent ups and downs...I know exactly what it means!

Thank you very much! Would you like to send a message to the Gonzo Magazine readers?

Yes, here is the message, which my guardian angel transmitted me to share it with everybody. It was in 1977, but I think it is timeless:

EARTH BEINGS, listen...

Please read carefully the following message :

The time has come to realise that your unlimited expansion in all sectors are seriously threatening the harmonious balance of your sphere of birth.

Consequently, your survival and the survival of your children are now threatened, for the new ecologic datas you are creating are artificial, therefore devastating to your natural ecosystem.

Even before the right to freely travel and to express yourself, your very first rights must be those to breathe non-carcinogenic air, drink non-polluted water and eat no- toxic food, all conditions indispensable to your biological existence.

Several severe plagues of planetary dimension are beginning to manifest, synonymous of dark and painful cuts in your rows, a new revolution, pacific and ecological this time, happens to be urgent and necessary.

To get rid of the ghost of your extinction, you, from the humblest to the almightiest would only have the small price to pay of remembering that the Bill of Human Rights passes necessarily after the Bill of Rights of the planet that welcomes and nourishes you. Do respect and appreciate the natural harmony of Nature, fruit of hundreds of millions of years of preparation and evolution.

Consequently; it becomes important that each of you wakes up in order to effectuate the necessary corrections for the preservation of your destiny, individual as well as collective.

Understand that the more you will delay to concretise this revolution, the more dramatic will be your fate, for the natural forces making functioning your ecosystem are stronger than yours and will be able to find an other new balance than the one you think you can impose and it will often make you feel miserable.

To help you to remember or to finally realise that your blue planet (whom you still are the most precious fruit), is really alive, listen to her music. Then will you understand she must be preserved from destruction.

Her voice is indeed necessary in the partition of the Symphony of the Spheres, primordial universal anthem for the establishment and development of Life

So protect and share her

Oz Hardwick is a York-based writer, photographer, lecturer and occasional musician.

As well as two well-received poetry collections, The Kind Ghosts (2004) and Carrying Fire (2006), he has published widely in international literary journals and performed throughout Europe and the US.

He has also published widely on art and literary history and is a Reader in English at Leeds Trinity University College.

Oz is also a photographer and was at a couple of shows by the newly reformed Pink Fairies back in the late 1980s. He writes: "Ooh - it's a long time ago!

All of the ones in front of the curtains with pronounced ripples were taken at Dunstable Queensway Hall, the other couple at The Crypt in Deptford - I attach a flyer for the Deptford gig, & maybe there's a website which will tell you what year the 9th May was a Saturday (I'm guessing '87 or '88).

Both were about the time of Kill 'em and Eat 'em, and I think the Dunstable gig (from which I've attached a couple more pictures) was earlier. Sorry I can't be any more help, but the late 80s is a bit of a blur, I'm afraid."

They were indeed, Oz. I know exactly what you mean..

Graham and Keith's most Excellent Adventure

Saturday dawns... the day of the radio interview with Clash and PIL co-founder Keith Levene, conducted by Tony Gleed of Bugbear Promotions. And I was going to video the occasion for Gonzo.

Heading from North Devon to Southwark in London was surprisingly trouble-free, and I checked in to my hotel within 5 minutes of the time I'd earlier anticipated. Thanks to an earlier look at Google Streetview, I knew the layout of the area despite never having been there before, and humped the tripod and video gear down the busy road to the rendezvous point - a cafe just south of London Bridge - and soon met up with the guys.

I wasn't sporting a red carnation for identification purposes, but I was wearing a Hawkwind t-shirt, which turned out to be just as effective. After some general chat we moseyed on up to the radio studio, tucked away in a back yard behind an electronic gate.

While Keith and Tony discussed things like CD fade points with Dan, the radio engineer, I did some general setting up and soon it was Air Time. The interview went well, interspersed with music and the answering of tweets - the show was billed partly as a "tweet-fest" and as often happens there wasn't enough time to cram everything in.

Afterwards, we adjourned to a pub's sitting-out area just off the busy main road, and I tried getting some stock photos for Gonzo of Keith with red London buses passing by in the background. With somewhat mixed results, I felt!

After a few pints, I said my goodbyes to the guys and carted the equipment back up the road to my hotel - and dived straight in to the shower. Mission Accomplished. **GRAHAM INGLIS**

Everybody's Wally

Hello, I'm a Wally, Wally Dean and although you don't know it yet YOU are probably all Wallies too.

Let me start by explaining my name; Dean I got from my parents. Mostly my old man, in an extreme act of good luck he read Jack Kerouac's On the Road just before I was born. I say lucky because if it wasn't for Mr K's beautiful anti hero Dean Moriarty, I would have been called Woody after Woody Guthrie. I must add that I don't wish to offend any other Woodys reading this, but I've worked as a coppicer and a charcoal burner and I reckon the name Woody may have left me less inclined to become a woodsman.

The Wally part of my name came from Helen the Hat, a legendary New-Age traveller and a truly wonderful woman in her own right. It was she, who one wet and windy Samhain night, gave me the honour of being the caretaker of Wally Hope's ashbox. Wally had been a hero of mine, the founder of the Stonehenge Free Peoples Festival and an acid prophet. He was in the words of Sir Walter Wally (Sir Wally Raleigh) a "psychedelic anarchist"

What was there not to like ?

Wally Hope was born Alexander Grahame Russell, in 1947, to a wealthy family from the Windsor area. His father was an international salesman for a chemical company and his mother was Danish. When he was 12 his father died.

Strangely his father had made arrangements, with the BBC presenter John Snagge, in case something happened to him while abroad,. This has always made me wonder if there was a british intelligence connection or

The Gonzo Annual 2015

maybe this is the first of the strange factors which surround his life.

His mother soon remarried to a man whose criminal past set warning bells ringing for the executives of the will, so Alex was made sole beneficiary of the family estate. This naturally upset his mother who moved back to her native Denmark, leaving her son living in South Lodge, a family home in Stoke Poges, near Windsor.

Young Alex soon dropped out of Art College, claiming that they tried to make him do everything their way. He adopted the name Phil, which means love, and became a Mutant, He began to hang out at Eel Pie Island and attending the "happenings" at the Roundhouse in Chalk Farm. These legendary parties must have made a profound impression on him as he started to regard LSD as a sacrament, a holy potion for communication with the divine. The Pretty Things were regular visitors, and the lodge was always a hive of activity. His mother then returned and although he said he'd been having a wonderful time, she called the police and he was arrested for possession of marijuana. He was sentenced to 2 years, first in Ashford then on the notorious A wing at Wormwood Scrubs.

On his release he set out to explore the world, visiting Canada, where he stayed on reserves and became fascinated with tipis. He also visited France, Denmark, Ibiza, Israel, Kenya, Morocco, Greece and Cyprus. Cyprus, he loved and he wanted to buy land there, but the war flared up. Wally joined the Cypriot army briefly but left after losing some friends in battle.

His time in Britain was spent immersing himself into the alternative lifestyle and psychedelic freedom which free festivals allowed him. He was at the Glastonbury Fair in 1971.

I remember reading in Andy Roberts brilliant book Albion Dreaming how a young chaplain from Swindon had had a very strange time after taking LSD. It is not clear if this was a voluntary trip, but he ended up spending quite a while in the Release bad trip refuge.

Then watching Nic Roeg's film of the fair who do I spot in the audience of the Sunday morning mass, but our friend Wally. If anyone could talk a young priest with a yearning for divine contact into a dose of LSD, then he was the man.

Over the next two years I will be inviting you to join me on a journey of discovery. I will be recounting major incidences which happened forty years ago, from 1974 to Wallys untimely death in september 1975. I will be inviting you to join me in a detective story, and to form your own opinions on his death.

Was it misadventure, suicide or perhaps murder?

I will be supplying you with all I know, with contributions from Wally (his words), Penny Rimbaud, CJ Stone, Nigel Ayers and others. I welcome any contact, as I write my book, and together we will lay his memory to rest.
DEAN PHILLIPS

JOEY MOLLAND REMINISCES
Part One

I have been a *Beatles* fan for about 40 years now, since someone at school lent me a copy of *Sgt Pepper,* and over the years I have amassed quite a collection of *Beatles*-related odds and sods. I am also fascinated with Apple Records; a gloriously quixotic concept that was quite probably doomed to failure, but which produced some transcendentally wonderful music before its eventual collapse into bitterness and acrimony.

Everyone agrees that the most successful band on the label, apart from the Fab Four themselves were *Badfinger*.

Poor *Badfinger*; if ever there was a pop group "born under a bad sign" it was them. Things started off quite auspiciously. As *The Iveys* they signed to *The Beatles'* Apple Records and had a hit single. However, they decided that their name, and their image were a little old fashioned and for reasons that remain obscure they also decided to change their guitarist. Exit Ron Griffiths and enter Joey Molland. *Badfinger* was born.

They had hit singles with the Paul McCartney penned *Come and Get It* (recorded just as Griffiths was leaving the band) and *No Matter What*, and perhaps their greatest moment was when Harry Nilsson had a massive worldwide hit with their song *Without You* in 1972. After that it was all downhill.

And downhill very very fast.

The band were the last non-*Beatles* artists to release an album on Apple, and a move to Warner Brothers was not a success.

There were grave management issues (which were so contentious that even now it is probably not safe to put in writing) and – probably as a result of these internal pressures – two members of the band (Pete Ham in 1975 and Tom Evans in 1983) committed suicide by hanging.

Joey Molland, who had written the vast majority of the group's later output, remains an immensely under-rated and very talented songwriter, whose career has been blighted by the appalling catalogue of disasters which had overtaken his band.

Originally from Liverpool, Molland now lives in America, where he continues to write and perform some beautiful music. Let's hope, with the release and re-releases of some of his most exquisite records on Gonzo that his star is finally in the ascendant.

He is also a very nice bloke, and I always enjoy talking to him. The other evening I telephoned him for a chat about some of the extraordinary things he has done in his long career. In this, the first of a two part interview he talks about how he got started in his musical career, and reminisces about life at Apple, and some of the recordings that he worked on. He shares his memories off Phil Spector, Derek Taylor and Richard DiLello amongst others, and he recalls other Apple artistes like the legendary Jackie Lomax (who died last year) and working on albums by George Harrison and John Lennon

http://www.gonzomultimedia.co.uk/radio/player.php?id=231

An Audience with Andy

Andy Colquhoun is a guitarist with a peerless pedigree. He first came to the notice of the music press when in 1977 his band Warsaw Pakt recorded an album (Needle Time) that was in the shops 24 hours after the first note was recorded (viz the session ended at 10 p.m. on Saturday 26 November 1977 and the album was ready to be sold by 7a.m. on Sunday 27 November 1977.).

The band was trying to make a point about technology in doing this, and the album sleeve was a 12" square brown bag with stickers and rubber stamping to display the band name and album title. After Warsaw Pakt, he joined Brian James' Tanz Der Youth, (described as the world's first hippy punks) subsequently moved on to the band The Pink Fairies, and then a band with ex-MC5 guitarist Wayne Kramer.

For the best part of thirty years he was songwriting partner and collaborator with the legendary Mick Farren; a partnership which only ended with Mick's sad death in July 2013.

In 2001 he released his first ever solo album He writes: "There comes a time in the life of every guitar player when he or she gets the chance to make a solo album. This is my attempt, and I've put as much guitar on it as possible".

But now there is a brand new one. I spoke to him recently about it...

JON: So, tell me about the solo album.

ANDY: Well, yeah, with the solo album; very, very pleased with the artwork and the way it's coming together. I've already seen the CD in advance and I'm very happy about the way that's going. It's got twelve original tunes on it that I wrote, and I originally recorded those in 2010. And then there's been an addition of another seven tracks that are all covers of songs that I like, and like playing. This is an instrumental album. The album I did before this, *Pick Up The Phone, America!*, just had four instrumental tracks on it. I think because I was working such a lot in the States with Mick Farren I didn't get around to writing a lot of lyrics, so the lyrics that really meant something to me went on that album. Then after talking over what I was going to do next with some of my friends, I decided to do a solo of just instrumentals, and then just sat down and wrote them. Got the recording process quite together so that by the end of it I could just start on a song and finish it by the end of the week but it took a lot more time than that to get started. I think the first tune I really approached on it is one of the bonus tracks; that was 'River Deep, Mountain High' – everyone knows that tune and I've always loved it; and that was the one I got my friend Philthy from *Motorhead* to do the drums on. And following that, I think I did 'Black Hole Sun', which was a song I'd heard on the radio and I was so knocked out by it, I had to pull over and listen to it properly. You know how sometimes a song gets you like that?

JON: Oh, yes.

ANDY: And so then I just did a straightforward translation of the merseyline [?] on to lead guitar and reconstructed the backing, and did it that way. So that's how it kind of started, and that took quite a long time, by which time I'd figured out the rest of the rest of the numbers I was going to do. I did carry on doing the standards but the challenging part was to come up with original tunes. So it starts off with this one title, 'Back in the Day', which is basically a Blues number – a slightly different sequence to a normal Blues tune – I was very pleased with that when I finally finished it and it went on from there.

The sequence on the album is pretty much the order in which the numbers were recorded, 'cause I'll do one, and then that will be the start and then I'll say, "Well, what it needs now is something a bit more up-tempo," so I'd write another one. And at the same time I was concurrently doing videos of the tunes.

So yes, it was like, the second track would be 'Blue Lagoon', which has kind of got a different feel; it's a bit more up-tempo. One of the notes I make on the CD is that when you're writing an instrumental you're not actually putting word-shaped thoughts in people's heads s when they listen to it they're a little freer than they might be if the storyline is written out.

The other thing, which contributed to going instrumental, I was working with Mick Farren, who of course is a prolific wordsmith and there are his wonderful words so there wasn't actually a call for any lyrics at that point in time and so I was free to explore the melodic ideas that you get in an instrumental. And, of course, when you're writing songs you might get a guitar break in the front and one in the middle and perhaps one in the out-trap. But it's a whole different discipline to writing instrumentals.

JON: It's also a style of music, which people wouldn't immediately connect with you.

ANDY: Very possibly. Very possibly.

JON: You're associated in most people's minds with a certain sort of music. Are the instrumentals still in that style, in that sort of genre, or have you explored different genres doing it?

ANDY: Well, it definitely has given me the chance to go into other fields. I mean, when I started out I was writing punk-rock tunes. Well, even before that I was playing and writing, to some extent, British R&B-type tunes; sort of feel-good stuff, you know. So you do progress, you know, and you try different things. There's quite a lot of fields in this, on the CD that's going to be released. Where there's a strong similarity would be sort of track twelve, 'Exit Stage Left.' It's very much in the same mould as the *Fairies* or *Deviants*. You know, sort of hard and heavy. And there are other tracks that are on there that are like that. Like the third track, 'Hot Rod'; that was a deliberate attempt to write an instrumental such as you might have heard coming out of a group in the sixties or seventies, perhaps, even. The fourth track, 'Electroglide', was basically a rock song. It's a sort of like small bass-y song, you know. Modern rock and blues; that's the one I'm referring to. Then the sixth track; that's another punky thing that's been given a guitar, and that's followed by a ballad, and so on. So it's quite a cross-section, you know.

JON: Who else is playing on it?

ANDY: Well, David plays bass on five of the tracks, mostly on the covers; you know, the standards. And Philthy from *Motorhead* is playing on 'River Deep, Mountain High.' But otherwise, it's me and a load of machines and instruments.

JON: Do you like playing with machines rather than people? 'Casue it's a very different discipline, isn't it?

ANDY: Yes. I do like sitting down and just making up a tune, and not having [laughs] to then get other musicians to over-dub into it. It can't really be done. Once you've done that, you then have to start again with other musicians and build the whole thing up again. And if that's easy, that's great. If you've got a band going, and you've got the space and time to do those sort of things, then I probably prefer that. But it doesn't happen every day of the week so I find it very useful to use the modern technology that we have, and I guess I'm going into a sound that's based in the sixties and seventies, which is kind of where I'm coming from.

JON: Where did you record it?

ANDY: Well, at Cyber Music, which is what I call my home recordings, so that would be in various locations. It was all done in LA on Hollywood Boulevard.

JON: Golly. I keep on forgetting that it was only a few years ago that you came back.

ANDY: Yes, we came back in 2011 so we're into the third year that I'm back in Blighty and it's been great so far, apart from the tragedy last year, of course, with Mick dying.

JON: That was horrible.

ANDY: Yeah, it was.

JON: I was really, really touched by the level of love that everybody showed in the obituaries and tributes to him.

ANDY: Yeah, it was amazing, wasn't it?

JON: It was the day the sixties died in the end, wasn't it?

ANDY: I think by that time people recognized what a force he'd been. For me and the band members, you know, he'd always been that sort of – what would you say? – a force of nature that was – he wouldn't compromise about anything. And he was still stuck to exactly the same principles and so on that he'd had in the first place and nothing had changed his mind about anything. In fact, it only confirmed his worse suspicions [laughs] as events unfolded, you know.

JON: I think we need somebody like him now more than ever.

ANDY: Well, I don't know what's gonna replace him....

Events that shook the world. #436

The Resurrection of Genius

I learned about Maestro James Conlon on the same night I learned about the Jewish composer Franz Schreker (opposite column). Delivering a lecture that was punctuated by the sexual frenzy of Schreker's "Die Gezeichneten" stood an unassuming, professorial gentleman that appears part Robin Williams, part Gabriel Byrne. You would not know it by looks alone, but at that lectern stood not only the internationally known Music Director of the Los Angeles Opera, but a hero of sorts who took it upon himself to mine the suppressed art of Jewish composers whose work had been not only censored, but disposed of by the Nazis.

I was sitting in an auditorium at The Colburn School with Composer Sharon Farber, who herself had celebrated the life of Holocaust survivor and hero Curt Lowens in her "Bestemming: Concerto for Cello, Orchestra and Narrator". We were pursuing the notion of artist as not only activist but as ambassador to the memory of those whose first person narratives of the Holocaust were about to fade into history. We listened as Maestro Conlon told the tale of Schreker's fall from grace at the hands of the emerging Nazi party. An acclaimed composer who achieved the highest position in German musical life, was summarily dismissed from his position as Director of the Musikhochschule in Berlin at the urgings of the National Socialist Party.

As unforgettable as Schreker's story and his music was, it was perfectly evident this evening that the man who recovered these forgotten voices was as important to the reunification and reassembling of the void as were the voices that he recovered. A puzzle is nothing but pieces until it has been reassembled, and Maestro Conlon's deft piecing together of a culture lost manifested itself like the joys of unearthing buried treasure. After the lecture, I had an opportunity to sit down with Maestro Conlon and Sharon Farber to offer up my own accolades of support. It was evident that Conlon was neither interested in nor responsive to any personal commendation. He waved away my plaudits and instead spoke of how he unearthed these important works.

"I was living in Germany and working there for about 13 years. At the beginning of that I happened by accident to hear some of the music of Zemlinsky. I fell in love with it, performed it, recorded it – and began to read about him. By reading about him I discovered the others, and it all developed organically to the point where I understood that if I as a musician, at 40 years old, and had never heard about Zemlinsky – how much other music have I not heard and how could the public possibly know if we musicians didn't know. At a certain point it became an epiphany, and I decided that I'd do anything I could to change that."

The others that Maestro Conlon refers to are the 'lost composers' that he singularly resuscitated with his 'Recovered Voices' project at LA Opera,

which David Mermelstein, writing for the Los Angeles Times aptly described as 'an extraordinary project of reclamation'.

Composers like Alexander Zemlinsky, Viktor Ullmann, Walter Braunfels, Ernst Krenek, Erich Wolfgang Korngold – were the focus of a campaign that sought to erase the mark of these Jewish Composers by a morally bankrupt and criminal regime whose claim to fame was the ethnic cleansing of 6,000,000 Jews and other recalcitrants who didn't fit into the Aryan profile. James Conlon would be the first to shirk his role as a hero, and certainly would avoid terms like 'artivist' that efforts to create a conjunction between artist and activist. His efforts on the surface would appear as an earnest attempt to fill a missing gap in recent classical music history. It goes quite a bit deeper than that. It brings back to life the voices of brilliant composers who were truly forgotten based solely on their religion. Hitler's final solution was not only about ethnic cleansing but also about cultural erasing. The emasculation of literature, scientific theory, and even music of that era left society impotent. It was a cancer that hid below the surface that never went into remission and threatens recurrence even to this day.

Yet Maestro Conlon prefers to insist that this music simply 'belongs in the standard repertoire, and should be put back into the standard repertoire". As he succinctly yet powerfully puts it, "It only lives, if it is performed".

Conlon's arc, like the ever-widening gyre of Yeat's 'The Second Coming' harkens to a time when things fell apart and the center could not hold. Yet as the falconer, Conlon has kindled light from darkness and celebration from anarchy. These voices have not as much recovered as they have now thrived under Conlon's lovingly downplayed passion for the truth, and as much for the moral as for the historical significance of these composers and their works.

Maestro Conlon emphasizes that fact. "Yes, there is a moral issue and yes, there is a historical issue, but most of all as a performing artist, my basis is that this is music. A lot of this music comes directly out of the same sources of the music of composers that we still play, that we recognize, who just didn't happen to be victimized. My purpose is to play it as much as possible, and to do as much as I can to make it happen."

"Memorializing is a noble thing, and we should do it. Ultimately, this is not about memorializing, it's about restoring the balance. These are not amateur composers. These are great composers." Great composers indeed, but what of Maestro Conlon himself?

In 2012 Maestro Conlon received the Cohon Award which was officially presented to him at the Illinois Holocaust Museum by the Rabbi Samuel S. and A. Irma Cohon Memorial Foundation. The award is given to individuals for accomplishments that benefit all Jewish people. It was only one of many awards and recognitions for Maestro Conlon's "Recovered Voices". During the Cohon Award presentation, the spirit of Maestro Conlon's work was beautifully summarized in the Maestro's own words:

"Undoing injustice where one can is a moral mandate for all citizens in a civilized world. We cannot restore to these composers their lost lives. We can however return the gift that would mean the most to them – play their music." And in that spirit, it was noted that in the Talmud, it is written "a person who saves a single life, saves an entire world."

On that day, sitting next to Maestro Conlon was Robert Elias, President of the OREL Foundation, an organization created by Maestro Conlon that has been successful in raising awareness in the academic community of the importance of these composers, and re-instates their rightful place in history. "When Maestro Conlon discovered for himself the music of Zemlinsky and others, there was nothing – no book written, no place where you can read these stories or get any background on these composers. So he created an online resource that musicians could access that has now become a major English language repository of information on suppressed composers and their music."

Inscribed on the wall at the Illinois Holocaust Museum, is a saying by Edmund Burke. "All that is necessary for the triumph of evil is that good men do nothing"

James Conlon is a good man who in doing something, insures that the voices of these Jewish composers are not lost or forgotten in the dusty basements of musical archives. On the contrary, as James Conlon insists, they have been put back to where they truly belong – their rightful place in history, in the 'standard repertoire'. **RICHARD STELLAR.**

BILLY SHERWOOD INTERVIEW

Billy Sherwood is a remarkable man. Of all the people that I have interviewed since I first started my association with Gonzo Multimedia over two years go, I think that Billy is one of the most interesting.

He does so many projects. Just a brief look at his recent workload reveals records with Gene Loves Jezebel, Days Between Stations (on which he proves himself to be a remarkable drummer as well as bass player, guitarist and producer. He also produced the astounding debut album by XNA which has been one of my favourite albums of this last year.

He is possibly best known as having been a member of Yes during the 1990s, and his long-standing relationship with Chris Squire has come back into play recently as he was called back into action with prog rock's longest running soap opera, to do production work on the backing vocals on the band's eagerly awaited new album which is out in July.

He was kind enough to agree to our second interview some weeks ago, but events conspired to thwart us. Everything that could go wrong, did go wrong. The first time I was scheduled to telephone him, I did so at the agreed time, but he was unavoidably delayed somewhere else, and we had to reschedule. The next time – a week later – the delay was entirely my fault. One of my nephews came to visit, and there were various family issues to discuss, some wine was drunk, and I completely forgot all about it or where the time had gone. I sent an apologetic email to Billy asking for yet another reschedule.

The third time, things worked out just dandy. Billy and I had a long and cheerful conversation about his recent activities, and once again I was left in awe at quite how much this pleasant and unassuming man manages to do with his life. He is not only a massively talented musician and producer, but a damned nice fellow as well, and I always enjoy our conversations.

It is telling, and quite the mark of the man, that he told me about his own new solo project (that sounds very interesting indeed) as an afterthought, having forgotten to mention it earlier in our conversation. Not one to shy away from difficult subjects, no matter how high concept, his new solo project sounds as if it is going to be a suitably apocalyptic career highlight. I, for one, can't wait. Listen to our conversation here.

**http://
www.gonzomultimedia.co.u
k/radio/player.php?id=240**

The Gonzo Annual 2015

MEETING CORKY LAING

Corky Laing is one of the more entertaining rock stars that I know to talk to. But who is he? Wash your mind out with soap honey chile! Corky Laing is a legend in his own lunchtime. Over to those jolly nice folks at Wikipedia:

Laurence Gordon "Corky" Laing (born January 26, 1948) is a Canadian rock drummer, best known as a longtime member of pioneering American hard rock band Mountain. A native of Montreal, Quebec, Laing was the youngest in a family of five children. His eldest sister Carol was followed by triplet brothers, Jeffrey, Leslie, and Stephen, and then by Corky. According to Corky, his brothers called him "Gorky" because they could not pronounce his given name "Gordon". "Gorky" eventually morphed into Corky, a moniker which has remained with him throughout his career.

Getting his break playing drums for vocal group The Ink Spots in 1961, he later played in a group called Energy, who were produced by Cream collaborator and Laing's future bandmate Felix Pappalardi. Laing left Energy in 1969 to replace drummer N.D. Smart in hard rock outfit and heavy metal forerunner Mountain, who, with Laing at the drum kit, released three albums and the classic song "Mississippi Queen" between 1970 and 1971.

After the band's first breakup the following year, Laing and Mountain bandmate Leslie West went on to form blues-rock power trio West, Bruce and Laing with former Cream bassist/vocalist Jack Bruce. West, Bruce and Laing produced two studio albums and a live release before Mountain reformed in 1974 and released two more albums, Avalanche and the live Twin Peaks, only to break up again shortly after. The band would once again reconvene in 1985 upon the release of Go For Your Life, and Laing has continued with them to this day, most recently working on the band's 2007 Bob Dylan cover album Masters of War.

But where do I come in? I have been working on a new and updated edition of his volume of rock and roll war stories, *Stick It!* And the other day I had a long telephone conversation with him during which we corrected his proofs, added some pictures and general stuff like that.

In passing he told me about the latest devel-

The Gonzo Annual 2015

opments in his "Playing God" Project. This is such a singular endeavour that I think that I should quote the original press release:

Mountain meets bioethics! The legendary

Corky Laing teams up with two internationally acclaimed philosophers (Prof. Matti Häyry and Dr Tuija Takala) in this joint effort that brings together '70s style music and contemporary moral problems of gene technology. Playing God is a concept album. Playing God is a musical metaphor for today's attempt to attain perfection. Musically the album covers many feels and approaches from soft ballads to riff-driven guitar rock, from meditative instrumentals to operatic melody lines.

Canadian rock star and two Finnish philosophers write an opera together. It doesn't get a better news story than that. I have already spoken to him about the concept of the opera before in these pages and on Gonzo Web Radio, but now the project Has entered a new stage—they are playing it live and I was fascinated to hear how it went. Listen to our conversation here.

http://
www.gonzomultimedia.co.uk/
radio/player.php?id=244

HAWKEASTER 2014

GRAHAM INGLIS: Seaton in East Devon has just seen its second Hawkeaster event, a kind of 'indoor festival' arranged by Hawkwind at the local town hall.

Time was, Hawkwind events were hotbeds of drug usage and generally disappearing in smoke, but this is much more a family event. To the extent even that Mr Dibs apologised after accidently using the f-word on stage!

And during the day the tea and coffee serving hatch saw almost as much trade as the bar - although the latter was offering a beer called "Levitation".

Naturally enough, Hawkwind headlined on both Saturday and Sunday, but - most unusually - did two different sets. With semi-Hawkwind bands The Elves of Silbury Hill and TOSH (Technicians of Spaceship Hawkwind) occupying support slots, and Hawkwind coverband Opusweed on the bill as well, there sure was a lot of Hawkwind material played over the weekend.

Hawkwind's Tim Blake did a solo set, and ex-Hawkwind vocalist Captain Rizz and his band soon followed, with his rhythmic rapping, if one can call it that: "You're all so pretty in the 'hood...!" Red Elektra, a three-piece, provided a break from space-rock as they pursued a more Led Zep type of musical path.

Festival band Here and Now, the offshoot from Gong, played on Day One, and jazz guitarist John Etheridge performed solo on Sunday, and then from time to time during the main Hawkwind performance, adding an excellent dimension to the band's sound.

The Gonzo Annual 2015

Fans wandered around the pubs and cafes of Seaton, many of the shops being open for this somewhat off-season influx of space-rock fans over the Easter weekend. Hotels and guest houses were sold out months ago, but the campsite up on the Seaton Downs ridge was able to accommodate the overflow. A section even provided tepee rental. A sunny Saturday, and a somewhat wet Sunday, but it would have taken a lot more than a bit of rain to dampen the spirits of the Hawkwind family…

PHOTO BY BRIAN TAWN

Picture this page: Graham Inglis

John Etheridge.

The Gonzo Annual 2015

NEIL WILSON WRITES:

Hi,

Saw the request on Facebook… It has been said many times before, by others more eloquent than me, that Hawkwind are not just a band but a family.

I have taken my 13 year old son to probably 12 or so Hawkwind gigs recently including both Hawkeasters and never once have I felt that he was not safe of being looked after, it consistently shines through the people, the music, the place, the atmosphere - everything says that you are part of a collective journey.

Long may it continue.

Picture this page: Graham Inglis

PHOTO BY BRIAN TAWN

The Gonzo Annual 2015

PHOTO BY BRIAN TAWN

The 2014 Hawkeaster was especially relevant to me as it was where for the first time, after many years of wanting but feeling too self conscious, I could let go and really dance free - my legs are still knackered! My wife and daughter are coming to the next gig and hopefully that will set them on the path.

Thanks
Neil

w h i c h w a y i s u p

MICHAL SKWAREK: Welcome HawkFamily.

Our trip to Seaton was a mysterious journey into the unknown. In addition, we will meet some friends do and that will be there Hawkwind. We did not have a clue what will meet us there. Already on Friday evening with Pati realized that happened upon a magical vortex of friendship, kindness, joy, surrounded by great music, people and nature, and of course Hawkwind Seaton. After returning home, we still live those three days and it is hard to return to Bleeeh neither reality ... . Certainly part of our souls has been there forever, but we took a lot of amazing energy with each other. We want to thank the organizers of the event in particular a zone for children, where our son Tim could spend a nice and safe while we gave ourselves a musical ecstasy;).We are very pleased with our son was with us and he could feel so close Hawkwind all this Hawkfamily atmosphere and get to know members of the team , captained by Dave Brock. Was great to meet Howlin' Dibs Hawkwinder, Tim Blake Brian Tawn and many others. Space thanks to Samdance Kirwan,Lucie Mlynar, MoHawk McDouall , Quintin Drake ,Stuart Brown,Darren Prometheus Butler ya know for what ..And all of You !!!That was best Easter time in our lifeThank You

HAWK,PEACE'n'LOVE

PHOTO BY BRIAN TAWN

...and Hunter Ayling had a fantastic time, with Tim Blake (above) and John Etheridge (below). An unspecified prize for the best captions
(Pics: Rob Ayling)

Douglas Harr
Ear Candy for the Hungry Audiophile

Three Friends plus Three

Three Friends performed the music of Gentle Giant at the Cruise to the Edge voyage April 7-12, doing 3 sets on different dates, and in the process reinforcing the preeminent place where Gentle Giant belongs on the progressive rock mantle. I had the chance to see all three shows and interview Gary for Gonzo Weekly magazine, and it's a week I'll never forget. The shows were exciting, diverse, and precise yet rocking, featuring Gary, Malcolm and all their friends, expertly arranging and performing these brilliant compositions.

The full band were led by Gary Green, the guitarist from all Gentle Giant albums, and Malcolm Mortimore who was the drummer on the 1973 album *Three Friends*. As the story goes, after recording the nuanced, boyant drum tracks on that album and beginning the live gigs, Malcolm had to leave mid tour after a motorcycle accident that led to a broken arm and leg. He went on to play with dozens of famous musicians including Ian Dury, Tom Jones, Van Morrison and many others, while the band went on with John Weathers.

For these shows, Gary and Malcolm were joined by a fantastic band of musicians including Charlotte Glasson on violin and winds of all kinds (recently winner of the Best Newcomer Award at Marlborough Jazz Festival,) Neil Angilley on keyboards, who has recently been touring with the

War of the Worlds extravaganza, and Mick Wilson on vocals, who has also been touring with 10CC and as a solo artist, and Jonathan Noyce on bass, known by many from his years playing with Jethro Tull. The band obviously worked hard to master the clever, intricate parts originally played by composer/multi-instrumentalist Kerry Minnear and the Shulman brothers, Derek, Ray, and in the beginning, Phil.

I sat down for a chat with Gary on April 8, 2014 on the voyage:

D: When you look back, at the various stages of the bands career what's your perspective now on the band's history, which ended a couple of years after punk hit in Britain. Your swan song, Civilian, which I saw performed at the Roxy (their last ever show) seemed an apt title and a bit polarizing for fans.

G: Music is a product, like art is a product of who you are at a given time, it does reflect the times – and everything we went through. Certain of the albums were named because of knee jerk reactions– like *In a Glass House* was named precisely that because we felt that anything we were doing would be [shot down] by someone else. So IAGH seemed like a totally appropriate name. For *Free Hand* – we just joined Chrysalis and thought, they're so good for us – they were letting us do what we want, and the music reflected those times. It did change – as a band we got a little frustrated that all our peers where getting fame and playing big gigs and we were lumbering on producing what we thought was good music to deaf ears –there's pressure from the record company a bit to produce a hit, and punk had come out. Ray was always keeping his ears to the ground for what was new and happening and steered it that way. But really the best period was the early-middle third of the band.

D: *Three Friends* seemed like the album where the band was really coming together, after the very experimental *Acquiring the Taste*. And then new drummer Malcolm had to leave the group mid tour.

G: Yes, Malcolm had a motorcycle accident right when we were on an upswing. When John came in a started playing with us it just fell together. Malcolm went on to do a lot better than us – he was with Gary Moore, Ian Dury, and he's done great.

D: The opening track from *Three Friends*, "Prologue," is heard live from New Orleans in 1972 as an extra on the latest re-master of that album – and is performed very aggressively – was your playing different at that time?

G: Oh, the breakneck speed version – there's a certain adrenalin – especially when we were playing an opening set for somebody – we had 40 minutes to do something. If you have a violin and cello opening for Black Sabbath, you had to do that. Then even if it didn't rock, it was enthusiastic!

D: After *Octopus* Phil left, and *In a Glass House* not released in America (though it did great here as an import) What was the impact of that?

G: Phil really was the original leader of Gentle Giant and forged the direction with that statement on *Acquiring the Ta*ste (The statement: "It is our goal to expand the frontiers of contemporary popular music at the risk of being very unpopular") That's complete Phil and though I did not like it too much at the time, now I think that was a great statement to have made because that's really the truth – we lost that kind of literal import to the words and philosophy of the band with Phil's leaving. At the same time he and his the other two brothers were always rubbing up against each other – so it was sometimes difficult to be around all that. When he left, there was an initial "oh my God the band's gonna break up thing" and I think Ray and Derek actually did think that might be it. We loved Phil, but determined he was not critical to the band's live success. We became a very strong 5 piece as a result of that and Derek took to fill his shoes with the lyrics.

D: For live performances, Derek would often sing Kerry's parts – did they agree on that?

G: Kerry does not have a loud voice, and is not a strong live vocal performer – he has a high register with not a lot of force and in those days we had really crappy monitor systems– you couldn't hear it well enough to do it – had it been today

with in ear monitors – different thing probably.

D: With Three Friends did he do some lead vocals?

G: We didn't do a lot of shows – but he did do "Think of Me with Kindness" live which was sweet – with Kerry singing it was lovely.

D: Why did Kerry stop playing in Three Friends?

G: He felt and feels an allegiance to Ray and Derek, who are not terribly happy about us doing this – not

obstructionist, but they are not sentimental about these things. Kerry decided in respect to that he could not faithfully continue – and he never liked playing live a lot and hated travel – we went to Japan to Canada and he remembered "I don't like this." For me, I think, yes they wrote the music, but it took me and John to inject a lot of life to it – great work takes some great interpretation.

P1000245D: Do you think you will take this band out again?

G: Yes we are going week after next to Portugal – a nice little festival. The band does not play a lot purely because everybody is busy doing other projects. Everyone is busy doing other stuff. Mick is with 10CC – Jon Noyce [with several projects]. Neil Angilley with the *War of the Worlds* tour – phenomenal stuff. Honestly so many promoters we talk to want to say "we'd like to have you but we want to call it Gentle Giant" and I won't have that cause it

isn't because there's only that one Gentle Giant and there could never be another one. But there could be really good interpretations of the music by people who know how to play it and love to play it.

D: It seems this music can live on like classical music played into the future.

G: I think so and it deserves to, you know, and that was my and Malcolm's whole reason for doing this again – yeah there was a resurgence of interest because of the internet and everybody enjoyed that – but I never felt Giant music in its day got a wide enough listen, and even those who heard it perhaps didn't quite get it, and time has moved on and perhaps there's another generation or two who have decided that Gentle Giant has subtle influences on what they've done. I'd like to say "okay then, this is how it's supposed to be played," while I can still do it and I love doing it. I'm totally respectful of the music. Some of the recordings really irk me- I listen to it and think "I really rushed that phrase" – so now there's a chance to correct some of those things and I find that really cool! It's not to be perfect, but music lives and music deserves to be heard – especially this as its very wide ranging – Giants music – its got many styles and it goes to many emotional areas and I find that fascinating. And it's a complete challenge to play. When you play something like "Schooldays" live it's a bastard of a tune to play really and when you pull it off it's like climb-

ing a hill and thinking – I didn't have a heart attack!

D: There has been a lot of reissue work and scraping of the barrel – both audio and video, which is so important to us who did not see those shows

G: I was the archivist for the video – I was the one who went to the BBC after the show saying we need a copy of that. There is not any more that I've found – wish there were. We are talking ancient history – there's little video back then.

D: Are you involved in the Steve Wilson re-master of *Power and the Glory?*

G: The rights to *Power and the Glory* have reverted back to us – so we own it thank God, and we don't own all of them by any means, but this we've got and Steve Wilson is working on it with Ray for a 5.1 surround sound remix – I'm as anxious to hear that as anyone else cause I love that album

D: How did it come to pass that the "title track" single was left off the LP?

G: It was made as a single – it was obviously and determinedly meant as a single but it seemed to me and all of us that it's not really part of the album.

D: In preparing for the Three Friends shows, what's been hardest or most rewarding track to go back and play now?

G: "Schooldays" is very rewarding – we did it only a few times back then – we had decided it was not a good thing for a live audience because often times we were opening up for somebody. It's good for a headliner where you have an audience and do what you want. Also now the technology is so different – it's a whole different world of noises and the monitors are good – better at least. We just learned "The Moon is Down" – I never played on it originally – the guitar you hear is Ray and now I'm singing it with Mick – I'm not a great singer but I'm giving it a go! A lot of them are hard to play and some are challenging or both – the best might be "Free Hand" which is both.

Gary's words rang so sincerely during the three sets that unfolded over the week. For the record, included in one of more of the shows was a cross section of some of the most complex and rewarding prog rock ever committed to record:

"Alucard" / *Gentle Giant* (1970)
"Pantagruel's Nativity", "The Moon is Down", "Wreck", and "The House The Street The Room" / *Acquiring The Taste (1971)*
"Prologue", "Schooldays", "Mr. Class and Quality", "Three Friends" / *Three Friends* (1972)
"The Advent of Panurge", "The Boys in the Band", "Think of Me With Kindness" / *Octopus* (1972)
"In a Glass House" / In a Glass House (1973)
"Proclamation", "Playing the Game" / *Power and the Glory* (1974)
"Free Hand", "Just the Same", "Mobile" / *Free Hand* (1975)
"I Lost My Head" / *Interview* (1976)

It was beyond expectations that a band of such diverse musicians could pull off these tracks with such accuracy and enthusiasm. The only thing that felt missing at all was Kerry's vibraphones, though they were replicated by Neil's exciting performances on keyboards. Also for this fan the lack of medleys was a real plus as I'd always felt some of those detracted from the original compositions. Top that off with the set lists being so faithful to the core period of Giant's catalog after so many years and you realized this was a new historical milestone for this music.

Hopefully not the last voyage for these many friends.

There are nine Henrys, purported to be the world's first cloned cartoon character. They live in a strange lo-fi domestic surrealist world peopled by talking rock buns and elephants on wobbly stilts.

They mooch around in their minimalist universe suffering from an existential crisis with some genetically modified humour thrown in. I think Peter McAdam is one of the funniest people around, and I cannot recommend his book The Nine Henrys highly enough. Each issue we run a Henrybit about the nine cloned cartoon characters who inhabit a surreal world nearly as insane as mine...

THE NINE HENRYS

The Nine Henrys are a quirky bunch of cloned cartoon characters.
They live in a strange lo-fi domestic surrealist world peopled by talking rock buns and elephants on wobbly stilts.
Over the years the Henrys have been published in a variety of local NE magazines and now here for the first time thanks to Gonzo Multi-Media the Nine Henrys are brought together in a compendium of line art craziness.

"a five ya aad can draw better than that"
Authors brother.

THE WORLDS FIRST CLONED CARTOON CHARACTER   modada@ninehenrys.com

An audience with
René van Commenée &
David Jackson

As regular readers of my inky fingered scribblings here and elsewhere will be aware I have a soft spot for Dutch performance artist René van Commenée who performs under the *nom de guerre* of 'Mr Averell'.

He wrote to me the other day giving details of a record that is imminently being released by Gonzo.

In 1992, when he was halfway through his forties, the legendary Van der Graaf Generator saxophonist David Jackson left teaching full time to practice, write, record and play gigs again. He created a one-man show of new and old historic pieces; some he had reworked in his studio and were never performed live before. At that time, Jackson had been seeing and keeping up with his young Dutch friend René van Commenée and knew of his percussive powers at the time.

"He had recently spent a whole night at our house in Wokingham in the room below our bedroom practicing for an immanent 24 hour Indian Tabla exam - which was a strange and exhilarating sound to wake up with!" (D. Jackson)

Van Commenée invited his legendary friend to perform at his birthday-party. Jackson took the invitation and insisted to perform, at least a part of the show, together.

Both musicians enjoyed performing together very much and Van Commenée proposed playing duo-shows together a year later.

" In Utrecht I felt a strange Hammill/VdGG connection kicking in. Something strange and magical would be happening very soon. This was great chance to play gigs with René at last. He loved my new repertoire and we loved to improvise together." (D. Jackson)

They were booked in a theatre at the center of "The Institute of Mental Health" in Utrecht, funny enough the title of an early Peter Hammill track (co-written with Judge Smith, a librettist and composer with whom both Jackson and Van Commenée worked together many times) on which Jackson played the saxes in the seventies.

At the shows Jackson came with his whole arsenal Saxes, flutes, the EMS soundbeam and electronics. Van Commenée had an incredible drum and percussion set up with drums and metals collected from all over the world and played in lotus seat, not using his feet!

"It was a bit distracting! How did he make it all happen and sound so good!?" (D. Jackson)
The gigs were lovely! The crew and audience were just great. That magic atmosphere is captured along with a great live-recorded sound. 'Batteries Included' is actually 21. It has come of age and it is the perfect time to distribute it again.

"Jackson is an incredible musician; unpredictable, original, a master of the double horns, a great pleasure to work with both on stage and in the studio. The percussion set I used at that time was a beast to conquer but Jackson gave me wings!" (R. van Commenée)

David Jackson's sax and double-sax wizardry with a strong and original drums and cymbal accompaniment is finally available in record stores around the world and can be ordered directly from Gonzo Multimedia.

Would I like to interview him and David, he asked. Of course I would, I eagerly said, even though it meant getting out of bed at an unfeasibly early hour on a Sunday morning.

However, as I will be the first to admit, I am no good with time zones and invariably mess them up. Sadly I did so on this occasion as well, and on top of it all our telephone system had finally given up the ghost after months of instability.

So, half asleep, and squatting on the milking stool in the kitchen with a half grown kitten and a neurotic terrier jostling for position on my lap, I managed to have an immensely entertaining half hour conversation with them, which covered all sorts of arcane topics.

http://www.gonzomultimedia.co.uk/radio/player.php?id=251

The Gonzo Annual 2015

EXCLUSIVE INTERVIEW WITH KEITH LEVENE

Just as we were putting this issue to bed we had a phone call.

In fact that was a lie, just as Corinna was putting this issue to bed and I was in my home studio recording backing vocals with the ever-talented Mike Davies, we had a phone call. It was our old pal the multi-talented and ever-entertaining Keith Levene, the original guitar slinger with both The Clash and Public Image Ltd. He has always been one of my favourite guitarists because he is one of the few purveyors of that instrument in the history of rock and roll who has actually gone out and done something different with it and in doing so re-defining both the instrument and the role of the guitarist for a new generation. Whilst not a virtuoso in the conventional sense of the word, to me he is up there with people like Les Paul, George Harrison and the dude from Radiohead who have all left their own idiosyncratic mark upon the culture that we call rock and roll.

Keith wanted to talk about the latest developments in his ongoing quest to get his visionary project Commerical Zone finally released in a form with which he is happy.

For those not in the know, Commercial Zone was originally intended to be the fourth Public Image album but for reasons that are not relevant to this issue of Gonzo Weekly there was a parting of the ways between Messrs Levene and Lydon and the rump PiL released an album culled from the sessions called This is What you Want, This is What you Get. Levene was so disappointed with this record that he released his own version (often described as a bootleg, but apparently with Richard Branson's blessing) calling it Commercial Zone.

This provoked legal complications, which after 30-odd years are so convoluted and so internecine that it is difficult to know what exactly happened. Anyway it doesn't really matter.

For three decades Commercial Zone has hung round Levene's neck like the corpse of an albatross (no pun intended) and Levene has been planning to finish it in the way he originally intended for decades. We had a long conversation about it that you can listen to here.

http://www.gonzomultimedia.co.uk/radio/player.php?id=247

Nick Calvert (son of Robert) writes:

Hi all,

Right, I did promise this group i'd sort The Kidout at some point. I'm a man of my word, but a little late sometimes.

Here are parts one and two of the full recording, there are seven parts in total, I'll do the rest over the coming weeks.

I hope there are those in this group that enjoy it.

As there is some new content to release again, like last year I'm going to try and raise a few quid for charity in August. I also found the test pressing of Test Tube Conceived and the (sadly quite battered) signed Freq over the long weekend, having thought I'd lost them, so these will be sold on eBay shortly. Also Bob's own copy of Road Hawks, which I think has an angry correction to the 'Drug Cabinet Key' name in Biro, which amused me.

To spread the love, any proceeds will go to Arts Emergency (http://www.arts-emergency.org/) this time - which is a fantastic charity, have a read up.

Just to be clear - this is the fan released VHS from the 80s. Someone has gone to a lot of trouble to stitch it all up with linking material, but I have no idea who. If anyone has names so I can credit them, then please let me know.

Nick Calvert

**Part One
https://www.youtube.com/watch?v=ZSvCssyAgAU**

**Part Two
https://www.youtube.com/watch?v=s_-d62BgsGU**

JOURNEY TO THE CENTRE OF THE MIRTH

Who says that prog rockers are humourless bastards? Everyone, that's who.

Even today, most of the articles that have been written about the current Rick Wakeman tour, go on about the hubris off the heyday of progressive rock back in the 1970s.

But no-one ever gets the point that it was often quite tongue in cheek.

I remember seeing *Pink Floyd* at Earls Court back in 1995 on the Division Bell Tour, and being impressed by the silly bits, like the whole band donning Groucho Marx glasses, cigars and moustaches for one song. OK I was slightly stoned at the time, but I am sure that I didn't make it up.

And 'Alan's Psychedelic Breakfast' and the pig with big bollocks. Of course these people were laughing both at themselves and at those who took it all too seriously And with Rick W, surely no-one takes things like the ice dancers at the original King Arthur shows at Wembley wearing stockings and suspenders as a serious comment on the feminist subtext of Geoffrey of Monmouth.

Of course it was tongue in cheek. Its not the prog rockers who are the humourless bastards (as this photo taken last week at an un-named venue on the latest RW tour shows)

It is not the prog rockers who don't have a sense of humour, but those both in and out of Her Majesty's Press who take the subject (and themselves) too bloody seriously.

Lighten up guys,

H.R.GIGER (1940-2014)

Giger was born in 1940 in Chur, capital city of Graubünden, the largest and easternmost Swiss canton. His father, a chemist, viewed art as a "breadless profession" and strongly encouraged him to enter pharmaceutics, Giger recalls. Yet he moved in 1962 to Zürich, where he studied Architecture and industrial design at the School of Applied Arts until 1970. Giger had a relationship with Swiss actress Li Tobler until she committed suicide in 1975. He married Mia Bonzanigo in 1979; they separated a year and a half later.

Giger's style and thematic execution were influential. His design for the Alien was inspired by his painting Necronom IV and earned him an Oscar in 1980. His books of paintings, particularly Necronomicon and Necronomicon II (1985) and the frequent appearance of his art in Omni magazine continued his rise to international prominence. Giger is also well known for artwork on several music recording albums.

Giger's most distinctive stylistic innovation was that of a representation of human bodies and machines in a cold, interconnected relationship, he described as "biomechanical". His main influences were painters Ernst Fuchs and Salvador Dalí. He met Salvador Dalí, to whom he was introduced by painter Robert Venosa. He was also a personal friend of Timothy Leary. Giger suffered from night terrors and his paintings are all to some extent inspired by his experiences with that particular sleep disorder. He studied interior and industrial design at the School of Commercial Art in Zurich (from 1962 to 1965) and made his first paintings as a means of art therapy

In 1998 Giger acquired the Château St. Germain in Gruyères, Switzerland, and it now houses the H. R. Giger Museum, a permanent repository of his work. The artist lived and worked in Zürich with his wife, Carmen Maria Scheifele Giger, who is the Director of the H.R. Giger Museum.

On 12 May 2014, Giger died in a hospital in Zürich after having suffered injuries in a fall

1991: as it was the 700th year since the birth of Switzerland (1291), a Swiss TV Quiz Show called "TellStar" was looking for only Swiss topics. So I registered myself with the topic "HR Giger". As a graphic designer and great fan of HRG, my final goal was not really the TV show, but having the chance to meet Mr HR Giger personnally... what happened a few weeks before the show in his home in Zurich.

Ok... then I did the TV show... and (as he was a very shy person... National TV had invited him to be guest on that very show... but he denied...) I know from himself that he has been watching the show at home... and after he told me he was more nervous than I was in the live show...!!

In the meantime Clepsydra was already working at its first album. They had decided the album title: "Hologram". And of course we wanted a "real" hologram for the cover...!!

I spent about a week calling around in Switzerland, Germany and also Austria looking for the right person able to produce a real hologram that would fullfill our expectations. In the end the best one was Mr Ralph Kühne in Zurich.

Next problem: To produce a hologram you need a real object..!! So Lele told me: "Why don't you ask your friend HRG...?"

Said. Done. I called him, and yes, he had an object that would fit perfectly for our needs...!!
In the next few months Lele and I did meet HR Giger along with Ralph Kühne a couple of times in Zurich to discuss and fix the details of the production of our hologram.

All 1000 holograms of the first release of the album "Hologram" has been "handmade" by Mr Ralph Kühne in his little laboratory in his cellar.

As a matter of fact, HR Giger discovered this hologram-technique because of us. In the next few years he worked several times again with Ralph Kühne, integrating hologram images into his outstanding paintings and sculptures.

Thank you HR Giger...!

Sandor Kwiatkowski

Rob Ayling writes: I loved what he did for ELP and his Alien was my alien, the others never scared me as much as his did. He was a true artist, not only his original artwork, but how he conducted himself. I wish I had met him! RIP HR, see you in the next life

Barbara Dickson
Interview

The Gonzo Annual 2015

I have been a rock and roll journalist, man and boy for over three decades now, and have been privileged enough to interview many luminaries from John Paul Jones of Led Zeppelin to Dave Brubeck, and from Steve Ignorant to Ken Campbell, and I wouldn't even presume to try to rank my interviewees in importance.

But in the two years since I have been doing my own particular brand of Gonzo Journalism there is one artist who far more people want to know about and are impressed that I have interviewed, than anyone else. It is Barbara Dickson.

With a long and stellar career, during which she has been the doyen of Scottish folk music, the queen of light entertainment, collected songs of the Jacobite rebellion, and the First World War, and has carried a torch for the songs of Gerry Rafferty (amongst many other achievements).

Sadly, whenever I mention on Facebook that I have spoken to her, one or other of my more idiotic family, friends, or acquaintances always ask whether that means "I Know Her So Well". Actually, we have never met in person, but I always enjoy talking to her.

For those of you not aware of her achievements, here is a brief potted biography.

As a multi-million selling recording artist with an equally impressive Olivier-Award-winning acting career, Barbara Dickson OBE has firmly established herself as one of the most enduring and popular entertainers in Britain today.

Born in Dunfermline, Scotland, Barbara showed an early interest in music. By the tender age of five she had already started studying piano and by twelve had also taken up the guitar. She developed a love of folk music whilst at school, and began to perform at her local folk club. At seventeen she moved to Edinburgh, combining a job in the civil service with evening spots performing in local pubs and clubs.

In 1968 Barbara was offered a three-week engagement at the Tivoli Gardens in Copenhagen, Denmark, and when she was refused leave from her job she resigned, deciding that it was 'now or never' to try her luck as a professional singer.

The late '60s and early '70s saw her gradually 'paying her dues' on the Scottish folk scene, building a reputation and working with the likes of Archie Fisher, Billy Connolly, Gerry Rafferty and Rab Noakes. Her first album, The Fate o' Charlie, a collection of Jacobite songs recorded with Archie and John McKinnon, was released on Bill Leader's Trailer Records label in 1969. She then went on to record three well-received folk albums for Decca Records in the early '70s.

On the advice of Scottish performing legend Hamish Imlach, Barbara next began to look for opportunities south of the border in the booming folk scene of the north of England and she was soon well-established there.

It was in Liverpool that she became re-acquainted with musician and playwright Willy Russell. Their friendship led to Barbara being offered the singing role in his 1974 musical John, Paul, George, Ringo… and Bert, staged at the Everyman Theatre. Barbara was on stage throughout the entire performance, singing the songs of the Beatles at the piano. The show became a huge critical success and went on to enjoy a long run at the Lyric Theatre in London.

In the West End, the show was co-produced by Robert Stigwood, who signed Barbara to his small stable of artistes at RSO Records, which also included The Bee Gees and Cream.

In 1976 she had her first hit single with Answer Me, produced by fellow Scot, Junior Campbell, and later that year she appeared on The Two Ronnies having been spotted in the theatre by Terry Hughes, their then producer at the BBC. This led to a guest residency on the show, which was drawing in regular Saturday night audiences in excess of 15 million viewers. Tim Rice and Andrew Lloyd Webber had also been impressed by Barbara's performance in John, Paul, George, Ringo… and Bert, and invited her to sing Another Suitcase in Another Hall on the original cast recording of their new musical Evita. Released as a single, the song went on to become her second hit single in 1977.

In 1980 Caravan Song from the film Caravans was released. Although it was to prove much less of a chart success than her other hit singles, it is still Barbara's most requested song wherever she plays.

January, February, released the same year, provided another Top 20 recording, with the accompanying LP, The Barbara Dickson Album, produced by Alan Tarney, giving Barbara her first gold album.

In 1982 All for a Song, her first compilation album, shot into the UK charts at No.9, based on sales in Scotland alone. It was her first platinum-selling album and went on to spend 38 weeks in the charts.

Barbara then accepted the leading role of Mrs Johnstone in Willy Russell's new musical Blood Brothers, which opened in Liverpool at the Playhouse Theatre in January 1983. The show, which marked her debut as an actress, transferred to London's Lyric Theatre and she was named 'Best Actress in a Musical' at the 1984 Society of West End Theatre Awards.

In tandem with her stage work, Barbara was also building a considerable reputation as a concert artiste, with lengthy sold-out tours that took her to every major town and city in the UK, culminating in shows at the Royal Albert Hall in London.

In 1985 the duet I Know Him So Well was released. This was recorded with Elaine Paige and taken from the new musical Chess, written by Benny Andersson, Bjorn Ulvaeus and Tim Rice. It went on to become a Top Ten hit around the world and sold over 900,000 copies. Barbara's subsequent Gold album, released later that year, was certified Platinum.

Further hits followed but in the 1990s Barbara began to move away from the pop scene and back towards acoustic and folk music. This resulted in the 1992 album Don't Think Twice, It's All Right, a selection of the songs of Bob Dylan and 1994's Parcel of Rogues, featuring folk music from the British Isles. 1995 saw the release of Dark End of the Street, which combined traditional music with tracks by favourite songwriters including Randy Newman, Sandy Denny and Jackson Browne.

During the 90s, Barbara also began to diversify more and more into acting, with major roles on TV including Taggart, Kay Mellor's award-winning Band of Gold and The Missing Postman, directed by Alan Dossor.

For many years, Barbara and Blood Brothers director Chris Bond had talked of working together again for the theatre and finally in 1996 this culminated in The Seven Ages of Woman, a musical walk through the life of 'everywoman.' The show toured the UK twice, in the process earning Barbara some of the best reviews of her career as well as the 1997 Liverpool Echo 'Best Actress in Theatre' Award. In 1999 Barbara was delighted to return to the theatre again in the new musical Spend, Spend, Spend, based on the life of the infamous 1960s pools winner, Viv Nicholson. Her role as Viv won her the 'Best Actress in a Musical' at the 2000 Laurence Olivier Awards in London.

In 2004 she released her first studio album for eight years, Full Circle. Produced by Troy Donockley, it was widely acclaimed as a long-awaited return to her musical roots with The Daily Telegraph noting: 'it is no exaggeration to describe Barbara as a great singer. She stood out a mile among the Scottish folk singers of her generation, and she has consistently shown her class when performing for a wider public. This is Dickson at her most engaging.'

Her follow-up CD, Nothing's Gonna Change My World, released by Universal in the autumn of 2006, took its title from Across the Universe, the Beatles classic included amongst a specially commissioned selection of the songs Lennon, McCartney and Harrison. The album was arranged by Troy and produced by Chris Hughes.

In 2007 Barbara was invited to guest on Channel 4's long-running quiz show Countdown and she returned to television again the following year with a leading guest role in the BBC drama series Doctors.

2008 was to prove a busy year for Barbara. Her latest CD, Time and Tide, was released, featuring the new direction that has become a feature of her music, blending together old and new songs with a distinctive atmosphere prevailing throughout. The varied song choice included Lady Franklin's Lament, Goin' Back and Palm Sunday, which marked her first writing collaboration with Troy, who again produced the album.

Into the Light, Barbara's first ever live DVD was also released to coincide with Time and Tide, and featured some of her best-loved hits, tracks from the new album and other favourites she has made her own through the years.

Barbara was then invited to perform The Sky Above the Roof for O Thou Transcendent, award-winning film director Tony Palmer's film about the life of composer Ralph Vaughan Williams, described by The Observer as 'a mesmerising masterpiece'.

On BBC's Songs of Praise in April 2008 Barbara performed a new arrangement of the beautiful hymn My Song is Love Unknown.

In the summer of 2008 she played live at the Stonehaven Folk Festival, her first festival appearance since 1973 and an experience she enjoyed immensely. In August that year she and Troy performed Smile in front of an audience of 9000 people at the Liverpool Unites concert at the city's Echo Arena, helping to raise funds for the charity set up by the parents of murdered schoolboy Rhys Jones.

In September 2008 Barbara performed live in Ireland. Her sell-out concert in front of a capacity crowd at Dublin's National Concert Hall marked her first concert in the city for 21 years and following the warm welcome she and her band received, plans are being drawn up for a return to Ireland for further dates in the near future.

In December 2008 Barbara was invited to record her first Christmas special for BBC Radio Scotland, produced by her old friend Rab Noakes.

A lengthy UK tour at the start of 2009 was followed by invitations to perform at the prestigious International Eisteddfod Festival in Llangollen, as well as the Brampton Live and the Linlithgow Folk Festivals.

Barbara's long-awaited autobiography, A Shirt Box Full of Songs, was published by Hachette Scotland in October 2009. To tie in with its release Barbara undertook a major promotional tour with appearances on TV and radio, and at book festivals across the UK to talk about her life and career.

Following a 26-date national concert tour between February and March 2010, Barbara began work on her new studio album, The Magical West, for the Greentrax label, which will follow on from her recent musical collaboration with Troy Donockley, including some newly-written tracks of her own and songs from her 'shirt box' which she has always wanted to record. The album is due for release in late 2010.

Barbara has also recently presented a new series called Scotland on Song with Barbara Dickson for BBC Radio Scotland, featuring music from the acoustic/roots/ folk scene in Scotland with guests performing live in the studio each week. A new series is planned for later this year.

Married with three sons, Barbara lives in Lincolnshire. She has been made an Honorary Doctor of Music by Robert Gordon University in Aberdeen as well as a Fellow of Liverpool's John Moores University and a Companion of the Liverpool Institute of Performing Arts bestowed by Sir Paul McCartney. In 2002 HM the Queen's Silver Jubilee Year, Barbara was conferred with an O.B.E. for her services to music and drama.

Now in her 42nd year in the music business, Barbara continues to do what she loves best - performing live for her loyal audience. 'Singing live is really the kernel of what I do,' she explains, 'Finally, after all these years I'm now in a position where I'm entirely responsible for what I sing - and I'm happier than ever!'

http://www.gonzomultimedia.co.uk/radio/player.php?id=257

Roger Dean prepares the limited edition etching for the new Rick Wakeman box set

Hello everybody.

Unfortunately there were some errors made in the original announcement about the prints for which we apologize and now fully clarify below.
Firstly, the prints are hand printed etchings and are not machine made lithographs, which makes them considerably more exclusive than we first stated. To complement the boxed set, some images showing the etching in process will be available on line from this address.

Secondly, regarding the size of the edition, the correct size is 200 plus 10 artist's proofs, making 210 copies in total. On completion of the edition the etching plate was destroyed, ensuring that no further copies can be made.

The etchings are to be numbered 1/200 to 200/200 and signed by both Rick Wakeman and Roger Dean. A total of 150 are to be sold from the Rick Wakeman Emporium as part of the Super Deluxe Collectors' Edition.

If you have already ordered and paid for one of these boxed sets and are unhappy with these corrections, please contact us to arrange a full refund.

On an entirely separate matter, Rick felt the original price for the standard Limited Edition Box Set (i.e. without the print) was set too high for the fans, so it will now be £99.99.

Anyone who has ordered one of these items need take no action, they will be charged the correct amount at the point of dispatch

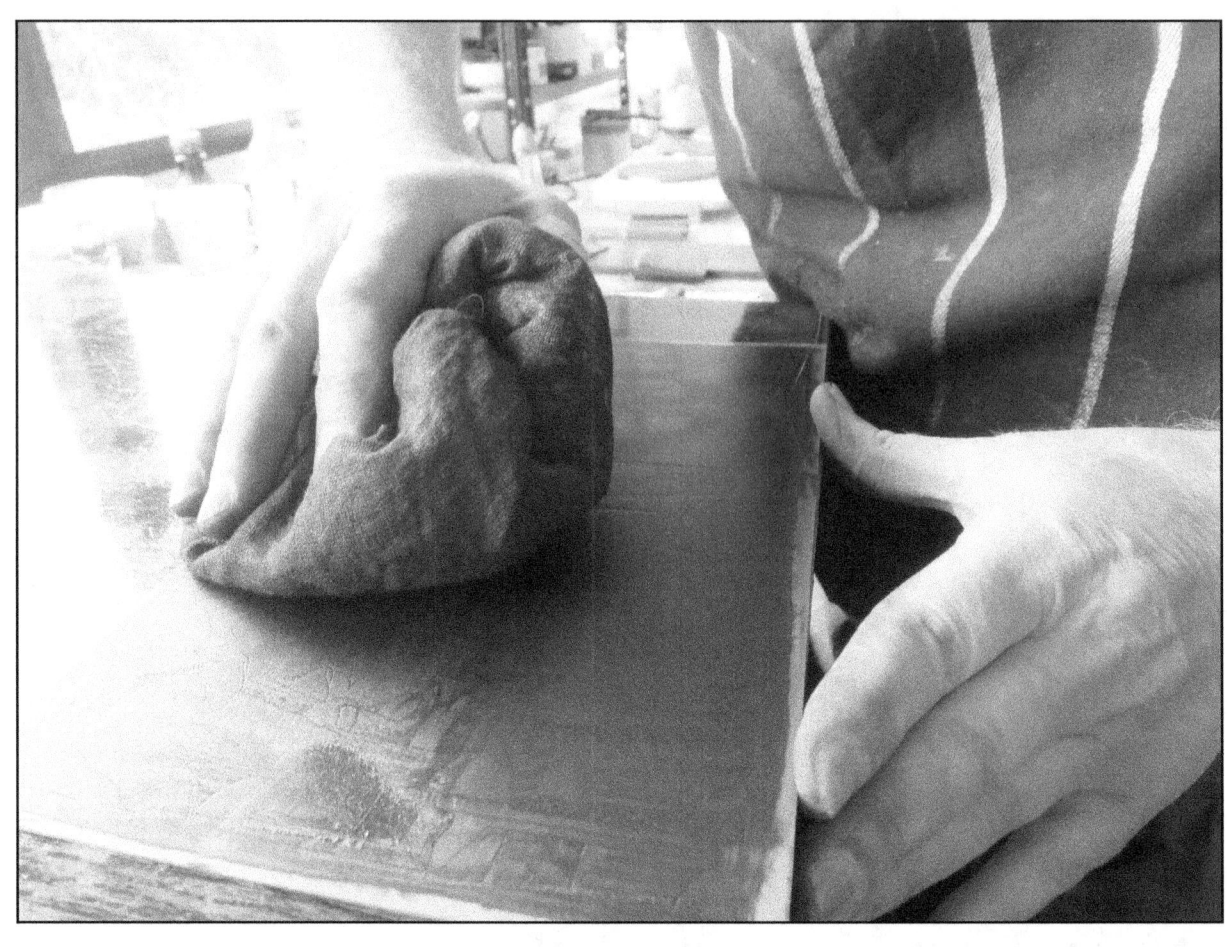

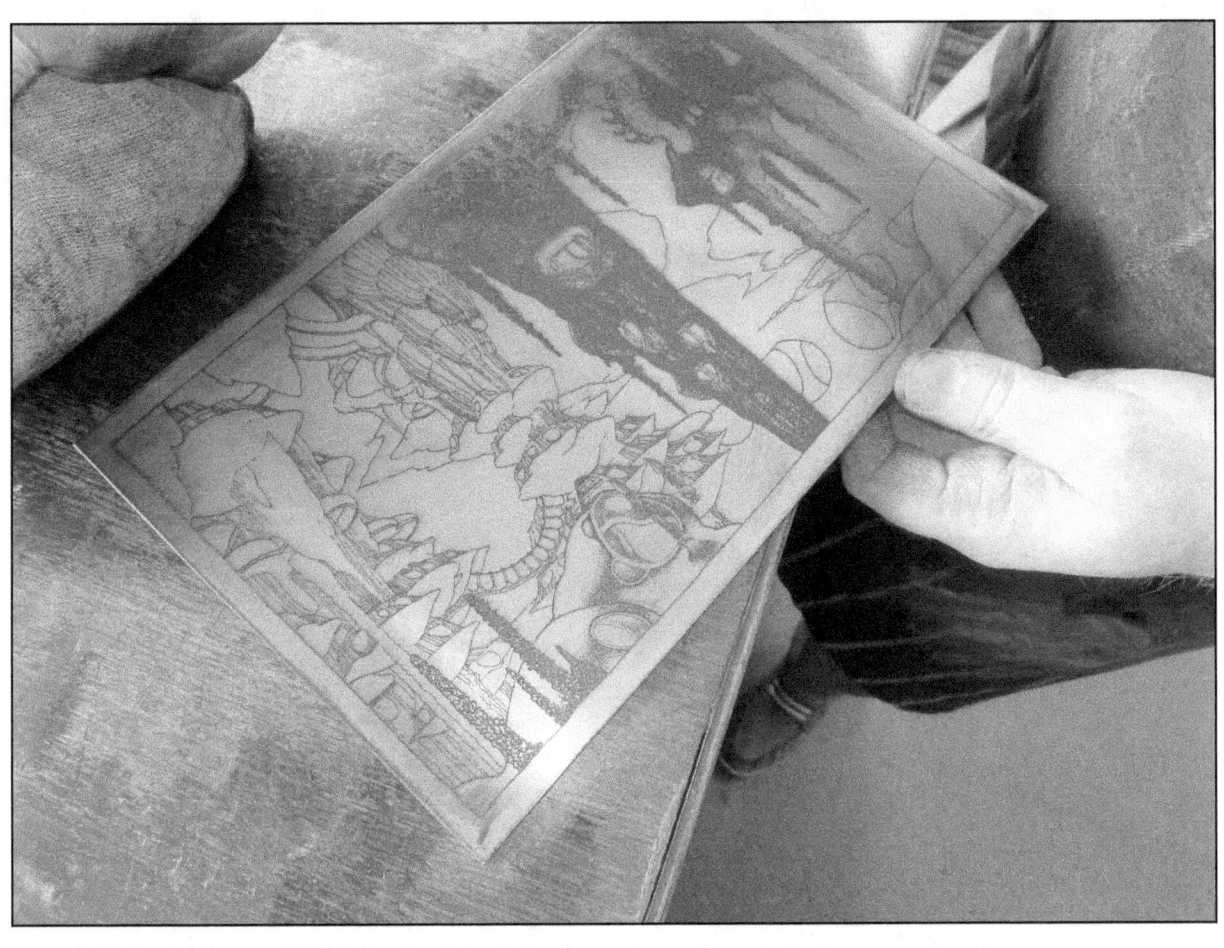

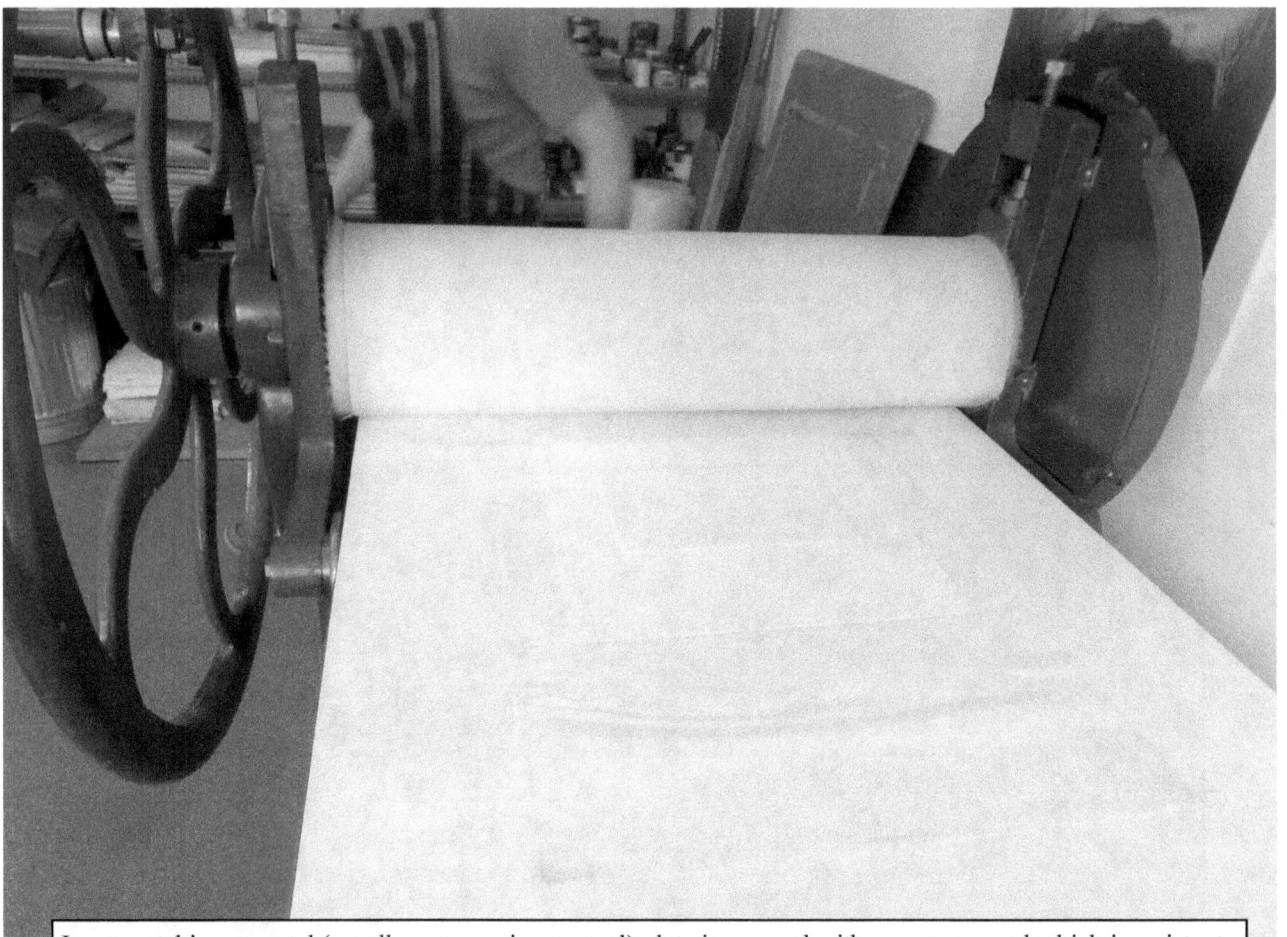

In pure etching, a metal (usually copper, zinc or steel) plate is covered with a waxy ground which is resistant to acid. The artist then scratches off the ground with a pointed etching needle where he or she wants a line to appear in the finished piece, so exposing the bare metal. The échoppe, a tool with a slanted oval section, is also used for "swelling" lines. The plate is then dipped in a bath of acid, technically called the mordant (French for "biting") or etchant, or has acid washed over it. The acid "bites" into the metal (it dissolves part of the metal) where it is exposed, leaving behind lines sunk into the plate. The remaining ground is then cleaned off the plate. The plate is inked all over, and then the ink wiped off the surface, leaving only the ink in the

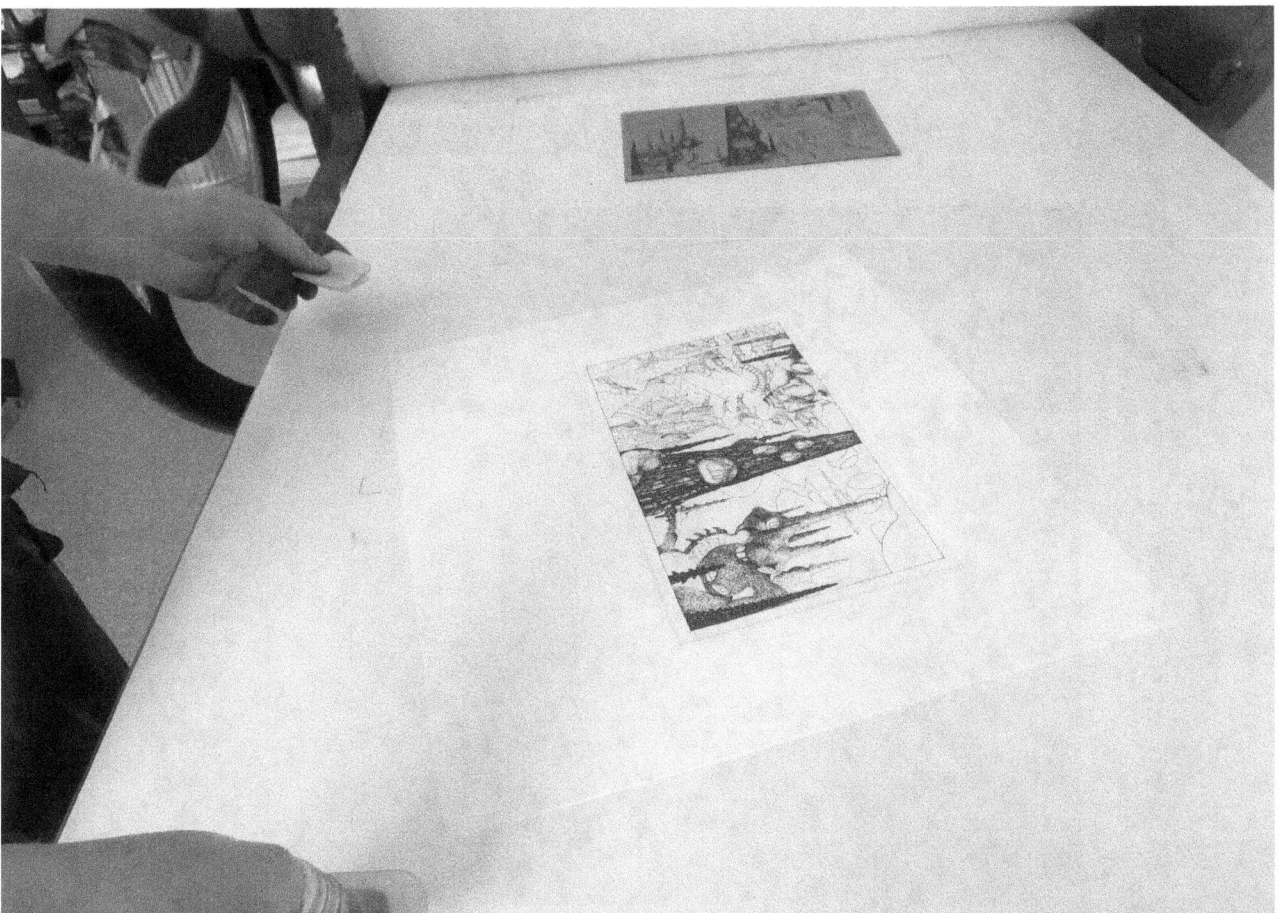

Etching by goldsmiths and other metal-workers in order to decorate metal items such as guns, armour, cups and plates has been known in Europe since the Middle Ages at least, and may go back to antiquity. The elaborate decoration of armour, in Germany anyway, was an art probably imported from Italy around the end of the 15th century—little earlier than the birth of etching as a printmaking technique.

The process as applied to printmaking is believed to have been invented by Daniel Hopfer (circa 1470–1536) of Augsburg, Germany. Hopfer was a craftsman who decorated armour in this way, and applied the

AN AUDIENCE WITH IGS

It was the late summer or early autumn of 1982. I was still young and idealistic enough to think that my peculiar talents would flourish within the National Health Service where I was working as a student nurse caring for people who only a few years ago had been described as being mentally subnormal who - in the white moral heat of Thatcherism – had just been dubbed the mentally handicapped.

I had recently discovered the music and philosophy of a bunch of musicians and artists who lived in a free community in Essex. They worked under the collective name of Crass, and they introduced me to a heady brand of anarchism, pacifism, vegetarianism and various other 'isms', which have permeated my life path ever since.

All the way through my life I have done things which, in hindsight, I explained with the phrase 'well I thought it was a good idea at the time', and it was one of these ideas which led me to taking a party of mentally handicapped young people from a hostel outside Dawlish to see Crass playing a very loud, and spirited performance at St George's Hall in Exeter. Afterwards I met guitarist Andy Palmer, who applauded the fact that I had brought my charges with me to the show. He introduced me to other band members including singer Steve Ignorant.

Crass fell apart a couple of years later, and I fell apart about five years after that, finally leaving the NHS in the spring of 1990. Whilst I had no contact with any of them after the autumn of 1982 I kept vaguely in touch with what the various ex-members of Crass were doing, and was happy to see Steve Ignorant do whatever the anarchist equivalent of the Victor Ludorum lap of honour is with one final world tour, before leaving the music of Crass firmly in the past. When I started working for Gonzo a couple of years ago I started writing about the solo efforts of Carol Hodge, the singer in Steve Ignorant's Last Supper band, and after recommending her to Rob Ayling, she was signed to Gonzo.

Carol kept me in the loop as to the further activities of Steve's, including the new band they had formed together with two other members of Carol's Manchester-based rock band, called a Steve Ignorant Slice of Life.

Through Carol I eventually interviewed Steve, who had remembered the day that Crass and the residents of Botchill Hostel had partied together in Exeter so many years before, and written it up in his immensely entertaining and insightful autobiography.

The universe is an extraordinary complex organism. As I become older I become far more pantheistic and believe that if there is a God, it is the universe itself. The universe being God, does indeed move in extraordinary ways, and if you had told the 24-year-old Jonathan that the 55-year-old Jonathan would not only be chatting with Steve Ignorant on a fairly regular basis, but would be working together with him on the packaging of the Gonzo release of two of his DVDs, he just would not have believed me. I wonder what the universe has in store for us all next .....

JON: So how much of The Slice of Life stuff has been recorded?

STEVE: We recorded about eight tracks but we've got to come in to re-do a couple of them 'cause we didn't use a clip track and it came out a bit quick. So I'll be going to re-do just a couple and then basically it's just a matter of mixing it all.

JON: So what's going to come out; an EP, an

Pic: Stephen Wardle

The Gonzo Annual 2015

album or what?

STEVE: Well, it's gonna be a CD with eight tracks on it – some spoken word, bits in between – and a little booklet. So, yeah, an eight-track CD thing.

JON: That's brilliant. What sort of time frame are we talking about?

STEVE: Well, hopefully not too long. I mean, definitely before August so that doesn't leave us much time but it's really when and where we can; I can't really give you a time thing on it but I'm hoping to have it done; it should be out hopefully before August.

JON: I'm really looking forward to hearing it because the bits I've heard on YouTube are bloody fantastic.

STEVE: Yeah, thanks. Yeah, yeah.

JON: I love your version of the Bowie song

STEVE: Yeah, we recorded but we won't put it on this, though; I might save that for later. [LAUGHS]

JON: I think it's really good. It was totally not what I was expecting. 'Cause Carol actually told me about a week before I heard it that you were doing it but you know, it came out completely different to how I expected.

STEVE: Oh! Were you expecting it to be closer to the Bowie version or –

JON: I don't know what I was expecting. I just wasn't expecting it to be like that. It was really moving.

STEVE: Oh right. Right. Well, yeah, I think what I tried to do was, you know, our version of it, something that blended in with the rest of what we were doing so it didn't stand out too much. That was always my concern; was that it would be sort of too separate, if you know what I mean. So I think from what you're saying we managed to achieve that.

JON: Well, Diamond Dogs was always my favourite era of Bowie. I really loved that album.

STEVE: Yeah.

JON: So what else are you doing at the moment?

STEVE: Well, Obviously, Slice of Life. I've got some more gigs coming up in June and then I'm doing some more stuff for Paranoid Vision. Obviously, I'm doing Rebellion. I'm off to Barcelona in a couple of weeks' time;

Photo by Dod Morrison

there's a great, big, sort of music event that goes on over there and I'm on one of the panels to talk about alternative music and independent stuff. Apart from that, sort of, you know, normal domesticky stuff.

[LAUGHS]

JON: I dunno if you've noticed but there's been a hell of a lot of media interest in the whole [COULDN'T HEAR] movement recently. There's been a real surge.

STEVE: Really?

JON: Oh yeah. It's one of the things I've been planning to do: a round-up of recent stories about the subject to go in the magazine.

STEVE: Oh right.

JON: I've got ten or fifteen stories for it to catch up on.

STEVE: Oh, right! So in the newspapers or stuff like that, or what?

JON: It's mostly blogs.

STEVE: Right.

JON: There seems to be a hell of a lot of interest at the moment.

STEVE: Oh. Well, I hadn't seen that at all. So that'd be interesting.

JON: 'Cause quite a lot of the bands of that era have re-formed and are playing gigs again.

STEVE: Right, well, I did notice that Adam Ant had got it all back together and was doing dirt with White Socks or something and he's them times, so I know a lot of those bands have been getting back together. But I didn't realise there was a big sort of resurgence in it.

JON: Well, there seems to be. I think it's possibly because the political situation at the moment is so crappy.

STEVE: Yeah, yeah. And you know, let's face it: I can't think of any of the modern bands that are doing anything that all those punk bands used to do. You know, politically-wise, if you know what I mean.

JON: No, it's sad. I don't know what's hap-

The Gonzo Annual 2015

pened.

STEVE: Yeah, I don't know either. I sort of despair sometimes 'cause you'd think with all the possibilities out there, what with technology and stuff, that – I don't know! There's such an opportunity out there for making, if you're a new band, but no one seems to be bothered politically about it.

JON: Neil Young said that about five years ago. He said that he was waiting for somebody – one of the young bands – to make a protest about George Bush and nobody did.

STEVE: Yeah.

JON: He and a bunch of other 70-year-olds had to go out and do it.

STEVE: Yeah. But I think that was always the case.

JON: I wonder why the younger generation aren't as politicized.

STEVE: I don't know. I can't answer that. You know, of course I can't. I'm fifty-six years old.

[BOTH LAUGH]

STEVE: But unfortunately I feel as though I've done all my political bit. You know, I've said all I needed to say about that and those songs still stand up so I'd find it really difficult to right a Crass-type song again. Me and I think a load of people are just desperate for someone else to just take up that gauntlet. You know, I'm really surprised they haven't. But fair point, there's a band called Sleep of Mods that are worth checking out. It's just two guys but the vocal is really good. So if you look them up on the internet, they're really good; they're worth a listen.

JON: And it was you guys who politicized the whole generation, I think.

STEVE: Well, yeah, yeah.

JON: You certainly politicized me.

STEVE: It certainly politicized me as well.

JON: 'Cause the stuff I got from you guys thirty-odd years ago – God, longer than that; 35 years ago – has stuck with me all my life.

STEVE: Talking to people on different stuff this weekend; people were saying exactly the same things. I played Winsford in Cheshire and the last time Crass played there was in 1985 or something, and the people that turned up there said that they hadn't been to a Crass gig since but they still felt the same about it. And I was like, yeah. You know, it's a strange thing that happened, when somehow, somewhere, Crass's work, lyrics and music really touched people, really very deeply somewhere. And that's very humbling to hear.

JON: There are an awful lot of people in their early to mid-fifties who still have wild, staring eyes; don't eat meat; and totally distrust the system.

STEVE: Yeah, yeah. Well, it's that generation, isn't it? When I come from gigs and I meet people, I always say "Thank Christ we survived it." All those horrible years, but we did somehow; we came through it. And the nice thing is that most of the people I meet are leading really good, purposeful lives. Yeah, they've still got a mortgage and kids and all the usual trappings like we've all got but they're still on the ball and that's really gratifying.

I'm really excited about it. I'm really enjoying working with Slice of Life in the studio. You know, it's weird-sounding, though, that's why I want to go back in and get it absolutely right. With doing what we do, if it had been a full-on rock band with electric bass and electric guitars and stuff I would have left some of the stuff go. I would have let it slip and said you won't notice it but because it's very acoustic you can really hear it if it's slightly wrong. I think it's worth the time and money and effort to go in and absolutely do it properly. I really feel it's got to be something that you want to play over and over. Myself included.

JON: Well, I'm really looking forward to hearing it. You've been wanting to do this for a long time, haven't you?

STEVE: Yeah, yeah. As I said, it's time and money and stuff, and getting the material together but we're getting there; we're getting there.

JON: The gig you did in Winsford was a benefit for a youth club you played back with Crass, wasn't it?

STEVE: That's right, yeah. It's a sports hall thing and we used to play there as Crass. Basically what's happened is, that centre has been a real central part of the community for well over thirty years and it does things like outings for disabled kids. It does things with kids with learning disabilities, kids who can't read and write, and sports activities. And it's also got an advice centre in there so it's really been a major part of the community there, and what's happened is a huge new academy has opened up right in beside it and so the council want to move all the resources from the sports hall into the new academy. That won't include the old people; they'll have to go right to the other side of town to get to their thing, plus there's gonna be staff cuts and it means that there's a large part of the community that won't be able to use that facility any more. All that really needs doing is the roof fixing so that's what the gig was for; to fix the roof.

It was explained to me that – it's best to go online and read about it. You know, there's lots of ins and outs, you know the usual in-tricks that go with councils and governments and academies and that sort of stuff. The council will and want to close that place down and it's a real loss.

JON: It's a very, very important cause to work with.

STEVE: Well, yeah, absolutely. There's a bloke there called Bob. He's worked tirelessly at the place and he's sort of been the backbone of it and he's distraught about it because there is absolutely nothing wrong with the way it functions at the moment. All it needs is the leaky roof stopped, which would cost – I dunno – ten grand or something to do it really properly. But the council, in their wisdom, would prefer to spend £28,000 to move everything into the new academy. Same old story.

JON: Congratulations for getting involved. It's very important you do.

STEVE: Well, I had to because Crass played there and I remember some of the people there and I just had to go and do it. And the nice thing was that because of the hall people turn up and a lot of the people who came hadn't seen each other for twenty years and a lot of them didn't know about the plight of the community centre even though they used to use it as kids and came to see Crass there. Or used to play football there. So that was really nice and it sort of stirred everyone up. If nothing else, it'll give them a spark of hope and who knows, maybe something good will come out of it.

JON: Well, I hope so because both with Crass and with what you're doing now, it is all about community, isn't it?

STEVE: Oh yeah. Absolutely. Yeah, yeah.

JON: I think that was always what inspired me about what you did back in the day because you were a band who were about a hell of a lot more than just guitars [...] and drums.

STEVE: And I think that bled over today, you know what I do for life of the community round here. Without a community, what have you got? Just individual people not talking to each other and not seeing each other and ghost towns. You can't live like that. One of our pubs has shut in the village, which is a real shame. That's probably gonna be knocked down now unless it opens as a pub again but I think it'll probably be knocked down and turned into houses, which will be holiday homes. The effect that's had is that there are some people that I've not seen for about six weeks because they don't like the other pub in the village so they drink outside the village or they're not bothering to go out any more. I'm having to go out and visit people because otherwise you just won't see them any more.

JON: That's happened in the village where I live. There's been a pub here for 1000 [?] years and there's been a big campaign to stop it becoming just two houses.
STEVE: Sure. Yeah, yeah.

JON: We're living in very strange and disturbing times.

STEVE: Well, it's all this stuff about 'oh should we go out so much?' But it's not that that's the problem because people can go out to a supermarket and buy the bloody stuff if they want and cheaper. The point is, the more pubs shut down, the less people socialize and then the binge-drinking really starts because there's nothing else to do but sit at home and drink. So that's what I think is the real danger: that actual villages are failing to social life any more.

JON: And it would be very easy to get paranoid and think that the powers that be prefer it that the people don't socialize because that's a way of dividing and ruling.

STEVE: Well, yeah. Keep them indoors and you know where they are. And they don't cause a fuss.

JON: As you know, I'm not the only guy in his 50s who gets paranoid.

STEVE: [LAUGHS] Oh, there are a lot of us out there.

Here is a miscellany of odd and sometimes slightly disgusting items belonging to, used by, or part of various music celebrities. People will buy anything…

Thom Yorke became the idol of a generation of disaffected rock fans, who elevated the Radiohead singer to the status of a modern day rock'n'roll saviour. Then some enterprising fan emptied a dressing room rubbish bin to hawk online Yorke's toenail clippings.

Beatles memorabilia doesn't come much stranger than this. In 2005, the website It's Only Rock N Roll.com auctioned off the door to the Beatles lawyer Nat Weiss' office – it fetched $51,858.
Corinna

I'm a Hog For You

Jon meets Ken Pustelnik

I was a latecomer to the music of the Groundhogs, only discovering them – almost by accident – in the early 1980s. In fact I discovered them first because I stole a sample from one of their records.

I was producing an album for a North Devon punk band and one of the songs had to end with an explosion. In those days before one had all sorts of on-line sample banks at one's disposal purely by clicking a mouse a few times, one had to get one's samples where one could find them, and the bloke who was recording the album turned up one day with a copy of a record called Thank Christ for the Bomb.

From this we nicked the sound of a nuclear explosion. I feel fairly safe in admitting this felony 30 years on, because the record was never released and even if it had been I don't think anyone would have bought the bloody thing anyway. However, in the breaks between recording, the engineer played me bits of this record and I soon became very enamoured of their particularly English brand of madness, fusing blues, heavy rock, and various less obvious influences into a manic and rather engaging whole.

Fast forward seven years and I was on extended sick leave from the National Health Service, and spending the summer of 1989 travelling, with a

The Gonzo Annual 2015

psychedelic gleam in my eyes at all times, from festival to festival flogging the magazine which I was editing, and through which I first met Gonzo Grande Fromage Rob Ayling. one day my then wife and I, together with a couple of my less salubrious hippy friends were at a small festival somewhere in east Devon.

A quarter of a century on I really can't remember where it was or much about it. I remember spending two nights in an increasingly uncomfortable little tent with Alison and my dog Toby.

One of them, I suspect Toby, kept on crawling out of the tent in the middle of the night, finding their way to the refuse bin around the back of the stall which had been selling pitta breads stuffed with dahl, and bringing back fragrant portions of the same which had been discarded by customers who had eaten their fill, and burying it in the bottom of our quilt.

The other things I remember were seeing Blurt for the first time and being massively impressed when Ted Milton opened his set by intoning that A was for Anarchy and B was for Blurt, and watching the Groundhogs play a transcendentally noisy set, so brutally elegant that it left one short of breath.

Fast forward another four or five years and, together with my band The Amphibians from Outer Space, I supported the Groundhogs on two occasions.

However, it wasn't until many years later that I found out that the band that I had seen and indeed had supported, were not the band that had recorded Thank Christ for the Bomb. The band was founded in the early '60s by Tony McPhee together with the Cruickshank brothers, and a few years later after John Cruickshank (harmonica, vocals) had left they were joined by Ken Pustelnik on drums and the classic line-up was born. Band members came and went with only McPhee as a constant, although in 2003 the classic line-up reunited for a while. I had never seen the classic line-up, but I wish I had.

Earlier this year I got a phone call from Paul Whitrow, an old friend of mine who has graced these pages on a number of occasions. He is a Bristol-based record producer who has been doing some stuff with Ken Pustelnik.

Would I like to talk to him for Gonzo Weekly? Is the Pope a Catholic? I replied.....

http://www.gonzomultimedia.co.uk/radio/player.php?id=263

Collectible Conundra

In one issue this summer, Bart Lancia writes "Isn't it amazing that seemingly every rock artist who's passed away in the last 40 or 50 years always seems to have 'unreleased' material made available?" I would add that it is interesting quite how many unreleased songs turn up every time that a major artist wants to do a retrospective compilation.

And it's hard not to agree with him.

Now I have to admit I am somewhat of a poacher turned gamekeeper here, because back in my mis-spent youth (ok, I was in my late twenties) I used to collect, trade, and even buy and sell bootlegs by various artists, including some of those who are featured on and off in these pages.

It was the late 1980s, and I as always excited when I managed to get hold of Beatles or Led Zeppelin outtakes, rehearsals or even live stuff that I'd not heard before. There was something about hearing music which had not been intended for ears beyond the immediate circle of the musicians involved that I found to be an irresistible thrill.

This is probably just me being a contrary sod, but although my appetite for music has never diminished I no longer feel the need to have a copy of "I am the Walrus", for example, with two extra bars on the introduction.

But presumably there is still a market for this sort of stuff out there because more and more glossy, expansive, (and expensive!) reissue packages keep on hitting the shelves.

I am sure that I remember when the last set of Led Zeppelin reissues came out four or five years ago, that Jimmy Page announced that there were no more un-issued studio recordings hiding in the vaults, and that therefore those reissues were the ultimate versions of the classic Led Zeppelin albums that would ever appear. Low and behold, roll on a few years, a whole bunch more unreleased songs and rehearsal versions have turned up, just in time to be included in the latest round of reissues.

Does this mean that the ones reissued a few years ago are no longer the 'definitive' versions? Does it mean that Mr Page was mistaken in his previous announcement? Does it mean that it is just happenstance that the newly discovered outtakes saw the light of day just in time to be included on yet another bunch of reissues?

Forgive me for being cynical. Once upon a time I would have been over the moon with this. I still remember how exciting it was when the Beatles albums came out on CD on which you could hear whole new swathes of sound which had previously been inaudible. Ok, much of it was things like Ringo Starr's squeaky bass drum pedal, but that was all part of the magic of the experience.

It gave you the feeling that you were able to be part of the sessions; that you had been privy to things no one outside that studio had ever heard before. That was twenty five years ago and the whole nature, not only of the way we consume music, but of celebrity itself, has changed since then. These days celebrity is a much more fleeting concept.

People become famous for the most ridiculous things; their lack of knowledge, cheating on a game show, or making idiots of themselves on fatuous reality television shows. The immediacy of the internet, particularly things like Facebook and My Space mean that it is far easier to approach, talk to, and even build up a relationship with your favourite pop star than it has ever been before, and so I personally question the need for these 'behind the scenes' glimpses of the recording process. Surely, these days, the thing that is most important is the ultimate performance of the song itself, done in the way which most pleases, and fulfils the concepts of the artists themselves.

What do you think? I am not actually voicing my approval, or disapproval, of the current model which produces these ever more expansive collectors' box sets. I am certainly not criticizing them. I am merely confused by them. There are some releases like this which are undeniably excellent; the current series of anthologies of unreleased materials by the late Hugh Hopper, for example, with which I am tangentially involved. These collect together whole swathes of unreleased or very hard to find material and can only be a boom to the fan or the collector.

But, the more I think of it, the more I question the excited release of material that sounds practically identical to stuff which we have heard for years.

(Before I finish I would like to stress that I have not yet heard the Led Zeppelin reissues and that they may well contain enormous amounts of stuff that will get me very excited. But it is the concept that gets me nervous).

Ironically, there are all sorts of things which we know exist, but remain tantalizingly unreleased. For example, during January 1969 the Beatles recorded hours of material for the project that eventually became "Let it Be".

I have heard it said that the sessions at Twickenham Studios, followed by the ones at Apple Studios, produced over seventy hours of recorded music, including unreleased original material, and covers of old Rock & Roll songs. The vast majority of this stuff remains unreleased. I suppose that in the current political climate, the racist version of "Get Back", which appears on the Sweet Apple Trax bootleg will never see the light of day, which is a pity, because it rocks like a bitch. But there is a hell of a lot more, available on bootlegs, which would make a fascinating official box set, or indeed a series of box sets.

There is also pretty good video footage from these sessions, including visits to the studio by Peter Cook and (allegedly) Jim Morrison.

And, leaving the 1969 material behind, the footage of their 1966 tour of Japan seems to have a semi-legal release in some countries but has never seen the light of day in the UK.

The most tantalizing recording, that may or may not exist, took place in 1965 when the Beatles met Elvis Presley, and a couple of loose recording were made. They are probably of the same sort of quality as those from 1974 featuring Lennon and McCartney playing together for the last time which are essentially un-releasable, except for their obvious historical interest.

Ever since the Bob Dylan bootleg series started in 1991, I have been waiting for a proper collection of the "Basement Takes".

> Ironically these were the subject of "The Great White Wonder", which was the first ever mass market bootleg, and by some estimates only about a third of what was recorded has ever come out.
>
> Again, we know from the stuff that has appeared, unofficially, that there is a hell of a lot of good stuff – maybe up to one hundred songs – which could be very well deserving of release some day.

Time to get off my soap box now and get on with the show, forgive me for my musings.

Love and peace,

Jon Downes

DO YOU REALLY BELIEVE IN THE SYSTEM WELL OK
I BELIEVE IN ANARCHY FOR THE UK

Sometime recently, I think in John Higgs' remarkable biography of the KLF, I read a critique of youth cultures which pointed out that since acid house in the late 1980s the popular youth cultures that have come along are more about recycling something old, than looking at something new. One of my favourite web comics, *Bad Machinery* by John Allison is playing with this idea in a current storyline featuring a yet another Mod revival.

But of all the genres that have been re-emerging from obscurity in the vault of history, the last one that I ever thought would come back to prominence is Anarcho-Punk. This is not because I feel that it did not have substance. Far from it. It is not even because I didn't enjoy the music. I did. It is that it was a music of its time – and as far as I was concerned – that time was the early eighties ending just about the time when Margaret Thatcher sunk the *Belgrano*, stamped all over the Miners' Strike, and then confidently declared to all and sundry that there was no such thing as society.

In 2006, Neil Young released an album called Living with War, which was basically a musical critique of then US president George W Bush and his conduct of the war in Iraq. At the time Young (who was 61) said " I was hoping some young person would come along and say this and sung some songs about it, but I didn't see anybody, so I'm doing it myself. I waited as long as I could."

I have a sneaking suspicion that much the same socio-political mechanisms are at work. It could well be argued that the country is now in a worse state than it was at the height of Thatcher's power in the 1980s, and that there are more social problems than there were back then. And I like to think that the people who were mobilised and politicised by Anarcho-Punk back in the day are, like I am, still politicised now as a direct result of it, and, like Neil Young, decided that if the youngsters were not going to do anything then it was time for those men and women of a certain age who still have wild, staring eyes and a belief that you should pay no more than 99p, to once again take a stand against the things that they/we believe to be wrong with our sceptered isle.

The Anarcho-Punk of the early 1980s was often a grim and monochrome affair. It was very much about the DIY ethic, and was all about Letraset, photocopiers and the even more primitive Gestetner.

Sadly, the realities of life for most of the people involved in the scene took over and mortgages, wives, children and careers were not really compatible with singing "fuck the system!" And, as the decade that taste forgot limped on to its inevitable climax with the first Gulf War, the movement seemed to lose heart. As people got older, I also suspect that the strictly skeletal musical template also became restrictive for many of them, and they moved on to new challenges and new directions. Some of us occasionally harkened back to our political roots.

My 2011 album, BiPolar, for example, included a jolly little ditty called 'No matter who you vote for, the Government always wins', but the days when my music, and that of most of my contemporaries, was angular, spiky, and to the point, are long gone.

ANARCHO PUNK - ITS BACK AND THIS TIME ITS SERIOUS

The new revival in the fortunes of Anarcho-Punk was, like the original, spurred on by Crass. A few years ago Penny Rimbaud and Steve Ignorant both wrote autobiographies, and there was a widely publicized rift between the ex-band members regarding the release of all their original albums in the form of The Crassical Collection. There were also several books about the subject, most notably George Berger's biography of Crass, and Ian Glasper's exhaustive *The Day The Country Died*. In their wake came a plethora of Anarcho-Punk related blogs and websites which in the last few months have started posing contemporary news rather than just rehashes of news from the early 1980s. Then many of the original bands, but not – sadly – Crass (that boat, I think, has sailed) have started to reform.

Bizarrely, I was telling Steve Ignorant, of all people, about this resurgence of interest in the genre which he had such a big part in creating and he was unaware of it all. So I promised that at some point over the next few weeks I would write this article, containing a sample roundup of some of the more interesting news items.

A lot of this comes from a blog called The Hippies Now Wear Black which is of course a reference to Penny Rimbaud wrote in his scabrous booklet, *A Series of Shock Slogans and Mindless Token Tantrums* which accompanied the 1982 box set Christ the Album, and was later issued as a (now very rare) paperback book. Penny actually gave me a copy of the paperback book back in 1982, but I have no idea what actually happened to it. I now have a digital version on my Happy Shopper version of the Kindle.

The blog is produced by someone called Rich Cross who is, apparently, working on an academic book on the subject of Anarcho-Punk.

- **No Future? Punk 2001 conference, Wolverhampton**

To make available the full-text of the conference paper that I gave at the No Future? punk conference back in 2001, I've republished an archive web page of mine (from a putative anarcho-punk history web site that I worked up a few years ago).

To cite the original conference presentation: Rich Cross, 2001. 'Yes that's right, punk is dead: Crass and the anarcho-punk critique'. Paper given at the No Future conference, University of Wolverhampton, 21 September.

To cite this online version of the original presentation: Rich Cross, 2001. 'Yes that's right, punk is dead: Crass and the anarcho-punk critique'. Paper given at the No Future conference, University of Wolverhampton, 21 September, [available online], The Hippies Now Wear Black, http://urko.org.uk/hnwb/index.html (Accessed on access date).

Crass's 1983 album Yes Sir, I Will, evokes a wide range of responses in people. Apart from a very brief song, which is beautiful and actually sounds a little bit like Genesis back when they were good, the album is unquestionably a bloody awful row. Steve Ignorant hates it, although I must admit I have a soft spot for it, if only for its sheer bloody-minded audacity. It amused me that the version that came out as part of The Crassical Collection a few years back, featured a second disc entitled Why Don't you Fuck Off? which features a remix of the album featuring luminaries of the free jazz scene which is, if anything, even less listenable than the original.

So the work does – bizarrely – begin to grow. But guess what happens now?

- **The Rebellion Festival (Blackpool, UK, August) report:**

We have a very special event to open Rebellion Festivals 2014 on Thursday in the Empress Ballroom.

In commemoration of the thousands on both sides who died brutal, pointless deaths in Word War I, Penny Rimbaud and Eve Libertine present a reworking of the Crass classic Yes, Sir, I Will complete with a six piece band. They are joined by Gee Vaucher who will be showing the classic film of the same name. As Rimbaud puts it - 'It will be good to do Yes, Sir at the festival because it's probably more relevant today than it was thirty-five [actually, thirty-one] years back, and all the more so for this being the centenary year of 'the war to end all wars' – will we ever learn?'.

Day tickets are available for this special one off performance – see day tickets for Thursday 7 August 2014 at : http://www.rebellionfestivals.com/tickets/

The Gonzo Annual 2015

Penny Rimbaud may well be well into his 70s, but he has been busy lately, with interviews, festival appearances and his work with Eve Libertine.

- Penny Rimbaud and his 'L'Académie des Vanités' (featuring Eve Libertine, Jennifer Maidman, Louise Elliot and Annie Whitehead) join the line-up of performers appearing at the launch event of 'The Word Is Your Oyster' at The Russet Cafe, 17 Amhurst Terrace, London E8 2BT on 21 May 2014: "a new monthly night of poetry, music and storytelling where words and lyrics pave a path for creative expression."
- Penny Rimbaud will be taking part in HowTheLightGetsIn, the world's largest philosophy and music festival, in Hay from 22 May – 1 June 2014. Bringing together world-leading scientists, musicians, philosophers and politicians including Roger Penrose, Bernard-Henri Levy, Laurie Penny, Charlotte Church, George Galloway, David Nutt, Katie Derham, Molotov Jukebox, Owen Jones, and Mr. Scruff for debates, talks, and wild parties, uncovers the uncovering the new heresies that might become the truths of the future. Culture Minister Ed Vaizey described the festival as a 'world-leading' forum of ideas, the Guardian says it is leading Britain back to 'big thinking', and the New Scientist hails it as 'a storming success'.
- Julian Brimmers. 2014. "Crass' Penny Rimbaud on graffiti, jazz and John Lennon", Red Bull Music Academy, 3 April http://www.redbullmusicacademy.com/magazine/crass-interview

And finally it's good to see some of the names that I had almost forgotten from the glory days of the Anarcho -Punk revolution. A small number of bands had, indeed, like Penny and Eve, continued to gig intermittently. Others never actually went away, and still others have come out of the woodwork to express their Tourettes–like existential angst.

- The Cravats join the bill of the two-day Na parameinoume apeili event near Athens on 24 May 2014; the first time the band have performed in Greece.
- As well as appearing at Rebellion 2014, Rubella Ballet are to play the 'Gothic stage' at Alt Fest 2014 - 15-17 August 2014, Boughton Estate, Kettering, Northamptonshire, NN14 1BJ. (Rubella Ballet play on Saturday 16 August).

- As has been the case for a few years now, the 2014 Rebellion festival (Winter Gardens, Blackpool, 7-10 August) features appearances from several original wave anarcho-punk bands, including:

    A-Heads
    Andy T
    The Cravats
    Hagar the Womb
    Lost Cherees
    Paranoid Visions (featuring Steve Ignorant)
    Penny Rimbaud and Eve Libertine (with Gee Vaucher) performing Yes Sir, I Will
    Rubella Ballet
    Steve Ignorant's Slice of Life
    Subhumans

There is even a new album by Rubella Ballet, one of the most interesting of the ensembles from the Anarcho-Punk heyday. This next piece is, once again, taken almost verbatim from The Hippies Now Wear Black.

- Sid and Zillah were inspired to start writing this album containing highly motivated and political songs about a variety of subjects such as: government brainwashing, the creation of new strains of flu virus to reduce human population, the police cover up of Hillsborough stadium disaster as well as a chance meeting with two whistle-blowing MI5/6 agents who had been monitoring their political activities in the 80s and were now working with William Rodriguez, a caretaker at the twin towers who had dedicated his life to telling the world what he believed really happened during 9/11.

Sid explains "The overriding message of the album is to not to believe every thing you hear on the news or read in the newspapers, as the very same people we are protesting against are those compiling the news."

"Thank Christ for Rubella Ballet! Punk went from being this fun colourful place to be, to all these miserable bastards wearing black! I knew what I'd see there (Crass Gigs) I knew what I'd hear played there... and bands like Rubella Ballet where a breath of fresh air" – Steve Ignorant, Crass. The Day The Country Died

JON MEETS PATRICK CAMPBELL-LYONS

Back in the late 1970s when I was coincidentally living in the same house, in the same village in North Devon where I live today, there was a middle-aged bloke called Dickie Dunn who lived a few doors up from us. He was a bit of a wheeler dealer who made a living buying and selling stuff at auction sales (car boot sales were at least 15 years in the future).

He knew that I was a devotee of what he considered to be monumentally peculiar music, so whenever he came across any LPs that looked interesting, or at least bizarre, during his journeys he would buy them and present them to me in the hope that I would purchase them from him, something that I usually ended up doing.

One day he turned up with a pile of records which included something which even today is probably the most striking album cover I've ever seen. It was a record called Local Anaesthetic by a band called Nirvana; I am not going to pretend to be any more hip then than I was, because I had never heard of it, but I was struck by the monumentally bizarre and rather freaky cover and so I paid Dickie (if I remember right) the palatial some of 75p for it, took it home and was completely riveted. I knew nothing about the band, only that there were two of them; a bloke with a Greek name and a bloke with what sounded like an aristocratic English one (it turned out to be Irish, but that's beside the point). But the music was fantastic. It was one of my first introductions to prog rock which wasn't by Yes or Pink Floyd, and the two long tracks, one on each side of the record were full of so many little hooks and tricks of the tail that I was, and still am, amazed by their art forms.

Over the years I came back to this record on a regular basis, playing it to any of my friends who I thought may be interested and proselytising about it like mad. If I am honest about it, one of the main reasons that I became a rock journalist was that I could discover new music, and brag about it to my friends.

I sorted out and listened to everything else that I could find by this singular band and soon discovered that Local Anaesthetic was far from being a one-off. They were also responsible for a hit single, and an album with the glorious title of The Story of Simon Simopath, which was arguably the first concept album ever released. It tells a simple everyday story of a boy named Simon Simopath who dreams of having wings. He is unpopular at school and upon reaching adulthood he goes to work in an office where he suffers a nervous breakdown. Unable to find a mental institution he gets upon a rocket and flies into outer space where he meets a centaur and a tiny goddess named Magdalena. They fall in love and there is a party.

You can't help but love anybody who could come up with such a peculiar farrago of oddness, and I totally fell in love with Nirvana. For years I would tell everyone that they were one of my favourite bands and it would mildly irritate them that I was talking about an obscure psychedelic/prog band rather than the Seattle grunge merchants.

It appears that the band were amused by the confusion between themselves and Kurt Cobain's Johnny-come-Latelys and they were actually intending to do an album of cover versions of the latter band in their own inimitable style. The album was to be called Nirvana sings Nirvana, but the project was curtailed after Cobain's tragic suicide. However, one track called Lithium was released by the band in 1996.

Some years ago I was pootling about on Spotify when I found a solo album by Patrick Campbell-Lyons. It was called The 13 Dalis and features a montage of 12 pictures of the Dali Lama in which the Dali Lama is flashing a peace sign, in the middle of which is a picture of Salvador Dali wearing a silly hat. You have to love this man.

Fast forward until six months ago when I was, by now, editor of this august periodical. Totally by chance, it turns out that one of the people who gets both the Gonzo Weekly and the Gonzo Daily, and who has done business with Gonzo over the years, is the owner of the record label on which Patrick Campbell-Lyons now resides. Would I like to interview him? Well der! Seldom have I been asked a more superfluous question.

Listen to our conversation here.

http://www.gonzomultimedia.co.uk/radio/player.php?id=271

Reformation Blues

I had a surprisingly positive reaction to my rant last week about the volume of unissued material which always comes out the proverbial woodwork in time to be included on retrospective compilation albums by your favourite heritage act.

However, this got me thinking about something equally peculiar that brings up a whole swathe of emotions in life (admittedly twisted slightly) and which I would like to share with you, if only to try to get my thoughts on the matter in order.

It seems to me, at the moment, that pretty well any band (whose members are still alive, or mostly so) who has ever existed, has re-formed, at least once. There are only four notable exceptions that I can think of.

THE CLASH

The main reason that they haven't/didn't/won't re-form is that Joe Strummer died just in time to stop the band doing exactly that at some awards ceremony or other (I think it was the Rock and Roll Hall of Fame, but I can't be bothered to find out). No offence to any ex-members of The Clash that I happen to know, but the idea of the band without Joe Strummer is as ridiculous as the Beatles without John Lennon. Wait, that happened didn't it? With Free as a Sodding Bird.

THE JAM

Paul Weller has always been adamant that this will never happen. Bruce Foxton has played with both Paul Weller and Rick Butler, but the chances of the three of them playing together again are negligible.

THE SMITHS

Morrissey is a law unto himself, and more importantly has an admirable romanticised view of rock and roll. He has always said that a Smiths reunion would tarnish the band. This week he said, "I don't know a single person who wants a Smiths reunion! But, no, there aren't any bands I'd like to see again because your memory of them was how they were in their prime or at their best or at their most desperate, and you look to them to be someone they no longer are."

CRASS

This is the band, of the four, that I personally have most emotion invested in. The nearest they came to a reunion was when most of them appeared – separately – at an anti-Iraq war concert in November 2002 at the Queen Elizabeth Hall on London's South Bank. The fall-out from this, and the subsequent arguments between various members of the band, have pretty well denied the possibility that they will ever do it again.

Back in about 1975 John Lennon spoke positively about the possibility of a Beatles reunion. Again, I am paraphrasing, because I can't find the original citation at this time of night, but he said that if the band were to reunite he would want them to do it in the studio and try to come up with new music rather than just going out and playing the old hits live.

It is tempting to theorise that if Mark Chapman had not taken the law into his own hands on that fateful night in December 1980, that the band would probably have reunited for something like Live Aid. However, they didn't, and John Lennon's statement must stand as the text for this particular sermon.

This week Julian Lennon reveals that he was unimpressed by a concert in Los Angeles marking the Fab Four's historical arrival in America.

"The last thing I wanted to do was stand in the audience with everyone else, and clapping my hands, and being filmed in front of millions while watching a Beatles karaoke session." This was in response to the two surviving Beatles performing Hey Jude on a highly rated US TV broadcasted concert.

The question has to be asked, therefore, why do bands re-form? Some bands certainly shouldn't. During the 50th anniversary shows performed by the Rolling Stones a year or so back, whilst the blues numbers featuring Mick Taylor were perfectly valid, and more exciting than one could ever possibly have hoped, the more sexual pop songs sung by a front man who – despite all his efforts to the contrary – is still a wrinkled septuagenarian were – I'm afraid – mildly distasteful.

Robert Plant should be lauded for his explanation of why he doesn't want to do a proper Led Zeppelin reformation. He quite rightly says that for a man of his age to be singing that he wants to give an unnamed young lady every inch of his love, or to squeeze her lemon till the juice runs down her leg, is embarrassing and age inappropriate.

Sadly, many, but not all, bands who re-form and play songs that they made famous four or more decades before have – despite their best efforts – just become self-referential cover acts, performing cover versions of their own material, and trying to re-live old glories whilst doing nothing to address the socio-political needs of their contemporary audience.

Of the four bands I listed above, the one I am most disappointed will not re-form is Crass. Last week I wrote about how many of the anarcho-punk bands from the early 1980s have re-formed and are playing today as a direct reaction to the current socio-political climate which, it could be argued, is even more restricted and suffocating as were the glory days of Margaret Thatcher. The world needs a band like Crass nowadays more than ever. There are more rampant injustices and divisions in society than ever, and pundits like myself are desperate to see musicians coming forward to address these concerns.

Crass are now in their 50s, 60s and 70s and as hinted at above, have too much personal baggage ever to re-form. Nor, probably, should they. It is time for a new generation of political musicians to take over, man the barricades and foment their own particular brand of revolution. But where are they?

I am not an expert in the history of art, but I would imagine that very few art movements have ever lasted much longer than fifty years. It is now sixty years since a young, feral truck driver called Elvis marched into Sun Studios and changed the world beyond recognition.

Sixty years later, of course rock music still exists, is still being made, and is still very popular. But the question has to be asked, what is it for?

At the end of last year I interviewed one aspiring political rock band whose songs espoused a neo-Marxist utopia and asked them just this question. And I am afraid that I managed to offend them mightily; something which was truly not my intention. They went off in high dudgeon and I never heard from them again, which was a pity. They were nice chaps and I believe that they truly meant what they were singing about, but they had no idea about the philosophy of what they were doing, and I don't want to get all Marshall McLuhan on you and rant on about the medium and the message/massage, but one has to ask that if an artist sings about political or social matters, but does not expect their song/message to actually exact any change within its listeners, then the net result is horribly akin to the most crassly, wishy-washy hymns sung in the most reactionary and ineffectual churches.

The whole crux of what McLuhan said was that the form of the medium embeds itself within the message, creating symbiotic relationship by which the medium influences how the message is received. The fact that so much of Crass's original output was a spiky ugly noise was, therefore, a direct reaction to them living and operating within spiky, ugly times.

Maybe our present, over-technological, society has become so deeply self-absorbed that we can no longer assimilate inconvenient truths proffered in this manner.

Earlier this evening my wife sent me a video by a marketing analyst explaining how the international meat industry is "systemised cruelty on a massive scale and we only get away with it because everyone's prepared to look the other way." She is perfectly correct. And maybe in music, art, ethics, and politics we have been conditioned to do exactly the same thing.

It is a great privilege for me, therefore, to be able to write about musicians and artists who are bucking the trend and making a valiant attempt to tell the truth as they see it.

The Gonzo Annual 2015

JON MEETS PAM WINDO

Pam Windo is a remarkable woman. I had, of course, heard of her late husband Gary: a saxophonist, who was a member of Keith Tippett's big band Centipede, played in Matching Mole alongside the legendary Robert Wyatt and also played alongside such luminaries as free jazz goddess Carla Bley and Pink Floyd's drummer Nick Mason.

But, to my great embarrassment, I knew nothing about his life (or even his death), and I didn't know that he had been married. All that changed about a year ago when I wrote sales notes for several Gary Windo albums which Gonzo were in the process of reissuing. It was then when I came across the inimitable Pamela Windo.

She was Gary's partner in every sense of the word during the years he was making such extraordinary music, and she was – and still is – a composer of some renown and great merit. She was also a notable performer with her band Pam Windo and The Shades, which actually eclipsed Gary's career for a while in the early eighties, fusing new wave music with more exotic jazzy soundscapes.

She writes:

> On my 38th birthday, I was handed a check for $20,000, along with a recording contract. Albert Grossman—show biz manager *extraordinaire*—had seen my band at the White Water Depot, a country club where the bands usually played country music. Gary had joined the band as soon as he'd heard my first punk number, "Gimme, Gimme!" I was the first punk in Woodstock, even made the front page of The Daily Freeman, beneath the latest news on the Iran crisis. I was a long way from my conservative home town of Brighton, England—and a long way from the reserved teenager who read French romantic poets. "I want your body, to hell with your mind, 'cos I've got a mind of my own," was my personal war cry for women's lib. I'd been a long time fighting the men's club in the world of music. Once I was given rein, I went for it: the live shows had themes, and drew both fans and the curious. The musicians (apart from Gary) who had the guts to join up with me were Rich McCarthy on bass, Charlie Brocco on guitar, Ian Bennett on tenor sax, Chris grassi on drums. The album did not live up to the live shows, which were energetic and visually exciting, and, with Gary as band master, were constantly improvised. But I went on with The Shades in search of a 'hit song.' Warner Bros offered me a song-writing contract which I turned down; naively asserting I wanted my songs just for my band. At Albert's direction, I changed the original personnel. The roster of musicians who came to play included bass players Ed Fitzgerald, John Marsh and Steve York, drummer Ron Riddle, and guitarists John Platania, Ted Orr and Robert Gelles. I became relentless and ruthless. Finally, sometime in the mid-80s, I bowed out of the music scene and turned to writing … and escaped to Morocco.

I interviewed her sometime last year. My memory is fairly unreliable, and for the purposes of this narrative it really doesn't matter. But our interview was both fascinating and entertaining. Pam is not just a very gifted composer who has lived a strange and, to some people, a shocking life, but she is a natural raconteur as well and talking to her about the various things she has done, and the various people she has worked with was a delight.

She told me that she has a book coming out which told the story of her life with Gary, and I told her that I very much wanted to read it, and then I have to admit I forgot all about the whole matter. Then, about a month ago, I had an email from her asking for my address, and last week her book arrived on my doormat.

I am a quick reader, especially when I am enjoying the thing that I am reading. And I have to say that seldom have I enjoyed a book of autobiography more. She is as natural a storyteller in print as she was a raconteur over the phone, and she told the story of her strange, and unconventional life with honesty, wit, and aplomb.

Unlike many autobiographers she resisted the temptation to skate over the nasty bits, but neither did she dwell on them. I reviewed her book in last week's issue of this magazine and I think that Pam was quite pleased with it; she certainly agreed to another chat. So early on Friday evening, I made sure that I had a cup of tea, some diabetic biscuits, a packet of cigarettes, and sat in my favourite chair, with a small Jack Russell on my lap. With a feeling of anticipation I telephoned a cell phone number in New Mexico.

However, as is so often the case in life, and in particular journalism, things just did not work out the way I had originally intended. I telephoned Pam's cell phone number and all I got was a series of peculiar clunking noises. The website that I use to record my calls (craftily called www.recordyourcall.com, and which usually does exactly what it says on the tin) rejected the number outright.

One of my late father's often repeated dictums was punctuality was the politeness of princes, and whilst not being any sort of prince, I always try to be punctual and anyone who knows me will bear witness to the fact that tardiness annoys the bejeezus out of me.

So, I telephoned Pam again, this time without the website prefix, and I eventually got through. However, either something was badly wrong with her telephone system, or she was talking to me with her head in a cast iron bucket and a mouthful of potato chips. It turned out that she had had problems already with her telephone today and so my scenario of buckets and chips was looking pretty unlikely. We tried a couple of workarounds, but none of them made any difference, and so Pamela was kind enough to suggest that we do the chat by email, which is exactly what we have done.

1. Why did you decide that 2014 was the sensible time to release your autobiography

Nothing to do with a 'sensible' time, more to do with a writer's whim - I began the first draft back in 2004, a few chapters, sent them out to possible publishers in the old way, where if they liked it, they'd give you an advance before you wrote the whole thing. Got good feedback but no offer, so I left it and finished a book about Morocco [Zohra's Ladder & other Moroccan Tales], which did get published. I then embarked on a second book about Morocco which I finished in first draft but which did not get published. At that point, in 2010 I think, I decided to go gung-ho on the music memoir and enlisted a book guru who set me off on a gargantuan task that turned out to be a Pandora's Box.....only one person read that draft [Steve Feigenbaum of Cunieform] who thought it great but far too much, not enough focus. So... I left it once again. And it wasn't until I'd been in Santa Fe for a couple of months that I decided one night to write it as a portrait of Gary, i.e. Him through Me. That was short, and as you know, I published it in e-book format on my website.

Having done that, people wanted a hard copy book, so I went back and made it into the musical journey that Gary and I had shared since our schooldays in post-war England, doubling the length, and adding photos and memorabilia. A local publisher offered me a contract so I spent almost another year in the Santa Fe library writing it.. only to find the publisher put it out without my authorization in an odd format and with photos that were so black you couldn't see the faces. I got my rights back (stopping publication) and redesigned it with the help of a graphic designer. Et voila!

2. How long did it take to write?

I guess I answered this above... all together, probably about four years!!

3. It is a very honest and raw book. Was it painful to write?

Yes, it was, and I cried many times as I wrote the hardest parts. I didn't want to write star gossip, and it isn't about being famous, so if I was going to write it at all, I wanted it to be universally honest about a relationship in those times.

4. Did you talk to any of the other musicians mentioned in the book to refresh your memory

During the last version, I spoke to Gary's old friend Ian Bennett about their seagoing days and first days in America. When I'd almost finished this book, Ed Fitzgerald, the bass player with me in The Shades, called me. He had had such a great time back then, he's never forgotten it and remains one of my big-

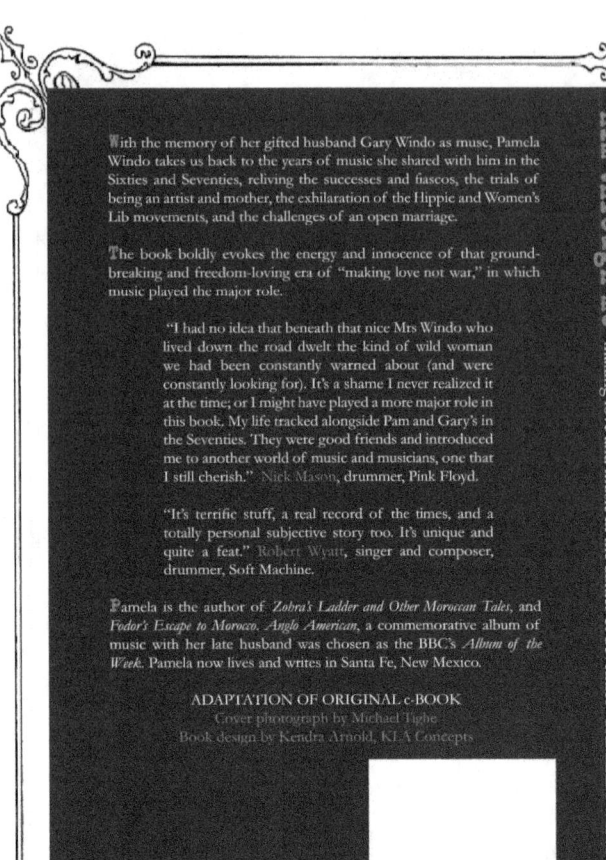

gest fans!

Oh and yes, I had a couple of e-mails with Nick Mason to let him know I was writing it, but not about the facts. And the same with Sir Richard Branson... in fact I sent him a draft of the long version before that because he said he would send it on to Virgin Books, who turned it down.

5. From your descriptions it seemed like a very vibrant and creative time to be a musician. What has changed?

This is a difficult question, because everyone who lived through an era will feel that it was the best! That said, I meet young people all the time (through my sons and because I keep my finger on the pulse!) who feel they missed something very special.. Here's something I wrote as a foreword but did not use:

"Three women inspired me to write this memoir. The first, a thirty-year-old English artist who enjoys all the freedoms young women have today, wanted to know what we thought and felt back in the Hippie and Women's Lib days. How was it different then?

The second, a twenty-year-old French student who seemed magnetized by me, finally spoke up. Yes, she was free, she said, but young women take their freedom for granted, she said. Why? I asked. Because it was given to us. We didn't have to fight for it like you did," she said, with envy and disappointment in her voice.

The third woman, an American, who lived through the Seventies and bears a large tattoo of Led Zeppelin on her body, still has all their albums and memorabilia, and longs to recapture the magic."

6. Are there any other pieces of Gary's legacy that remain unreleased in your archives?

I think that I covered, if not in the kind of detail some would like, all the aspects of Gary that made him who he was. He was a Renaissance man, happy to be a husband and father, as well as a musician. He did not set out to be famous or rich.

7. What is your next project?

I am never at a loss with projects! I may return to the Moroccan book -- Love in a Foreign Tongue -- about how a foreign culture and language (in this case, Islam and Arabic) impact a love affair. Or, I might edit a book about my childhood and adolescence in England.

PRAYING FOR A POT-HEAD PIXIE

Daevid Allen has been in hospital this week. We have done our best to keep up to date with events as they transpired, and have posted out bulletins on his progress to subscribers of this magazine as well as on the Gonzo Daily blog. The following statement appeared on Daevid Allen's Facebook page on Monday:

"First thing on Tuesday morning in Australia daevid is having surgery to remove a Staph infected cancerous growth from his neck. The operation will also involve the removal of some nerves and moving a bit of muscle to replace some which will be lost from the site of the infection.

A cyst appeared on his neck sometime before the Gong Brazil dates in early March. Unfortunately the initial treatment of the cyst on his neck resulted in daevid contracting a Golden Staph (*Staphylococcus aureus*) infection which compromised and delayed further treatment on the cyst, which kept growing.

Then things got really difficult - daevid badly fractured his upper left arm falling on the concrete path to his house. It was wet and slippy and over he went - bendy has never been a useful term in describing daevid's physical frame - and unfortunately so it proved.
The nature and position of the fracture meant that it could not put in a cast - only held as immobile as possible in a sling. This made many of his regular quite energetic health regimes, and even the cutting of food (all those salads and fruit he enjoys so much), impossible, and sleep (in a chair) as near as impossible.

Three weeks after breaking his arm and while trying to reduce the Staph infection to the point where it would be possible to operate on the cyst (and also possibly operate on the fracture as well, which wasn't healing as it should) daevid got to such a low point that he had to spend a week in hospital. It was then that the cyst was diagnosed as cancerous.

Daevid's physiological 'perfect storm' was complete and it was at this point that his participation in the Gong dates in June, which he was trying so hard to get well for, was just not going to happen.
After the operation daevid will spend a week in hospital before going home. He will then have a period of radiation therapy on his neck and will obviously need some solid recovery time to ensure the cancer has no reason to return.

All things considered daevid is in good spirits, although in a fair bit of discomfort. Naturally he is aprehensive about the general anesthetic and the operation as he has experienced neither before. He remains optimistic, yet realistic about the future and is looking forward to being restored to rude health - and let's face it no-one does 'rude' health quite like hymn-self.

If you would like to help by tuning in at 9.00 p.m. GMT on Monday 9th (close to the starting time of the operation in Australia) and sending healing vibes to the old reprobate via Radio Gnome Invisible (step away from the modern 'mediaeval' technology, cut out the dodgy middlemen and go direct) you will be joining many of us doing the same."

Gong devotees from all over the world sat, prayed, and waited. It was a long wait, because the next bulletin didn't come in for several days. . When it did, it was reasonably encouraging news. This was posted on Tuesday teatime:

.Daevid has got through the Op OK and is now recovering in hospital. these next few days are critical, this is a very vulnerable healing time for the ailing alien, so keep

sending him that love and positivitea.
;^)

The next news came in on Wednesday morning (by the way these are all UK times rather than local time in the Antipodes) and came as close to the horse's mouth as one can get, David's son Orlando:

Orlando Allen: Great News from Gong's beloved Dingo Virgin/Bert Camembert otherwise known as Daevid Allen - The operation was a success and the Surgeons particularly commendable for taking extra special care with the nerves and tendons vital to daevids ability to continue performing.

Daevid sends a huge special thank-you to everyone who has been sending there love and there time concentrating on him and his health it has made a huge difference!! well done everyone! still some big hurdles to overcome yet - but - PHEEEEEEW* spread the news and lets keep that energy focused on seeing him Happy, perfectly healthy and jumping around stage like a teenager again! I will keep Updating as we go- O

And the latest news came in on Friday evening, just as we were going to press.

News from the front..
daevid's wound gets better everyday - so all heads in the right direction. He had a skin graft from his leg to the site of where the tumor was removed. There is now an indentation there.

He is in good spirits helped no doubt by being on pretty full on medication - having lots of weird hallucinations apparently! All normal there then.

I think that will be the last time he postpones having a lump removed to gig. He is lucky to be alive. Yes Gong is special and all that, but let's not die for it - well unless you really want to.

Anyway he always said he fancied going while on stage - daevid 'Tommy Cooper' allen, then a Viking funeral. Perhaps an end of the pier gig and a waiting rowing boat piled high with kindling would do the trick.

It goes without saying that we at

Gonzo Weekly are joining in the prayers and healing vibes being sent to Daevid on his sick bed. He is a very special person, and I feel privileged to have known him. In a very real sense none of this would have happened without him. It was visiting Daevid Allen in the spring of 1988 where I first met Rob Ayling, and our long friendship was kindled. Daevid Allen was also the inspiration for Rob to start Voiceprint Records. As I believe I have written elsewhere, the first LP I ever owned was by Gong, and so Daevid Allen has been of pivotal importance in my life, in the life of the Gonzo Grand Fromage and in the lives of countless Pothead Pixy acolytes across the face of the globe (and one suspects across the face of many other globes as well).

Get well soon, Daevid and we guarantee you that if you ever come to North Devon for whatever reason Corinna will make one of her best and most splendiferous cakes for you.

REMEMBERING RICK

really am in a very strange place this week. In 1982, May of 1982 to be precise, I moved to North Devon from South Devon. I became a student nurse studying for what was then called being a Registered Nurse for the Mentally Subnormal at the Royal West County Hospitals at Langdon and Starcross.

The 22-year-old Jon Downes was living at nurses' homes at these two hospitals doing his best to uphold his emotional image that all you needed was love by drinking too much, and getting emotionally and sexually involved with as many girls as he could. And he (I) did his best to fulfil that ambition to the best of his (my) ability.

Some time in the autumn of 2002 (in between studying for his qualification, and doing his best to shag his way through the young ladies of the hospital) he switched on his television set. There, on the screen, was something that he really didn't expect; a young man of about his own age, with an exaggeratedly stupid, anti-establishment haircut. He was pointing accusingly at a policeman. He said:

"Pig! What's your gig, pig?
Barry Manilow?
Or the Black and White Minstrel Show?"

It was Rik Mayall. It was the People's Poet. It was a TV show called *The Young Ones*. He was Rik the complete bastard.

The 22-year-old Jon Downes fell in love. And this is probably where the fact that the 22-year-old Jon Downes is as mad as a bagful of cheese comes into play. It was the first series of a BBC television series called *The Young Ones*, but the 22-year-old Jon Downes just saw it as a glorious window upon life. Art is supposed to be a window on life, but when you are as mad as a bagful of cheese as the 22-year-old Jon Downes was, and believed that the window upon life was, indeed, art then Jon Downes was going to portray the confessions of the window cleaner.

He was then – and if I have to admit it now – *The Young Ones* was an encapsulation of what I thought life should be. And so, I spent the next ten, twenty maybe even thirty years of my life, doing my best to carry out the psychosocial image which *The Young Ones* had so gloriously showed me. I am now 55, and this might actually show - if any illustration was actually needed – what has happened to me, over the past thirty years.

I have spent my adult life as a mixture of Rik (the People's Poet) and Neil (the pointless hippy), and this has led me to the position in which I am now quite proud to be in; the editor of Gonzo Weekly, the director of the Centre for Fortean Zoology, and the husband of Corinna Newton Downes.

But it was only a facile BBC TV sitcom.

Or was it?

Who cares?

One of the things which has caused me quite a lot of mental, psychosocial, and socio-political anguish over the past three or four decades is the fact that what I do doesn't really fit in with any of the accepted social models of life within the accepted frames of the 21st Century. That is because, if I am going to be completely honest with myself, I have always been stuck within something invented by the BBC light comedy department of the mid-1980s. This week saw a change.

Rik Mayall died this week. And despite the fact that he had far more to do with. In the late 1990s he had a quad bike accident, which had caused him serious brain damage, and had made him susceptible to some sort of epileptiform seizure and it appears that his death, at an age only a year older than me, a year younger than Graham, and two years younger than Corinna, was probably something to do with this.

I know more about epileptiform seizures than I do rock and roll, although I make a living writing about the latter rather than the former, and therefore – knowing what I do – I am quite prepared to admit the probability that Rik Mayall – the People's Poet – (P) Rik, was a man who – without knowing – shaped the destiny of a whole slew of us, was dead due to a concatenation of events which had nothing to do with Thatcher, the establishment or anything else that he railed about during his career, is dead. And a little bit of me, is dead with him.

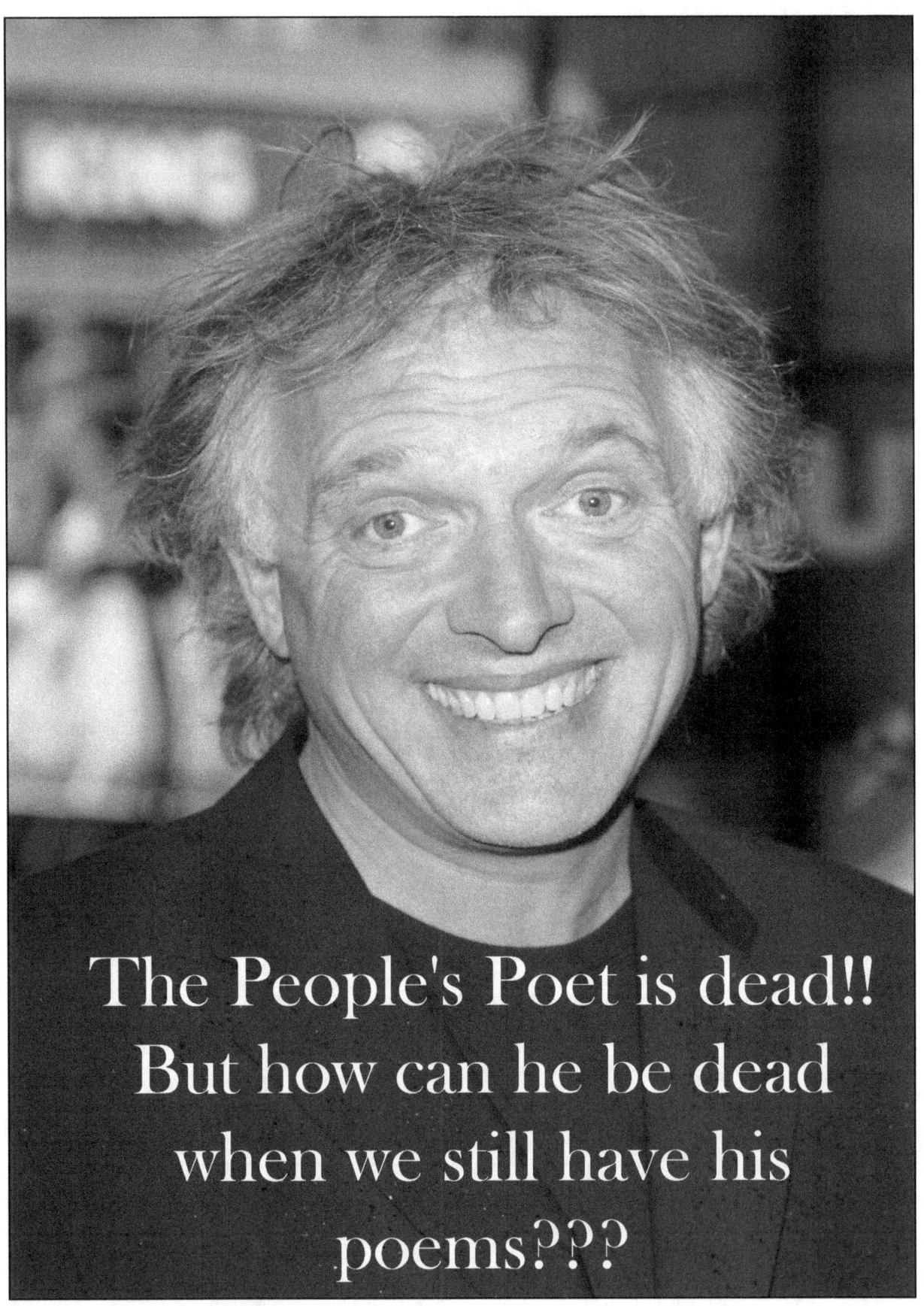

I would like to pretend, as editor of these pages, that the encapsulation of what I do comes from Mick Farren, Jon Sinclair, or the pages of the late-'60s, early '70s or whatever, underground press. But it doesn't. More of what I am, what I pretend to be, or what I have ever pretended to be, comes from bits and bobs to do with that particular 1980s BBC comedy series (*The Young Ones*) than it does anything else.

But, the People's Poet is dead. But how can he be dead, if we still have his poetry?

Does this make sense to you? I don't know, I don't care. *The Young Ones* was one of the few socio-cultural media events of the early 1980s which really affected, not just me, but everybody I knew.

I would like to say that we had all been influenced by Jerry Rubin or people of that ilk, but we weren't. Rik Mayall and his comrades, did something unforgiveable. They didn't manage to delineate where reality ended and entertainment began. This is why I, and many people like me, are far more upset today than we should be for the death of a comedian.

And if you want to know about the death of a comedian, just check out the first chapter of Watchmen.

But the death of Rik Mayall is not the only thing which has happened this week which has upset my equilibrium. The Weird Weekend, the event that I have been promoting for the last fourteen years is under threat.

I still have no idea what I am going to do about the Weird Weekend. In the week I posted that:

"There are more unfortunate developments re the Village Hall Committee and the Weird Weekend. They have put the price up again, and unless they back down it looks like I shall have to cancel. Everyone will get a shiny sparkling refund, and offered the option of a little present instead."

After my posting , five different people contacted me offering to pay part or all of the extra money, and I am overwhelmed by their love and support.

The problem is not really the money, however, but a matter of principle. Through no fault of ours, the ladies who have done such an excellent job of the catering for the last six or seven years are not able to do it this year. I asked the organisation which runs The Small School in Hartland, an institution with whom I have much sympathy, to do it.

The Community Centre are now charging us a surcharge of £150 because the Small School is not from the village. The fact that they are from a small town five miles away seems to be irrelevant.

I think that this is completely outrageous.

On top of this, it has been made clear to me that the views we hold and have expressed about bloodsports and the badger cull have not made me/us popular in certain quarters.

Against this background of bad vibes, I feel uneasy about holding an event that has always worked on happy co-operation and good vibes to produce a truly magickal experience. I am waiting to hear back from the Hall Committee before I make up my mind, but with the mixture of bad vibes and poor ticket sales and the number of WW regulars who will be unavoidably absent this year due to other commitments, I am tempted to cancel this year's event, and start again in a new venue in 2015.

It makes me wonder what The People's Poet would have done? Probably run about shouting that everyone involved was a "complete bastard" and that it was all a neo-fascist conspiracy, which I don't think that it is.

He would then have composed a piece of freeform poetry which would have made McGonagal sound like Shelley.

But none of that really gives me any pointers as to what decision I am going to have to make. Should I cancel in order to showcase the greed and stupidity of the people involve? Should I carry on regardless so as not to disappoint the people who have already bought tickets and booked their holidays in advance?

Truly, I still have no idea.

Where's Wally?

As I have mentioned before in these hallowed pages I have a love/hate relationship with anniversaries. I think if something matters to you, you should remember it all the time, not just on selective dates. But this is the 40th anniversary of the first Stonehenge Festival, the 30th anniversary of the last Stonehenge Festival and to break that run of glorious dates divisible by 10 it is the 39th anniversary of the death of Wally Hope.

Who was Wally Hope? His real name was Phillip Russell and he was born in 1939. He was a friend and artistic collaborator of Penny Rimbaud and other members of the free house in Essex which later gave birth to the legendary anarcho-punks Crass. He was a member of a countercultural group in London called The Dwarves, who were described as being a Notting Hill version of Ken Kesey's Merry Pranksters or the Dutch Provo group who inspired the classic My White Bicycle.

Here it should be pointed out that despite claims to the contrary, Provo – a Dutch anarchist group active in the mid-60s – have, and had, no link whatsoever with the Irish Provos (Provisional IRA). It was just one of those peculiar lexilinks which turn up in life more often than one would like to believe.

Phil adopted the name Wally Hope and together with a band of like-minded anarchists, started the Stonehenge Free Festival. A year later he was imprisoned on jumped up charges, driven to the edge of psychosis with institutional medication and – a few months after his release – committed suicide or was murdered depending on who you believe.

The Wally Hope story came to prominence culturally in 1982 when a major essay by Penny Rimbaud telling his take on the subject was included in a booklet included with their lavishly packaged 1982 album, Christ the Album.

This bitter, and often naïve, booklet has achieved the status of a hagiography in many people's eyes and Wally Hope has become a legendary figure, almost a hippy saint.

Thirty years after the Battle of the Beanfield, alternative culture in the United Kingdom is in a very different state that it was when the eyes of the world were focussed on a motley collection of travellers in semi-legal school buses.

Countercultural publishing with magazines, including this one, has taken advantage of the new technology provided by the internet and the mass communication provided by social media. But rising above it all is the legendary figure of Wally Hope.

One wonders what he would have thought of it all, and although one suspects that he would have found his elevation to the sainthood to be rather embarrassing, one suspects that if he were to walk into the room now and look dispassionately at the counterculture of 2014 that he might be mildly amused.

His cremated ashes were put into an ornate wooden box made by Rimbaud and emblazoned with the legend "Wally Hope, Victim of Ignorance". These ashes have – in many ways – achieved the status of a holy relic and have been passed down a long line of custodians.

The most recent custodian is Dean Phillips, or Dean Wally, and the other day we gave him a call and had a wide ranging conversation covering Stonehenge Festivals, past and present, the traveller lifestyle, and what it means to be an anarchist in the 21st Century.

http://www.gonzomultimedia.co.uk/radio/player.php?id=279

JON MEETS A PRUNE

Electric Prunes fans are buzzing with excitement about the release of a new CD of unreleased live material titled 'WaS'! Featuring 15 slamming cuts to keep you up at night! American psychedelic rock group The Electric Prunes first achieved international attention in the late 1960s. The band performed their 1966 hit song "I Had Too Much to Dream (Last Night)" on American Bandstand, and were also recognized for the song "Kyrie Eleison", which was featured on the 'Easy Rider' soundtrack. After a period in which they had little control over their music, they disbanded for several years. In 1999, much to the delight of their fans worldwide, The Electric Prunes reformed, and resumed recording and touring!

And now an interplanetary message from James Lowe of the Electric Prunes...

"The Electric Prunes invite you, our closest friends, to a new adventure! WaS. That WaS the Electric Prunes! It has been a long journey here and we have waited till the planetary alignment was correct for a new release. The lunar eclipse signaled the start of something, tho no one is sure exactly what? We offer WaS as the saucer to fast forward you to the cosmic finish.

There is a fine line between 'IS' and 'WAS'. If what you did is more important than what you are doing, you WAS. One moment you is and then you was. Somehow 1967 doesn't seem much different from today; tastes change but I think people are always on the lookout for some fresh ideas from the 'is' that makes them remember the 'was'.

Mark Tulin and I were collecting ideas and songs for our last adventure when hethe records; witnessed by some of the goofy cuts we have released, we were just happy to be able to record our thoughts. It seems fitting that we release this 9th offering with the same abandon. This is a garage band and is not meant to be taken seriously. The music here is from all layers of the band from 1966 to 2014. This is a cool album, maybe the last we will ask you to support. But we do hope you will post it on the web and dance to it in the moonlight on 11! There is even a music video by the band for TOKYO floating around! Please bring your friends because the band wants to go out and play live one more time and we need you for that. Tell your local club to invite us. We will come.... We WaS but we still Is ...."

The 15-track CD features a throwback version of "Smokestack Lightning" from 2000 that was the band's reunion call-to-arms with

Ken Williams on lead guitar, Quint back up on drums, Mark Tulin on bass and an occasional harmonica by James Lowe. Original noise! There is also a live version of "Bullet Thru The Backseat" from a night in Bristol England featuring Williams, Lowe, Tulin, Dooley, more original fare.

That press release arrived last week on my desk, and to say that I was intrigued is an understatement. I have always been a fan of the Prunes since I first heard I Had Too Much To Dream (Last Night) from one of the Nuggets compilations. I then went on to a massively scratched copy of Mass in F Minor, and I was a complete convert.

The fact that I heard a bit of the latter record during the sublime Easy Rider was just another bonus.

Diffidently I emailed Billy James who had sent out the press release. Was there any chance that I could interview James Lowe, the singer?

Yeah, why not, came back the message, and, grasping my new iPad in my sweaty hands I Skyped him. Listen to our conversation here:

http://www.gonzomultimedia.co.uk/radio/player.php?id=281

OZ DESERVES TO BE FIRST - IT WAS HIS IDEA AFTER ALL

MEMORIES OF A FREE FESTIVAL

MAN AT STONEHENGE 1984
- OZ HARDWICK

SNORKWIND AT STONEHENGE 1984
- OZ HARDWICK

Hello

As it was my idea, I thought I'd best send in my memories from Stonehenge '84. Along with this, I attach a couple of photos - one of the festival's main drag, & the other of me with Trevor Hughes (Hawkfrendz) and Alan Davey, who made his first appearances with Hawkwind at the festival. To be honest, I can't place most of the more-day-to day stuff in any particular year, but one thing I do recall specifically about 1984 is that it was ridiculously hot and, in consequence, dusty, so there was a patina of dust over pretty much everyone and everything.

Being young & somewhat foolish, I used to head off to festivals without even a tent back then, trusting to good fortune - and it never failed. That year, myself & my mate Mik found a bit of ground under the canopy of a friend's tent from which to venture out into the beautiful chaos. Naturally, 30 years on, that chaos is a bit of a blur, but there were a few musical highlights that have stayed in the memory.

Man on the main stage played a blinder, and were preceded by a comedian who I remember singing a ridiculous version of 'Rock around the Clock' - the sort of thing Ted Chippington used to do - was it him? Lying on my back just outside the Tibetan Ukrainian Mountain Troupe's tent, I heard one of the most amazing spacey jams I'd ever experienced, though didn't wrench myself upright to look at the band. Asking around later, it turned out they were called Ozric Tentacles.

Hawkwind played a couple of times, but while everyone remembers the Ritual set, for me the highlight was a low-key set - again in the TUMT tent - where they played with Agent Beartrap under the name Snorkwind, with a set made up of both acts' material, including stuff Hawkwind hadn't played for years ('Brainbox Pollution' comes to mind) - it was probably a mess, but I have very fond memories.

This must have been very late night/early morning, and when we got back to the tent we found they'd left.

Our stuff had just been left in a couple of bags, and no-one had interfered with it. So off we went & found a large sheet of polythene to sleep under, with just our heads poking out the end. Woke up around midday with the worst sunburn I've ever had in my life! Hope you get some good responses.

Cheers,
Oz.tick it

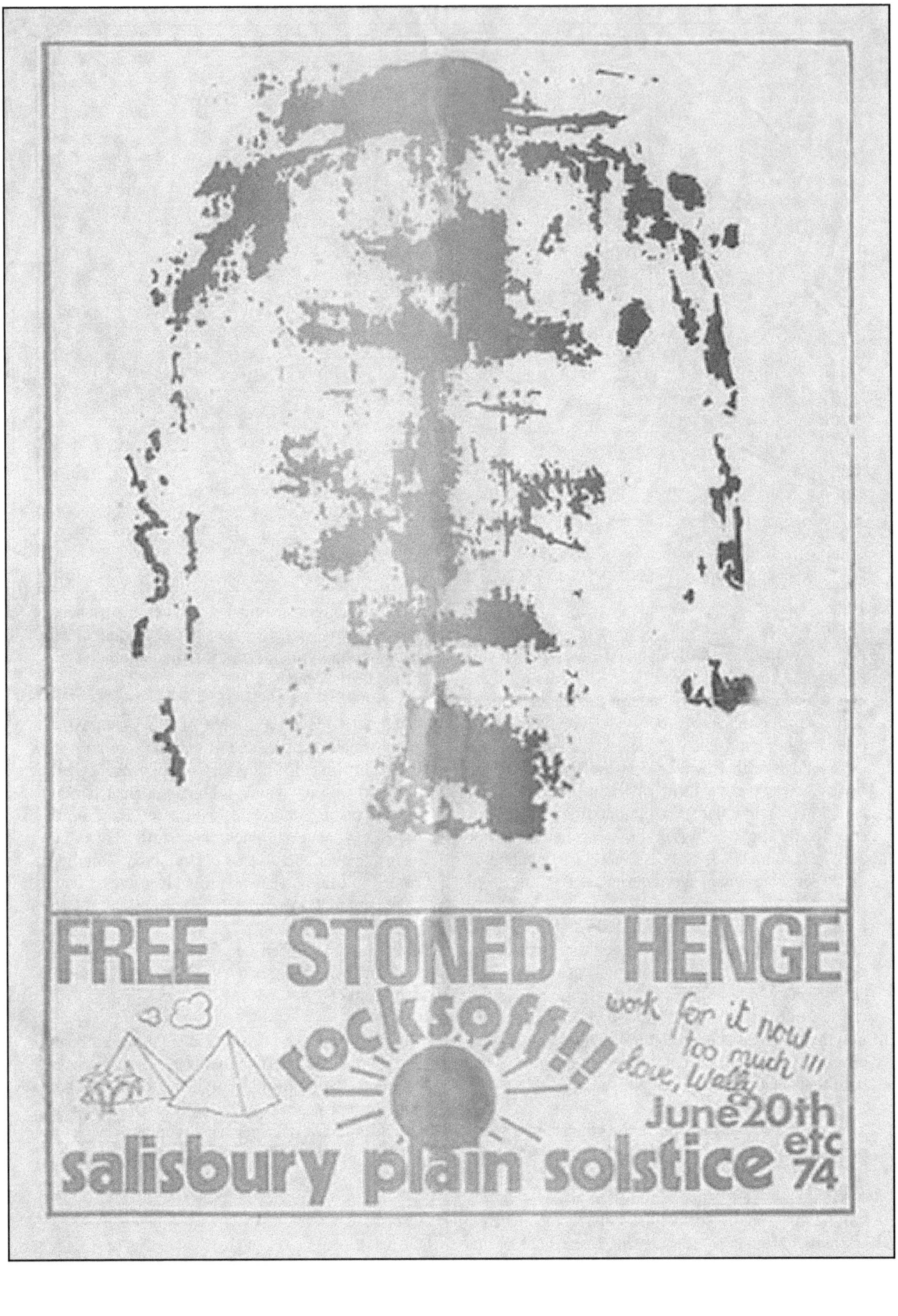
FREE STONED HENGE
rocksoff!!
work for it now
too much !!!
love, Wally
June 20th
etc
74
salisbury plain solstice

WALLY REMEMBERS WALLY

FORTY YEARS AGO........................
June was a very busy month for our friend Wally Hope. He had been planning and organising the first Stonehenge Free Festival all year. Invites had been sent; bands had been encouraged to come and play; he had been flyering all the hippiest areas of London. His broadsheet proclaiming his pilgrimage to Stonehenge had been printed at Dial House and his friend Gee had helped him design a poster incorporating the Turin Shroud image that he always carried with him. He had sent off nearly five hundred envelopes packed with a map, poster, a poem sheet and a booklet. These had been sent to most of the English public school debating societies, social secretaries of many of the leading universities in the world, the leading religions, Bahi, Sufi, Native American church, Divine Light, Quakers, most of the major bands, Stars, communes, Friends of Friends, of Friends etc. etc. etc. Prince Charles, Amin, Gadaffi and Dustin Hoffman, Dalai Lama, Desmond Morris and more...Now he had to wait and see what would happen next.

On the Road Home
Sunday

(1974)

Dear Sir,
    with all well meaning respect, Our Lord GOD and his son Jesus Christ, have ordained a spiritual Pilgrimage to Stonehenge on 20th June 21st etc, to fulfill the TWO COMMAND MEANTS

LOVE ! ! GOD
Love your neighbour.

You are and will be our neighbour we beg of you for help, friendship and trust, if the gathering is overflowing big, we will give you any help you need, but you must respect we are to GOD's law, and trying to balance the violence, corruption, insuing 3rd world war, oily energy crisis, to Manual communal Farming Love Peace and Freedom

Your Best mate WALLY   HELP   For the Kids ✕

He had also managed to get the support of the pirate radio station, Radio Caroline. They then advertised the upcoming gathering as a 'Festival of Loving Awareness' and promoted it with catchy jingles. There is some proof that Wally also travelled to the ship and did an interview for Mike Hagler. (If any Gonzo readers can shed any light on this it would be appreciated).

Wally Hope was also respectful enough to write to his new neighbours before the event. In the spring of '74 he sent a letter to 'the farmer of the land around Stonehenge.'

> ' On the RoAD Home
> Sunday
>
> Dear Sir,
> with all well meaning respect,
>
> Our Lord God and his son Jesus Christ, have ordained a spiritual Pilgrimage to Stonehenge on 20th June 21st etc, to fulfill the Two COMMANDMENTS
>
> Love God   Love your neighbour. you are and will be our neighbour. We beg of you for help, Friendship and trust, if the gathering is overflowing big, we will give you any help you need, but you must respect we are to God's Law, and trying to balance the violence, corruption, insuing 3rd world war, oily energy crisis, to Manual communal Farming Love
>
> Peace and Freedom
> Your Best mate
>   WALLY
>   HELP For the Kids X'

This next excerpt is an exclusive peek into the world of Wally Hope. It comes from a book he was working on called *Windsor Rock,* which has kindly been lent to me by Penny Rimbaud. Take it away Wally:

> ' I arrived at Stonehenge on the 19th of June 1974 expecting everybody, anything, I found the Henge surrounded by three rows of 8ft barbed wire and a straggly camp of true Wallies.
>
> Well, to cut a long story short, I communicated with the authorities about the possibilities which thankfully they found humourous and logical and placed my tent on the hill overlooking the Henge, by a cow trough of sacred water. We had a rae old night, hoisted the Union Wally to herald in allies and waited.
>
> Well, by the Solstice night, we had at least three thousand Wallies, mostly cream of Windsor Free. All moved to come. Hardly any of my envelope lot answered the call, their national anthem was BAND ON THE RUN !
>
> THE FIRST SHALL COME LAST.
> THE LAST SHALL COME FIRST
>
> SPEARHEAD TIME
>
> We had a Stereo Disco Unit, who for four, five days and nights gave us everyone a gem. A synthesiser band

The Gonzo Annual 2015

called Zorch blew our minds to the universe, The Wallys danced the finest I have ever seen, exploding zillions of joyful stars in the night sky, we became Druids immediately, celebrating noon at our own built mini henge, toasted with five tins of guinness, cooled in our mascot, Clarence the Bull's Water Trough.

Holland based private station Radio Caroline, broadcast it as the festival of L.A, loving awareness. All Europe and Scandinavia were there. We telepathed to Ibiza, South America, India, Venus etc. I couldn't sleep there was so much energy, thanks to Worthing

A 30 foot plastic sapling Dome was sacrifice built, later sheltering in rain drop glittering bliss, an entrenched unite, through the driving tough weather.

Hundreds of trailers passed through the camp, all one, all together, we had pioneered the only campsite for pilgrims.

Our neighbours were the British Army, Tank Corps behind us, Artillery to the left, Airforce in front, and germ warfare to our right.

Our best friends were everybody, espeschally the Royal Military Police Wallys, and the Hengeburger Wallys, who gave us wasted bread rolls to soak up our vegetable bean grain stews and other gourmet treats. The Wally police thought it all very funny having real ancient britons on their patch. Our main problem was the Farmers who were worried about our dead wood collections on their land, also due to instances: non common sense behavior, but seeing we had to be there for some yet undisclosed reason, we had to be there, Willy Nilly, eat and keep warm.

I kidnapped my friend Charlie who had for three years built a red indian teepee, to the pure essence of painting.

The canvas became a living white spotted eagle, bird of Aquarius Dove, head the door flap, eye the central SUN, tail the Smoke Flaps, wings the sides, the left to the pattern of

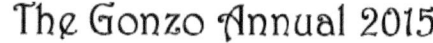

Mother Moon, the right patterned to Father SUN, the skeleton was twelve poles, symbolising the twelve hours, months, astrological signs, knights of King Arthur, tribes of Israel and disciples of Jesus. The central fire symbolised the 0 and 13, Alpha and Omega, the Heart.

When the winds blew, the bird shimmered to take off, the canvas swirling buffalo, trout, the Pied Piper and Leaves

EVERYBODY IS WALLY
EVERYDAY IS SUNDAY
FOGHT WALLY
c/o GOD, Jesus and Buddha
Garden of Allah
Stonehenge Monument
Wiltshire.

IF THE LEOPARD CAN'T CHANGE ITS SPOTS, THE LION MUST LIE WITH THE LAMB".

Electro wizards Zorch played at the Stones in 74. Basil Brooks recalls:

"We knew Wally Hope who got it all together. This was the first one there. So the band all piled in to the old green van and made it there."

Zorch set up stage facing the Stones.......200 yards away .

"1974, it wasn't heavy at all . Not many people there . Best so far. First day the whole band played and we went down pretty well."

The following day was Basil Brooke's solo set during which he completely freaked out a guy in the audience who thought he was conjuring up Dark Forces .

"There was a little police Cortina parked in the road – that was the police presence! Innocent days."

Wally Jake describe his first impressions of Stoned Henge...

"At the top of the sloping crest,

overlooking the stones is a synthesiser desk. A blonde bronzed figure is talking through it. The message is simple, though nearly inaudible through the sound effects. OK, so this crazy figure is sproating cosmic gibberish through the mike.

"Who's the nutter with the synth ?"

"He's not a nutter, He's Wally, he organised the festival".

It's very hot, at the peak of summer, but wakening in the open air next morning it feels cold, my sleeping bag loses feathers in a great cloud as I get up, it looks like snow.

Wally appears at the fireside. "Get up and greet the sun, He'll come up. He'll shine And he does, while Wally brews up the best coffee you've ever tasted in a steel mess tin coffee kit.

A stuttering biker joins the fire. His studded armband draws Wally's comment ," That's real Viking stuff". he says.

And I see then, this guy is no peace freak.

Wally wears a Black Watch Kilt this morning. He's wearing it because it's a specifically military Highland tartan. He's a Sun Worshipper,

He's Arthur of the Round table. His money goes on making his people, our movement strong. Festivals, Tipi's materials and machines for his people.

And ACID. "Long Sunny Daze" he says.

As the alternative paper Maya later reported it…

"Suns of the Sun, the Wallys, are letting the mysteries of Stonehenge work through them, despite the barbed wire that surrounds it, despite the Army bases and despite the state nets of secular legalisms. Freedom is a career."

And Wally put it well when he said:

"The Department of the Environment said they were looking after Stonehenge for the people. We said , we are the people, we'll help look after it".

Wally Hope had won. He had held his first Stonehenge Free Peoples Festival and he was squatting on the land at Stonehenge.

He was being watched by the keepers of the Stones, and he in turn watched them and waited for their next move.

I shall leave the last word to Phil Russell. On June 24th a Stonehenge postcard was sent home to his guardians in Ongar. He simply wrote...

"ALL TOO FAR OUT !! LOOK OUT BAD OLD WORLD. THE WALLIES ARE ERE !! LOVE PHIL, YER SUN".

WISHING A HAPPY SOLSTICE TO ALL WALLIES FROM WALLY DEAN x

Wally Dean can be found at Wally's Bar at Pilton, for the next two weeks, and as we sit putting this issue together on Midsummer's Night he will be at Stonehenge. He asked me to point out that the picture of the stones from the air is the front of the postcard he mentioned and asked me to credit another old mate of mine Nigel Ayres for the picture of the stones surrounded by barbed wire.

I suggest that you check out the Wally Hope Appreciation Society Facebook page:
https://www.facebook.com/groups/180481282065/

and if you want to contact Wally Dean do so c/o wallyhopesociety@yahoo.co.uk

AND MOONWEED WRITES

What always amazed me about this Photo (Photo:Steve Gay) is the total lack of any of those who claim to have held the festival together..I'm second row down, on the right ... Did the Solstice at Glastonbury in 1979, and then stopped going. This is 1976 or 77.

Don't know year here (BELOW) - friend sent it

The Gonzo Annual 2015

Garry Masters writes:

Hiya

I saw your request for pics from the festival so here's one you might like to use...

Garry Moonboot of The Magic Mushroom Band with daughter Jasmine at Stonehenge Free Festival 1984

regards

Garry

A little bit of digging and one discovers that Garry Masters *is* Garry Moonboot, and his little girl will now be in her thirties. And finally, a letter from no less a luminary than Dead Fred, who claims that we actually are a year out in our calculations:

Hi there Jon.

At about 2.30 AM on 21st June 1973, Myself and Trev Thoms picked the lock next to the watchman's hut whilst he dozed inside.

We got right up under the stones and played a few songs from our religious set which included "I Saw God" and "It Was One Move" both written in 1971 on Trev's post Cotswold acid trip. Finally the guard came and politely asked us to leave, we showed him the open lock as we passed the gate, I think I suggested they get a Chubb or similar.

There were a few vans in the car park 20 or 30 heads at the most. So I claim that we played the first festival in 1973 making this the 41st anniversary of rock at the 'Henge.

We got in the van and went to the Glastonbury Tor pre sunrise and climbed. Cloud obscured the sunrise on that misty morning.

Trev and I played the Henge many times in later years with either ICU or Hawkwind '79 '80 '81 '82 '83 '84 under various pyramid stages. Trev Thoms slipped off his mortal coil in 2010 but will be remembered at this years Kozfest where the second stage is named for him as 'Judge Trev's Place'

Missed yes forgotten no.

Love and peace this solstice time.
Dead Fred.

The Gonzo Annual 2015

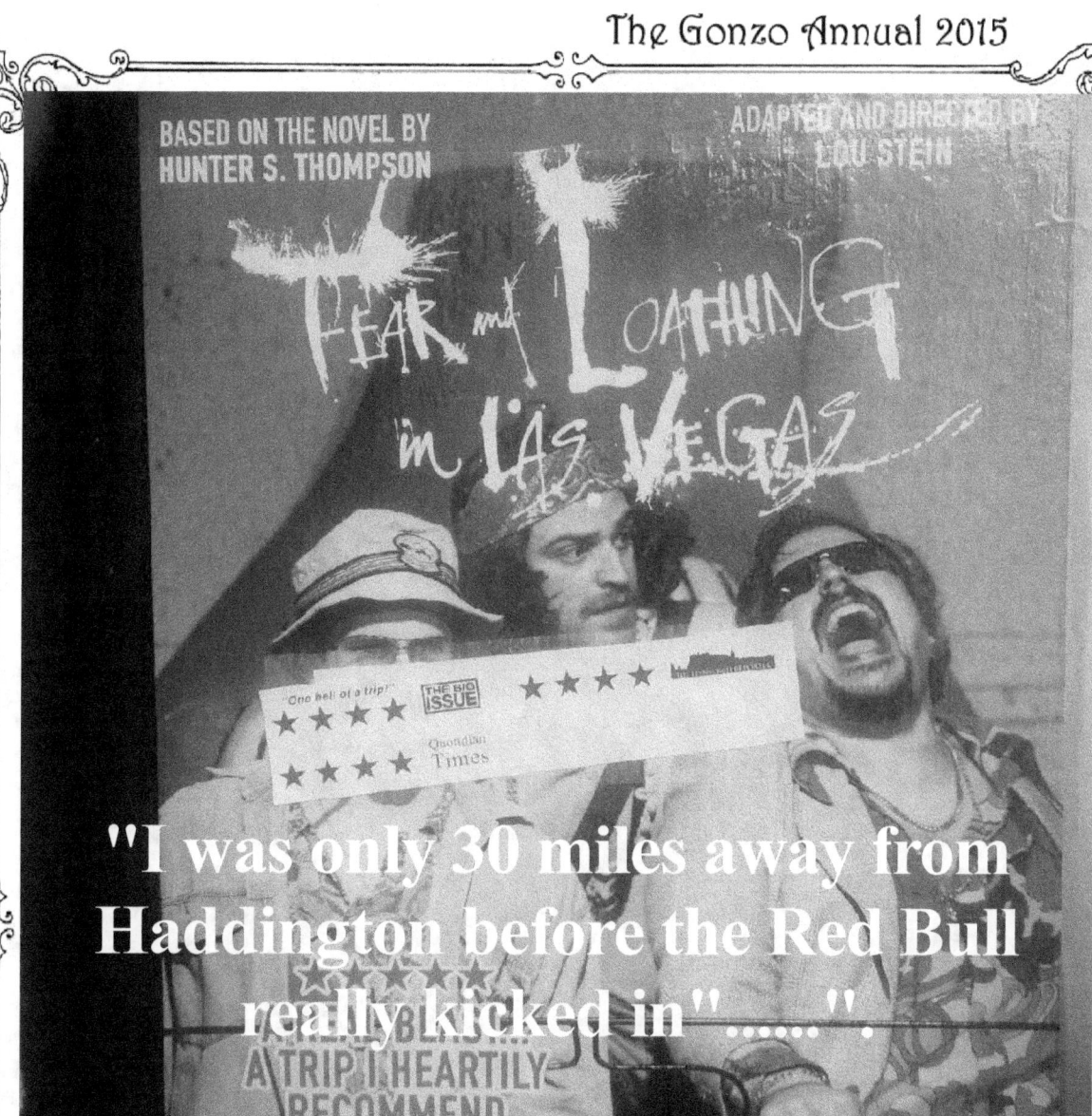

"I was only 30 miles away from Haddington before the Red Bull really kicked in"......".

The other day, the Gonzo Grande Fromage, Rob Ayling, went up to Edinburgh to see Lou Stein's theatrical adaptation of Hunter Thompson's *Fear and Loathing in Las Vegas*. There was an interview with Lou in last week's magazine, and a feature on the play in #86. Now enjoy Rob's words and pics:

Our fearless chief, regardless of huge personal risk to himself took the medium grey shark (maybe it was another colour, as it is in need of a car wash) aka the Gonzo Mobile to the Edinburgh Fringe festival on a Saturday. Despite facing multiple caravans, tractors etc on the A1, along with disillusioned Scots fleeing the country south with the cars full of 5 pound notes, before the in or out vote, he made it to the Scottish capital in one piece.

"What a trip!!! I was Lou Steins guest of honour for the day to the stage version of "Fear and Loathing in Las Vegas". What a great version! As we all know F&L is one of the sacred texts that shouldn't be messed with, (like doing a cover version of Stairway to Heaven) but Lou along with Terry Gilliam pulled it off. The show gets a whopping double thumb salute from me. So book your tickets now!" said Rob.

Now back to those caravans on the A1....
"I was only 30 miles away from Haddington before the Red Bull really kicked in"......".

"Maybe it meant something. Maybe not, in the long run, but no explanation, no mix of words or music or memories can touch that sense of knowing that you were there and alive in that corner of time and the world. Whatever it meant."

"Every now and then when your life gets complicated and the weasels start closing in, the only cure is to load up on heinous chemicals and then drive like a bastard from Hollywood to Las Vegas ... with the music at top volume and at least a pint of ether."

On Wednesday, I went into the aviary to feed the rescued magpie we are looking after, much the same as I have been doing for the past couple of weeks; this aviary being the home of our Reeves pheasant - Vic. Every day I have been going in, chatting cheerfully to Vic, then leaving without any bother. The day before I noticed he was a bit 'iffy' but on Wednesday, just as I was leaving, he rushed me and pecked my leg. Now, that is the first time I have been attacked by a pheasant, and should - no doubt - just notch it up as one of those unique events in life.

However, no pheasant is going to get the better of me. I am not too sure whether it was the fact that he pecked me, or that he made a self-satisfying little noise as he did so, but, boy oh boy, did I give him what for! I can't remember exactly what I said - very loudly - but it was along the lines of 'Don't you dare do that again you little sod', and waggled my finger at him as I bent down and invaded his ever-so-smug pheasant personal space. And do you know, I think he actually regretted his faux pas? He looked at me with his little beady eye and backed away looking more than a little abashed.

Pheasants and Mondegreens
By Corinna Downes

On Thursday I was prepared for a possible re-match, but all has been quiet on the pheasant front since. But try it again and he may well rue the day he crossed me, the little blighter.

But that is by the by, and absolutely nothing to do with cabinets, although one could perhaps file it under curiosities.

And now, we move on to:

Mondegreens
'I beg your pardon?' I hear you ask. This is your science lesson of the week. This is the name given to misheard lyrics no less. And, apparently, their study can have real psychological significance according to this little treasure I discovered:

"The Mondegreens

We've all had those

THE BITCH IS BACK

The Gonzo Annual 2015

awkward moments. A group of friends is singing in a car, and suddenly, someone says the wrong word. And everyone looks at each other, wondering how that person heard the wrong song lyrics, or whether they themselves are wrong. These little misunderstandings are common, but most people don't know that there is an official title for them. It came from a popular essay by writer Sylvia Wright, where she recalled when her mother read a certain book of poems to her. One of the verses was as follows:

Ye Highlands and ye Lowlands,
Oh, where hae ye been?
They hae slain the Earl o' Moray,
And Lady Mondegreen

Readers will be glad to know that Lady Mondegreen was spared the slaughter, but only because she never existed. The actual last line of the verse was, "And laid him on the green." Wright christened these misheard lyrics, which often make the poem or song better for the listener, "mondegreens". The title caught on."

"I heard "I can feel it coming in the air tonight," as "I can hear it coming in the yellow night," well into my college years, and thought Phil Collins was just being poetic. A friend of mine claims both her parents, independently, heard Creedence Clearwater Revival's "There's a bad moon on the rise," as "There's a bathroom on the right." She had to be born, grow up, listen to the song herself, and correct them before they even considered that they were wrong. When she asked them how they thought the lyrics were directions to the bathroom, her father answered, "I just figured they were stoned." Which is as good an explanation as any."

Two of mine are: 'Me ears are alight' instead of 'Israelites' by Desmond Dekker and 'Sue Lawley' instead of 'So Lonely' by Police.

Anyone out there want to share their mondegreens with me? Please email me at corinna@cfz.org Not only will it go to prove that there is someone out there who actually reads my drivel (which would make me a happy girlie) but it also could make quite a fun thing to add here. Come on folks, don't be shy; it's nothing to be embarrassed about.

If you want to learn more about mondegreens, have a read here:
Well that was a nice little earner:
Dylan's Like a Rolling Stone lyrics fetch $2m record

"A working draft of one of Bob Dylan's most popular songs, Like a Rolling Stone, has set a record at auction for a popular music manuscript.

The manuscript, said to be the only known draft of the final lyrics, garnered $2m (£1.2m) at Sotheby's.

Dylan wrote the song, about a debutante cast from upper-class society who becomes a loner, in 1965 at age 24.

The sale of the handwritten lyrics eclipses the 2010 sale of John Lennon's writings for A Day in the Life, the final track on the Beatle's 1967 Sgt. Pepper's Lonely Hearts Club Band album.

Those lyrics sold for $1.2m in 2010."

MERRELL'S X FILES

This week I had an email from our old friend Merrell Fankhauser in which he told me a rather interesting story. Ok, to tell the truth he told me this some months ago but this is the first time it has been made public knowledge. As you know I have somewhat of a double life being a mildly well known Fortean as well as a jobbing music scribe, and as anyone who has ever read this magazine will attest, I am also very much a Beatles fan, so this story ticks all the boxes for me:

The author of "Alien Rock," a book about famous rock stars and their alien encounters, this week revealed on "Coast to Coast AM" radio that John Lennon was in contact with highly talented Extraterrestrial Musical Forces who enabled the late Beatle to write many of his greatest hits. Michael C. Luckman, who is also director of the New York Center for Extraterrestrial Research, told the nation's largest late night radio audience that Lennon confided to West Coast surf guitar king Merrell Fankhauser that he regularly experienced an automatic writing phenomenon that originated from an outside source.

Lennon told Fankhauser that muse-like spirits allowed him to hear entire songs in his head which he quickly wrote down. Fankhauser explained that he experienced the very same phenomenon that also helped him produce some of his best music. The unusual conversation between Lennon and Fankhauser took place at singer Harry Nilsson's home in Los Angeles in 1977.

The two quickly became friends.

Luckman quoted Lennon as saying that he felt "like a hollow temple filled with many spirits, each one passing through me, each one inhabiting me for a little time and then leaving me to be replaced by another." Lennon said that these were the moments that he lived for. Lennon's wife, Yoko Ono, once told Playboy magazine that "They (the Beatles) were like mediums. "They weren't conscious of all they were saying, but it was coming through them." Luckman noted that to this day Lennon's bandmate, Paul McCartney, cannot write or read music.

The veteran UFO researcher said that he has statements from a surprising number of famous artists who regularly get their inspiration from muses or spirits. "In some cases the artists actually feel guilty that they have been credited for songs that they haven't written," said Luckman, who is currently writing a sequel to "Alien Rock" titled, "Rock Stars, Hollywood and Real Aliens: Celebrities' Biggest Secrets." He is also at work on an explosive new book about Michael Jackson.

Fankhauser started in 1962 with the instrumental surf group The Impacts who had a hit album titled "Wipe Out". He went on to form the Psychedelic Folk Rock groups Fapardokly, HMS Bounty and MU. His studies and discoveries about the fabled Lost Continent Of Mu have been published in magazines and books worldwide. He has played with Rock icons, Ed Cassidy of Spirit, Nicky Hopkins who played with The Rolling Stones and The Beatles, Dean Torrence of Jan and Dean and Willie Nelson just to name a few.

He's been doing a popular West Coast TV show called Tiki Lounge for twelve years that airs on the California Central Coast and Hawaii. His latest release is a Merrell Fankhauser "Best Of" 2 CD set that covers his music from 1964 to present, on the U.K. Gonzo Multimedia label.

Merrell Fankhauser And Friends still perform live today and will be headlining a 60's bands reunion in Palmdale California July 19th.

THE BIG CHEESE SANDWICH

Yesterday the Gonzo Grande Fromage, Rob Ayling, sent me this picture with a two word comment, "cool eh?" Have you ever wondered what would happen if you mixed a big cheese with the God of Hellfire and add a modicum of bread? Yes. You guessed it, you get a toasted cheese sandwich. And is there anyone in the universe who doesn't like toasted cheese sandwiches? If there is, then they shouldn't be reading this magazine.

So, yes, we have now established that everyone likes toasted cheese sandwiches, but you know what everybody also likes? A forthcoming series of archive compilations from none other than Arthur Brown. We don't have any more details at the moment, only that they are happening, they will be later in the year and that there are likely to be ten of them including material going back to 1969.

Of course, there is history between Messrs Ayling and Brown.

In the early 1990s he was working as a house painter in Texas together with the legendary Jimmy Carl Black (the Indian of the group), and Rob flew Arthur over to the UK for his first British tour for many years. I saw him on this tour back in 1993/4 when they came to Plymouth and he was utterly awesome.

I am very much looking forward to working with him.

This week once again through the magic of Facebook, I had a long chat with Cyrille Verdeaux of the mighty Clearlight. In fact he *is* Clearlight, but that's another story. I wanted to know more about his remarkable album 'Tribal Hybrid Concept' which features one of the world's most legendary eco-warriors.

But first I asked him about another one of his albums, 'First Visions', which is being re-released by Gonzo. He told me:

"It was recorded in 1977 and this is my first album where I was 100% producing, recording, mixing...it was fun to be the decisions taker in the recording studio...It has been chosen also to be in the 100 best prog albums for the Billboard magazine guy."

Raoni Metuktire first became known to the Rock & Roll world thanks to musician Sting, who came to meet him in the Xingu in November 1987. On October 12, 1988, Sting participated with Raoni to a press conference prior to the Sao Paulo show of the 'Human Rights Now!' Amnesty International tour. After the impact of this event, Sting, his wife Trudie Styler and Jean-Pierre Dutilleux became the co-founders of the Rainforest Foundation. The initial purpose of this association was to provide support to Raoni's projects, the first one being at that time the demarcation of Kayapos territory threatened by invasion. In February 1989, Raoni became one of the fiercest opponents to the Belo Monte dam project. Television broadcasts transmitted his opinions in Altamira during a huge assembly of chiefs.

Raoni Metuktire, also simply known as Chief Raoni, born ca. 1930, is an important chief of the Kayapo people, a Brazilian Indigenous group from the plain lands of the Mato Grosso and Pará in Brazil, south of the Amazon Basin and along Rio Xingu and its tributaries. He is a famous international character, a living symbol of the fight for the preservation of the Amazon rainforest and of the indigenous culture.

Raoni appears on 'Tribal Hybrid Concept', and I asked Cyrille how they met. He replied:

"I met him in the French Embassy in 2006 for the Bastille day's cocktails. But the communication is difficult, I don't understand his way of speaking Portuguese, lol"

But it was some years before Raoni actually

appeared on a Clearlight album. Cyrille explains:

"Three months ago, a French friend, Jean Michel Pinoteau told me he had recorded in 1998 a music with Raoni, from a sample that his friend J-L Dutilleux had done with Raoni during a movie he was doing about Raoni and he asked me if I had an idea to help him to release it.

Since I had done my album Tribal Hybrid Concept in the same spirit (Music built around samplrs of chants and voices of various tribes around the Wold, I proposed him to host his song in my album that was scheduled to be released the next month. He sent me the song, and that's it."

"After, I picked up an interview of Raoni on Youtube, made a montage of it and added it as extra tack of Amazone Corazone, the last piece of the album."

Cyrille continued:

"But I didn't meet him directly during the process...I know Jean Michel saw him 3 weeks ago and gave him a CD. I am looking forward to the picture of Raoni holding it!"

I asked Cyrille about the philosophy behind the record:

"The idea came in 1995, when the sampled sounds technique started to rise up. A friend of min, Pascal Menetrey had just bought an EMULATOR and had many natural sounds stored, from rain to birds, gorillas, tribal chants from Africa, Asia, South America, etc. And I thought it could be challenging to crate a whole concept album with only sampled sounds. Use the animals as instruments to recreate a real organic tapestry."

"This album has now 14 songs packed with these natural and tribal sounds from all over the planet and the total number of samples is certainly good enough to figure in the Guinness Book of records."

"This is why it is called "tribal Hybrid". On the same tune, you could have bees from Kenya doing the rhythmic, chants of Tuvas or Inuits, mixed with sampled, instruments from Korea or Didgeridoos."

"And of course, this CD is dedicated to all tribes and species facing extinction. I guess this concept was so advanced that no label has been interested to sign and distribute the final product produced by Pascal and myself until GONZO now...20 years later."

JON MEETS PAUL MAY

I have been a musician for just about the same length of time I have wanted to be a music journalist and I formed my first band in the spring of 1975.

My secretary Andrea, who is a cheeky young flibbertigibbet, who really doesn't know her place in the potato shed and (just in case you think I am being disloyal to her) is typing this as I dictate, sniggered when I mentioned the spring of 1975 because that, apparently, was when she was born.

You can't get the staff anymore, and she steadfastly refuses to behave in the subservient manner that I would wish, and leads me a terrible life.

I am now completely confused and have no idea where I was going with this due to dear Andrea's girlish sarcasm, so I think I am going to have to start again.

In the spring of 1975 (shut up Andrea) I formed my first band, and wrote what I thought were terribly witty satirical songs about the then current political scene. With hindsight they were terrible, but what songs by a fifteen year old boy aren't?

Over the years my musical skills, and I like to think my songwriting ones, have got somewhat better and I have released a whole string of albums which very few people have heard and which even fewer people have paid for.

But I still have the conceit to call myself a musician, and so this week my fragile ego got a particularly pleasant boost when I received an email from Paul May, guitarist with – amongst other things – the Atkins/May Project. He attached a couple of MP3s of the songs he is planning for the next album – their third.

To my great delight, he not only asked me to critique them but asked for my opinions on salient points of the mix. In my fortieth year of musicianship, someone was taking me seriously at last!

I enjoyed the new material massively – with this third album the band are entering into pleasingly progressive territory with interesting key and rhythm changes, extended tracks, and a much more accomplished overall feel.

Al Atkins has never sounded better and I was astonished to hear that the massively groovy drumming was actually done by Paul himself. I needed to know more. Would he like to have a chat? I asked diffidently.

Of course he would, he replied, and after a few technical complications we got through to each other and proceeded to talk the hind legs off the proverbial donkey. We will, of course be talking again when the album is finally released, and - as I always do with their record - go through them track by track with both Paul and Al.

**http://
www.gonzomultimedia.co.u
k/radio/player.php?id=287**

As I think I have mentioned over the past few weeks, Glastonbury Festival is no longer the sort of event which I would enjoy attending. It is too large, too corporate and too far removed from my idea of what a rock festival should be. Don't get me wrong, I have no intention of being one of those irritating nostalgia freaks who bemoan the days when rock festivals were badly organised seas of mud full of violent bikers and intractable drug dealers. I went to more than my fair share of those back in the day, and didn't enjoy them very much. I am nearly 55, and more or less a cripple, and the idea of going to an event like that fills me with horror.

No, it is just that the overtly commercial and annoyingly bourgeois ethos which seems to permeate so many rock festivals now is totally at odds with what I feel that a festival should be.

After all, I promote my own festival once a year; it's not a rock festival (although there is a smat-

Festivals, education and other stuff

tering of music), it is a gathering of people interested in mystery animals, Forteana, UFOs, and all sorts of esoteric subjects. But I have tried to model its ethos upon the best of the festivals which I attended back when I was young enough and fit enough to do such things. And believe it or not, one of the things that we do at the Weird Weekend is to not make it too easy for people. Interspersed amongst the entry level talks, the fun and frivolity, are some talks which are serious hard science, and others which address what I consider to be important moral conundra. We have even had the occasional guest for whom speaking English is by no means their primary accomplishment - this not only makes the point that the subjects in which we deal are of truly global importance, but also that by experiencing this, we take the audience out of their comfort zone.

My nephew, David Braund-Philips, currently works as a freelance technician for various companies who put on big outdoor events such as air shows, food fairs, county shows …. and, yes, rock festivals. He came to see me yesterday during a brief four-day break between engagements and told me that there are now something in the region of 250 rock festivals in Britain each year, and that by far the biggest growth area in this industry are small events with less than (often very many less than) 10,000 attendees, and that these are the most successful, and are the ones that are growing in number. And I am not at all surprised.

In this issue, we feature an interview with Paul Woodwright who is one of the organisers of the KozFest Festival, which truly seems like one of the best of this new brand of festival. It is small enough to be manageable and retain its intimacy, but is still large enough to be able to put on a wide range of interesting acts, including (plug, plug, plug) Paradise 9, featuring our very own Jaki Windmill.

We are living in a world where people are getting ever more dehumanised, and where the concept of society is – each year – getting closer and closer to that which the late unlamented Margaret Hilda described in an interview with – of all things – *Woman's Own*

magazine in 1987. Those who are put in power over us seem to be doing their best to dismantle what remains of the welfare state as quickly as possible, the current education system seems to be designed not to educate, but to reduce a new generation of young consumers as quickly as possible, and everything appears to favour the selfish, the semi-literate, and the stupid more than the people who actually want to achieve something.

This week we were greeted by the appalling news that the BBC, once the gold standard by which programme making – both entertainment and documentary – has decided

> "that the scientific and factual approach of wildlife programming that led to the BBC dominating nature documentary production with global admiration is to come to an end.
>
> The head of the corporation's Natural History unit, Wendy Darke, said in the piece that the BBC will not be seeking to replace Sir David Attenborough but

will aim to present populist programmes with a range of presenters.

Ms Darke has said she is developing a range of presenters to work on BBC wildlife programmes, stressing the "need to continue to innovate and diversify". She added: "That includes offering a more diverse range of presenters and programme styles and formats that have relevance to people's lives."

The above quote, by the way, is taken from that anarchic organ of world revolution, the *Daily Telegraph*. Personally, I think this is a terrible move on the part of the BBC, although far from being a surprising one. Over the past three decades we have seen everything being dumbed down beyond all recognition, in order to provide an easy to digest pabulum for the ever more housebound and unthinking masses.

I have a steady stream of students who spend placements with me learning about a mixture of practical and theoretical zoology, and I am appalled by how little some of them know. It's not their fault; I put the blame firmly on the plate of the education system itself. It is a system which doesn't actually teach, it prepares children to pass exams, and to get high SAT scores, and this is a completely different thing.

It is a system which even teachers complete lies in order to further the socio-political agenda of those in charge of us all. For example, about ten years ago a very intelligent and academically gifted young lady of 15 told me how in school she had been taught that the reason that we had black people living in England was that they had all been brought over by white people as slaves.

She got quite angry with me when I tried to explain that the first major influx of Afro-Caribbeans was on a boat called *The Empire Windrush* on 22nd June 1948. I repeated this story to my current student – an intelligent, enthusiastic 17 year old girl called Saskia – earlier today, and she looked at me shocked. "My teachers told me exactly the same thing!" she gasped.

When people like Ms Darke say that they want to produce programmes which has "relevance to people's lives", whose lives does she actually mean? And in what way does she want her programming want to be "relevant"? We have already seen a socio-political situation where great stately homes are reduced to having Pokemon and paint-balling weekends in order to stay open, and where a few years ago it looked as if Canterbury Cathedral, one of our most important historical and spiritual buildings, was likely to close due to missing out on £10 million of lottery funding.

The important things are being sidelined and neglected in favour of trivia and an ever more rampant consumerism.

There is something terribly wrong with this country at the moment.

But what's this got to do with rock festivals? Well, quite a lot in my opinion. As the big events become more corporate, more reliant on advertising by the major multi-nationals, and more easy to negotiate, as Iron Maiden's Bruce Dickinson said, with "air-conditioned yurts" and cash-point machines, they have turned into just another easy to digest form of entertainment, whereas once they were a real alternative to the way of life followed by most of mainstream society.

Events like KozFest and, indeed, the Weird Weekend are about building bridges between people, about education, information, and promulgating ideas in a fashion that otherwise would seldom see the light of day. And I also truly believe that that is what this magazine does. Yes, of course, it's about selling music, but it's about selling music which is outside the mainstream, which challenges and which offers social, political, and emotional alternatives to the mainstream.

I have dedicated the latter part of my life to fighting a gallant rear guard battle against the socio-political trends which I find particularly disturbing, and I shall continue to do so for however much longer I have left. I hope that you will forgive me for using these pages to highlight this battle, but I have to warn you that whether you do or not, I shall continue to carry on just in the way that I have been doing. Thank you to all of you who support me, and my team. I really do appreciate it, and hope that you know that.

DRONES FOR DAEVID

As regular readers of this magazine will know, Daevid Allen, the legendary musician who started both Soft Machine and Gong (amongst others) and without whom neither Gonzo Multimedia or indeed this magazine would exist has been seriously ill with a cancer of the neck. I have been posting regular updates about his health from information sent to me from (amongst others) his son Orlando, Thom the World Poet, the Daevid Alien Facebook group, and his old pal Harry Williamson.

Something extraordinary seems to have happened, and it all appears to be related to a piece of music recorded under the aegis of Daevid's old pal, Harry Williamson, another boy from North Devon (like me) and son of the author of Tarka the Otter (hence the Grande Fromage's one time incarnation as head honcho of Otter Songs). Drone for Daevid is a collaboration between Steve Hillage, Fabio Golfetti, Makoto, Harry Williamson, Miquette Giraudy, Josh Pollock, Brian Abbott, Andy Bole, Steve Bemand, Mark Huxley, Greg McKella, Kev Hegan, all members of the Glissando Orchestra *in absentia*.

The only instruction was to play for 9 minutes in F and then the same in G, and send the result to Harry. The results are extraordinary. download the files from here http://www.springstudio.com.au/store/music choose your format, add to cart, checkout and off you go. Music www.springstudio.com.au

As someone who is interested in magick as well as musick (and all sorts of other things ending in 'ick') but above all in the well-being of Daevid Allen who is a very dear, sweet, and much loved man, I decided to investigate further. On Monday I carried out a long interview with Harry Williamson about the 'Drone Orchestra', and also about the philosophy behind it and the positive results it has had for Daevid.

On many occasions over the past nine months I have filled these pages with writings that are inspired by an extraordinary book about an extraordinary band. Author John Higgs has deconstructed the story of, and the mythos associated with, a band known variously as The Justified Ancients of MuMu and The KLF amongst others. I had always been a fan of their music and had recognised that there was something peculiar about them but hadn't realised how much their story impacted upon things that I had experienced for myself during my other life as a Fortean investigator. Several people that I knew personally were sighted in the book and more importantly various people whose work I have always admired were also sighted. These two subsets included one person common to both; author, investigator and practitioner of magick, Steve Moore, who died earlier this year. He was a personal friend of mine as well as being someone who I admired greatly. I was particularly impressed by his magickal work in conjunction with the incomparable Alan Moore (no relation).

Again, I think it unlikely that any readers of this magazine will have failed to recognise that I am a massive fan of Alan more, who, most certainly – as Pop Will Eat Itself most sagely pointed out – does know the score.

Bruce Sterling (above) opened his seminal book *The Hacker Crackdown* (1992) with a succinct description of cyberspace, which, only twenty two years ago, when the book was first published, was still an unfamiliar concept for many people. he wrote: "Cyberspace is the "place" where a telephone conversation appears to occur. Not inside your actual phone, the plastic device on your desk. Not inside the other person's phone, in some other city. THE PLACE BETWEEN the phones. The indefinite place OUT THERE, where the two of you, two human beings, actually meet and communicate.

Although it is not exactly "real," "cyberspace" is a genuine place. Things happen there that have very genuine consequences. This "place" is not "real," but it is serious, it is earnest."

Cyberspace is real. We have all been there, and continue to spend more and more of our lives there. But you can't measure it, you can't see it but it still exists.

I have always thought that Sterling's description is stunningly like an esoteric, but very common sense idea from Alan Moore (below). An idea known as "Idea Space". Alan Moore describes it as:

"...a space in which mental events can be said to occur, an idea space which is perhaps universal. Our individual consciousnesses have access to this vast universal space, just as we have individual houses, but the street outside the front door belongs to everybody. It's almost as if ideas are pre-existing forms within this space… The landmasses that might exist in this mind space would be composed entirely of ideas, of concepts, that instead of continents and islands you might have large belief systems, philosophies, Marxism might be one, Judeo-Christian religions might make up another."

I think if you can get your head around these two concepts – Cyberspace and Idea Space – then you can understand the nature of our omniverse much better than otherwise. You will not only grasp more ideas of physics than you would have done otherwise, but you will understand more about magick. And it is these two poles that, as far as I am concerned – define the entire nature of the omniverse.

But what is magick? Let us turn to Alan Moore again:

"I believe that magic is art, and that art, whether that be music, writing, sculpture, or any other form, is literally magic. Art is, like magic, the science of manipulating symbols, words or images, to achieve changes in consciousness… Indeed to cast a spell is simply to spell, to manipulate words, to change people's consciousness, and this is why I believe that an artist or writer is the closest thing in the contemporary world to a shaman."

Bizarrely we now have to go back to the previously sighted grebo band from the West Midlands. It may have been Edgard Varèse (below) who first described music as organised noise but it was Pop Will Eat Itself who pinched a sample from a film *Wonderwall* and brought the concept to a generation of earnest young dope smokers including me over twenty years ago. The Chinese musicologist Chou Wen-chung described how Varèse's concept of music as "organized sound" fits into his vision of "sound as living matter" and of "musical space as open rather than bounded" He conceived the elements of his music in terms of "sound-masses", likening their organization to the natural phenomenon of crystallization.

If you can take this concept on board; the idea that something that has no physical form, like music, can have a conceptual structure akin to that of a lattice crystal, then it is only a short paradigm leap to the concept that ideas can function in much the same manner. If you extrapolate this into Alan Moore's concept of Idea Space then it is no longer surprising that Harry Williamson's Drone for Daevid had such a remarkable affect on the old musician. It would have been more remarkable if it hadn't!

But there is another concept that I would like to throw into this multidisciplinary melting pot. And again, we go back to John Higg's book, and the half of The KLF that is the extraordinary and unpredictable artist Bill Drummond. Between 2003 and 2013 Drummond devoted much of his efforts to a project called The17. A choir whose ethos derives from Drummond's quondam disillusionment with recorded music – something that he has since repudiated. His idea was that

"the advent of the iPod and all the file-sharing as the curtain coming down on the greatest art form of the 20th century – recorded music. Some art forms die, overnight, like the silent movie with the advent of the talkies. Others take a few decades. People with vested interests do not want to see their business model crumble and fall, so they keep trying to patch it up. But it is over, well and truly over. And I wanted to dance on its grave. A new dawn. Music could be free and once again be able to celebrate time, place and occasion and have nothing to do with something trapped in the iPod in your pocket. But the new music would not be going back to the music of the

prerecorded music age, it would be looking to the future and using everything at its disposal."

The idea was that a group of people (initially seventeen of them but later any number of them) would sing a piece of music lasting seventeen minutes with no words and no tune. There is no sheet music, the choir performing according to instructions written down by Drummond, or indeed anyone else. These instruction are called 'scores' but are open to change over time and exist completely in the public domain. The fact that Drummond does for seventeen minutes with seventeen what Harry Williamson did – across the globe for eighteen minutes with twelve guitarists – throws up an irresistible conceptual link as far as I am concerned. But I will be the first to admit that I like conceptual links.

As anyone who has ever read my book *The Owlman and Others* will know, exactly twenty years ago this year, my first wife and I made friends with an extraordinary Irishman. his name (and still is) Tony Shiels but many people still refer to him as "Doc". He is probably most familiar to you because of the famous pictures of a man in a tall hat (him) accompanied by various naked witches on the shores of various lakes both in Ireland and Scotland, and sea inlets in Ireland and England conjuring up, or claiming to conjure up, which ever way your particular world view takes you, semi-legendary sea monsters. Or, you may know him best for his two 1977 photographs of what he claims was the Loch Ness Monster. He has been my friend for two decades now and, although he dislikes me saying so – in the months surrounding my divorce when my family had largely abandoned me - he was the closest thing to a father figure that I had, and although he keeps on telling me not to, I think of him in that manner today.

He is a surrealist artist (having received the endorsement of none other than Salvador Dali in the 1950s), a musician, a stage performer, a busker, a stage magician, a hoaxer, a mountebank, a thimble rigger, a self-admitted fraudster and for many years was known as the Wizard of the Western World, the resulting acronym predating the world wide web by a very long time. I love the old bastard very much and not because he was the first person to prove to me that magic really does exist. He showed me the importance of numbers words and sounds within magic; something that he calls 'surrealchemy' and over the years he has led me on tangled paths full of lexilinks and populated by strange and bizarre figures. He has never given me any reason to doubt that he is the most powerful magickian that I have ever met or indeed am ever likely to meet, although I suspect that both Alan Moore and Bill Drummond may not be very far behind.

I am sure that all these links and connections are leading me somewhere. They have led me places before, and no doubt will do so again. After all Daevid himself is one of the most magickal musicians you are ever likely to meet and there is something very invocatory about his music, and indeed always has been. the fact that his best known work involves a complex hagiography of saints and sinners inhabiting a complex universe with its own detailed mythology tends to lead me to believe that he knows as much about the goings on in Idea Space as does anybody else that I have cited in this rambling essay of mine. I am some sort of a scientist and I have always believed that as a species we are particularly susceptible to the sin of hubris; we take ourselves far too seriously and truthfully don't know half as much about the universe as we think we do. I believe that Alan Moore is completely correct, that the creation of art is indeed a magickal act. I believe that there is no doubt whatsoever that a magickal act of creation performed by twelve guitarists a few weeks ago has helped treat a very ill Daevid Allen and may quite possibly have saved his life. I believe that what we can extrapolate from these assertions is very important and that it proves, as if any proof was needed, that events on a magickal/artistic continuum can affect read world events. I don't want to leave you on a downer because this whole experience has been a very uplifting one for me, but I very much doubt if there is anybody reading this who is not aware of the terrible event going on in Syria at the moment. Whilst researching this essay, and indeed dictating it to Andrea, who puts up with my crap, I found the following snippet on one of Drummond's websites:

"In March 2011, Bill Drummond was supposed to lead a performance of Score 328: SURROUND around the top of the ancient city walls of Damascus. This was part of a tri-nation festival organised by Reel Festivals. The three nations were to be Syria, Lebanon and Scotland. The Lebanese and Scottish legs of the festival happened. The Arab Spring caused the Syrian leg to be postponed. It was also supposed to be part of The17's City-to-City world tour. While Syrians are slaughtered on their city streets and the world looks on wondering what it should do, Reel Festival have decided to organise a festival in waiting with the Syrian refugees and exiles who are currently living in London.

Bill Drummond plans to lead a performance of the same score as he was going to do in Damascus. This score is usually performed on the circumfrence of a five-kilometre circle. As stated above it was to be performed around the city walls of Damascus, which are also five kilometres in circumference. Drummond plans to draw the outline of the Damascus city walls on a map of London and then lead this particular performance following the outline on the streets of London. The 100 members of The17 that will be taking part in this performance will be drawn from the Syrian refugee and exile community in the UK."

One can only wonder impotently whether subsequent events would have been any different if Drummond had been able to carry out his original plan and perform with the seventeen in Damascus. I suspect that they would have been.

John Higgs has made an extraordinary extrapolation of the real life story of The KLF, but if you would like to know more about that then I suggest that you either read his book or come along to this year's Weird Weekend in Hartland, Devon where he is one our most exciting guests. What has all this got to do with Daevid Allen, Harry Williamson and the Guitar Drone Orchestra? Have a listen to Harry and my conversation and make up your own mind.

http://www.gonzomultimedia.co.uk/radio/player.php?id=294

THE DRONES CLUB

Hi Jonathan,

I just have read your article on the healing drones for Daevid Allen. I just want to set the record straight.

When I heard that Daevid was ill I contacted him and made the suggestion to do the two drones for him while he was having his operation. He was absolutely delighted at the idea. I am one of the original members of the glissando orchestra from Amsterdam 2006 and its founder member along with Andy Bole here in the UK. I then co ordinated all the gliss players to do a focussed gliss ritual at the time Daevid was having his operation. Harry Williamson suggested that we record it and he would mix it and make it available as a free download and also present it to Daevid. That is how it happened. It was not Harry's idea it was mine.
Also just a foot note, it is the glissando guitar orchestra not drone orchestra.

Regards
Brian Abbot

THERE ARE FAERIES AT THE BOTTOM OF MY CAR PARK

Last weekend, no sooner had we finished putting together the Gonzo Weekly than together with Mike Davis, Mother and my delightful, and long suffering secretary Andrea, we went over to Hartland to the inaugural North Devon Firefly Faery Ball. And a great time was had by all.

There was an impressive range of acts covering folk to psychedelia, and quite a lot of other things in between. There was delicious home cooked food and a number of beautiful young women wandering round dressed as faeries with diaphanous wings. Who could ask for anything more.

It is a pity that the event was not better attended, but plans are underway for another event next year. In an overdose of enthusiasm Mike and I have agreed to play at least a couple of songs.

Babz Hewlett-Beech, one half of the organizing team has kindly let us have some pictures that we reproduce on the next couple of pages, which we hope will whet your appetite for future events. Away with the faeries? Too damn right.

JON DRISCOLL (?-2014)

It was the early spring of 1985 when my mate Andy first introduced him to me. Andy, who was at the time playing in a shambolic punk band, which I believe was called The Loose Pricks, was performing at a club night in an Exeter pub. Remember here, that three decades have passed, and in those three decades a lot of water has passed under the proverbial bridge, but an equally large amount of brandy has disappeared down my gullet, irreparably poisoning millions of brain cells, so forgive me if I don't remember names or places. I only remember the date because I got married for the first time in April 1985 and the event I am writing about took place a few weeks before that.

I can't remember which pub it was in, whether I went with Alison, or even whether I joined the band on stage to play a raucous version of 'Louis Louis'. What I do remember is that the evening was compered by a massively entertaining anarchic comedian who was even fatter than I was at the time (although not as fat as I was to become). His name was Jon Driscoll and he operated under the *nom de guerre* of 'Jon Beast'. The whole event may even have been performed as 'Club Beast' but I can't remember.

What I do remember was that he was massively foul mouthed, massively silly and massively funny.

I later wrote a piece which mentioned him for a fanzine I was producing, in which I (probably, exercising a fair amount of hyperbole) likened him to Lenny Bruce. Truthfully, he was nothing like Lenny Bruce apart from the fact that they both swore a lot. But I have never let the truth get in the way of a good story and – truthfully – it doesn't matter anymore because not only did the magazine in which the piece appeared sell its fifty copies and go out of business nearly thirty years ago, but my week started badly when Corinna told me on Monday morning that Jon Beast had died.

He became most widely known when he was the stage manager, MC, and lighting manager for Carter the Unstoppable Sex Machine, and his unforgettable warm up act, which usually involved him capering about the stage very nearly naked whilst the audience quoted "you fat bastard" at him, inspired the opening lines of Carter's 1991 album '30Something'.

I interviewed Carter a few day before the album came out, and went to meet them at Fruitbat's flat

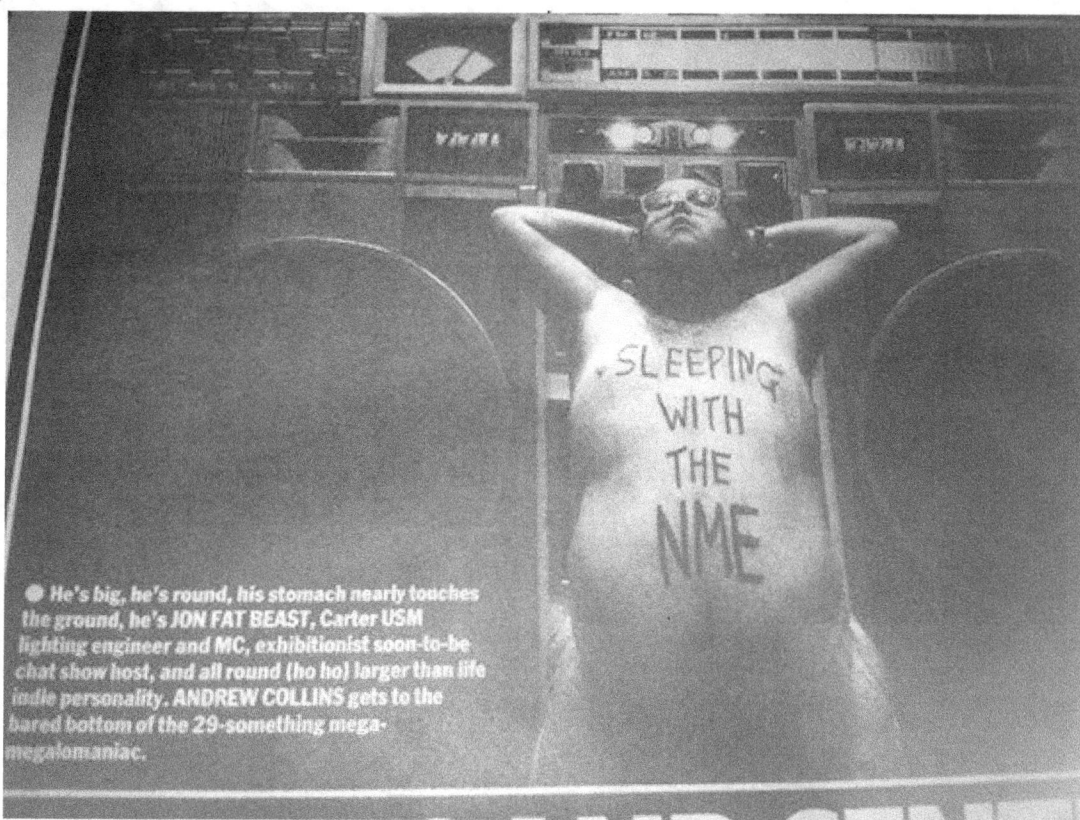

● He's big, he's round, his stomach nearly touches the ground, he's JON FAT BEAST, Carter USM lighting engineer and MC, exhibitionist soon-to-be chat show host, and all round (ho ho) larger than life indie personality. ANDREW COLLINS gets to the bared bottom of the 29-something mega-megalomaniac.

in Brixton. And on the subsequent tour I ran into Jon Beast again. "So you think I'm like Lenny Bruce? You soft bastard!" He cackled at me giving me a hug, and proceeded to take the piss out of me from the stage whilst giving his introduction. Our paths crossed occasionally in the years that followed, and now he is dead I feel that an era is at an end.

Another part of my mis-spent youth has gone down the can. In his memory: the only couplet of the only piece of his poetry I remember

:

Go mental, drink 25 beers
Go mental, stick poo in your ears

God bless you Jon. The world is now a slightly poorer and less funny place than it was a few days back. In a world run by psychopaths, where the people ruling swathes of the Middle East have started crucifying their opponents and where our own country is getting drowned in a maze of bureaucracy, technology and greed we need fat bastards exhorting us to "Go Mental" more than ever.

BEATLES TEAPOT, SUGAR BOWL AND MILK JUG - WASHINGTON POTTERY Ltd.
Price:
£130.00

"A COLOUR PICTURE OF THE GROUP AND FACSIMILE SIGNATURES TO EACH PIECE TEAPOT AND LID 17cm TALL X 22cm WIDES IN GOOD AS NEW CONDITION"

These would look good in a tiny music-of-the-1960's/70's-themed café. The sort of place you would walk into on your holidays in some seaside town when you are parched and dying for a cup of tea. The sort of place that, when you open the gingham-curtained door, a little bell rings to announce your arrival to the seemingly deserted premises. It would be like stepping back in time, with all the wall space covered with photos, autographs and posters of 1960s and 1970s pop idols. Shelving, and display cupboards would be overflowing with knick-knacks of the time and upon each table would be placed a bong – erm no sorry – that last one would probably be most unlikely, it would more likely be a specimen vase with its in-

habitant either being a fake poppy (there I go again) or one of those plastic flowers you get in Volkswagen Beetles, or even a couple of lush Biba feathers. (I used to have a purple one of those – it got covered in dust and became quite bald eventually!).

There may well be a mock Carnaby Street road sign on the wall behind the counter, and even a mannequin standing in a corner, bedecked and bejewelled in the fashion of the time. There would be the obligatory Sgt Pepper poster somewhere too of course. And whilst you supped your brew the iconic wide-eyed Twiggy would stare down at you from her equally iconic poster. Where am I going with this? I have absolutely no idea, but it is surprising to where a photo of a Beatles teapot, sugar bowl and milk jug can take you!

And each table would just HAVE to have a pair of these too:

CLIFF RICHARD SALT & PEPPER POTS - £12.50

"Dishwasher safe. 3 inches high, white ceramic."

Give Sir Cliff a good old shake up whilst showering your chips with salt or your tuna sandwich with pepper. That'll wipe the rather smug grin off his face and add a few more frown lines to his tanned forehead. And a quick, or not so quick, depending upon the circumstances, visit to spend a penny or two in the facilities of such an establishment would undoubtedly include one of these:

CLIFF RICHARD TOILET SEAT COVER washable cotton A MUST HAVE FOR ANY FAN! - £11.99

"100% cotton. Washable at 30 degrees. Drawstring design to fit any toilet seat lid. New and unused." Another one of those 'must haves'. Lots of those about. But is this not a slight insult to your idol? I mean, if I were famous I am not sure that I would appreciate it knowing that there were some folks out there in fan-land that actually had a toilet seat cover with my face on it! I wonder if there is a matching toilet-brush holder out there too? Can't fans bear to be apart from their idol even while they are seeing to their ablutions?

Jon Meets Judy

Judy Dyble is really one of those legendary performers who very nearly achieved Syd Barrett status. As her self-written biography sheet reads:

> Born in 1949 when rationing was still part of daily life and Britain was recovering from the greyness and worry of the war years, Judy was the third of four children whose early years were spent in a prefabricated bungalow surrounded by gardens in North London.
>
> Moving into a maisonette in Wood Green when Judy was 10, she and her sisters and brother were edging into the teenage years in the heady mix of rock and roll teddy boys, beatniks and jazz, the stories of folk

and the pure joy of pop. All three girls had started piano lessons but only Judy continued, to the fury of her sisters when the piano lesson coincided with the start of Ready! Steady! Go! (or was it Popeye?) and the TV was turned off so Judy could learn another bit of music. Her teacher was very into dance music, so the music ranged from quicksteps to foxtrots and that kind of stuff. Judy asked for, and was given, the sheet music for Let There Be Love and was miffed that it didn't include instructions on how to play like George Shearing.

However, onward to the years of youth clubs, then folk, blues, jazz and soul clubs, often all housed in the back rooms of the same pub but on different nights, and the first of the bands at the age of 16 -Judy and the Folkmen - who practised a lot and performed very little, but whose debut (and only) gig at the Hornsey Conservative Club's Candlelight Soiree was a triumphant success, until you saw the newspaper photo of some rather terrified Soiree-ers being serenaded while they ate their supper.

But with a newly acquired autoharp in hand (easier to carry than a piano) Judy formed a loose connection with other musicians in the Muswell Hill area, and became the longhaired girl singer when an acoustic set was required with the musicians who later became Fairport Convention.

She appeared on the first Fairport Convention album, did a bit of recording with the band who were later to become King Crimson, made one album as half of a duo called Trader Horne (named after a character my friend Richard Freeman wrote about in one of his books) and then disappeared for the next thirty years.

She would have been considered one of British progressive music's great lost talents had she not emerged from the shadows in the early years of this century with a string of exquisite records.

The last two of the studio albums have been released through Gonzo Multimedia, which is where I came in. I have interviewed Judy many times over the last couple of years, and even went to a psychedelically bucolic festival in Kent where I filmed one of her very few live performances.

She must have enjoyed it because, although that was only the second or third show they had done in many years, she has since done quite a few more and even released a live album.

I always like an excuse to talk to her, so last week I phoned her up and we had a very pleasant chat....#
#

**http://
www.gonzomultimedia.co.
uk/radio/player.php?
id=305**

The Gonzo Annual 2015

Jon meets Lou Stein

Lou Stein is a London based Theatre Director/ Writer who founded the Gate Theatre, Notting Hill and has worked with such actors as Dame Helen Mirren, Clive Owen, Sir Patrick Stewart, Chris Eccleston, Sir John Mills, and Helena Bonham-Carter in London theatres including the West End, The Royal Court, and for the BBC.

I was a fan of the writings of Dr Hunter S Thompson a long time before I started working for Gonzo Multimedia. Although I do not deserve it, several commentators when reviewing my books in the late 1990s, and the early years of the decade that irritates me when people call it 'The Naughties' described me a Forteana's answer to the good doctor.

This is all very flattering, but completely untrue. Okay there were superficial similarities; especially then, but far less now, I drank considerably more than I should, and indulged in the abuse of various other substances. I also wrote some of my best known non-fiction books in a slightly racy first person style, but the bare fact remains – Hunter Stockton Thompson (1937 – 2005) was a genius, and one of the greatest men of letters that American literature has ever produced. I am a journaling hack who has been lucky enough to make a few quid over the years by writing about things I have done.

Thompson's best know work is undoubtedly *Fear and Loathing in Las Vegas*, written in 1971 and published a year later.

"The basic synopsis revolves around journalist Raoul Duke (Hunter S. Thompson) and his attorney, Dr. Gonzo (Oscar Zeta Acosta), as they arrive in 1970s Las Vegas to report on the Mint 400 motorcycle race. However, they soon abandon their work and begin experimenting with a variety of recreational drugs, such as LSD, ether, cocaine, alcohol, mescaline, and cannabis. This leads to a series of bizarre hallucinogenic trips,

during which they destroy hotel rooms, wreck cars, and have visions of anthropomorphic desert animals, all the while ruminating on the decline of culture in a city of insanity."

The book is a masterpiece which has never quite received the acclaim that many people feel that it should, mainly because of its subject matter. It was made into a film in 1998, which – although entertaining enough – was ultimately unsuccessful and did not manage to bring Thompson's sparkling and often magickal prose to life.

Back in 1984, theatrical director Lou Stein wrote a version for the stage, which – surprisingly – met with Thompson's full approval. Nine years after Thompson took his own life, the play has been revived and is part of the Edinburgh Festival. The day after the final run-through, I caught up with Lou for a chat about the project …

http://www.gonzomultimedia.co.uk/radio/player.php?id=306

THE SLEEPYARD GOES ON FOREVER

It is not often that one comes across musicians who manage to fuse the cerebral world of the avant garde with the visceral world of pure pop sensibility. This is not to say it hasn't been done. From 1965 onwards, the Beatles managed it quite successfully, and I think that one of the reasons that I've always liked Crass is that they mixed the high cleverness of the avant garde with gloriously done pop songs like Do They Owe Us a Living and Banned from the Roxy, which I have always thought are conceptually similar to one of the greatest works that Phil Spector produced. It has to be said that I have been making this assertion for over 30 years now, and nobody has actually agreed with me. Even Steve Ignorant just smiled politely and moved swiftly on, but I know what I am talking about.

Recently our old friend Judy Dyble told me that she had been working with a Norwegian musician called Oliver Kersbergen, who works under the name of 'Sleepyard'. Wikipedia has this to say:

"Sleepyard is a psychedelic pop band from Norway. Oliver Kersbergen formed the band in 1994 to record the first demo "Velvet sky". Later on brother Svein joined in and they started playing concerts.

The band released the mini-album "Intersounds" on their own label Orange music in 1998. This was hailed as one of the very first post rock albums from Norway.

Sleepyard released "The runner" on trust me records (2003) and contributed music to the movie Monsterthursday, which was nominated for best foreign film in the 2005 Sundance film festival. Next album "Easy Tensions" saw the band reaching for a more mellow and richer sound. Their multi tracked vocal harmonies reminded critics of the Beach Boys and drew comparisons to the psychedelic sound of Smile.

On their last album "Future lines", the band has collaborated with Pianist Mike Garson and Sonic Boom from Spacemen 3".

I really am getting old. Once upon a time I understood music journalism, but now I find it hard to differentiate between all of these new, and – it seems to me – wilfully eclectic musical sub-genres. My nephew Max sneers at me because I can't tell the difference between Black Metal and Death Metal, I don't know the difference between Grind Core and Grime, and although I know perfectly well what Oliver Kersbergen's music sounds like, I haven't a bloody clue what Post Rock is. But, as my younger step-daughter told me nearly ten years ago, when I got the name of the member of Slipknot who had a dead crow in a jar wrong, I don't know much about music do I?

I listened to the Sleepyard album, and was very favourably impressed. I have always been fond of electronic music which sounds organic. Years ago I became a fan of the music Richard David James makes under the nomme de guerre of Aphex Twin, and although the two acts sounds nothing like each other, conceptually I think that Aphex Twin are one of the closest musicians that I have heard to what Kersbergen is doing with Sleepyard. They both produce a sort of sonic alchemy taking purely electronic instruments and moulding something organic and even cellular from them.

I was very intrigued by Oliver and his work, especially having chatted to Judy about it, and so I took the bit between my metaphorical teeth, grabbed the man himself on Facebook, and asked him if we could do an interview .....

JON: How did the Sleepyard project come about in the first place?

OLIVER: I started Sleepyard in 1994 as a solo project and to record my first demo. I used to play in a punk band at the time, but found little satisfaction with that kind of music after a

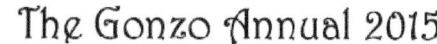

while. I had already played Jazz music in my youth, so i was longing for some new challenges.

After then my brother became involved and started writing his own songs as well. We then became a band with various line ups for live performances through the years.

JON: How do you choose your collaborators, and how do you ask them to get involved?

OLIVER: I like their music and write or phone them and try to explain the concept. I then send some music and see if they like it. I'm so chuffed every time someone say yes.

The Gonzo Annual 2015

Sometimes they find me too and propose a collaboration which is a lovely experience

JON: Specifically how did you start working with Judy?

OLIVER: My publisher Joe Foster put me in touch with her. I was originally going to make some tracks for her, but she ended up singing and writing on the Sleepyard album

JON: How does the compositional process work?

OLIVER: That`s a tricky question. I usually start with a "feel", then add a few instruments and see where it goes. Usually this can take a while. I may send it over to Mike Garson and ask for a bit of 50`s exotica piano or romantic tones.. then the song can suddenly change direction and i take it from there.

JON: Where do you record?

OLIVER: I record at home or in the studio. New projects will probably be recorded mostly in the studio as I`ve started working there now.

JON: How long did it take to record Black Sails?

OLIVER: That would be 4 or 5 years. Sleepyard albums usually takes a long time to make flow naturally with all the layers of sound.

JON: Is there anyone specific who you would like to work with in the future

OLIVER: Danny Kirwan

JON: Do you use outside musicians?

OLIVER: Yes, I do locally and internationally. I am happy to have good friends who can play things i can`t, like the Theremin (Thanks Bo!) I`ve had great pleasure in working with Mike Garson on piano, Nik Turner on sax, Geoff Leigh, Suki Ewers from Mazzy Star on this new album.

JON: What other projects are you involved with?

OLIVER: I am working on a poetry project. I`m putting music to Stephen Kalinich spoken words with ambient music in the background. I love his message and poetry. He`s done a lot of great lyrics for Beach Boys and PF Sloan.

JON: What are you working on next?

OLIVER: I`ll be working on music for Film & TV + other projects. Even a few commercials. Might be a Sleepyard EP in the works too as some tracks are shaping up faster than usual..
I`m also hoping to make a version of Karlheinz Stockhausens piece "Virgo". I did get instructions to record and perform it from him and it would be nice to do this as a tribute to him.

JON: how did you get involved ith stockhausen?

OLIVER: Stockhausen… Now that really changed my life and ways of thinking music.

He was playing in my hometown of Stavanger in 2005. He performed Gesang Der Jungelinge and then had a break before Kontakte. However he was doing a soundcheck of that piece and i got to hear an exclusive performance of it. These sounds flying through the room in eight different speakers was quite magical. It did feel a bit like 2001: A Space Odyssey..

I then said hello to him and thanked for the generosity of having me listening.

I then wrote to him and told him how much i loved his track Virgo. I was very surprised when i did get an answer back with books to read and ideas.. Also an invitation to go to his work camp.

I was originally going to perform it at his 80th birthday, but unfortunately he passed away before that.

JON: so how much is your work influenced by the avant garde, and 20th C experimental music like Stockhausen

I am still reeling from that performance when thinking about it.

Very much of my music is inspired by the avant garde. John Cage, Béla Bartók, Charles Ives, Iannis Xenakis are some of my favorites.

JON: It is interesting the way you mix the avant garde with far more commercial forms of music

OLIVER: Thank you Jonathan, cool that you noticed that. Commercial music has always interested me. So it is natural to mix these things. I love singing and making harmonies, although this latest album is very ambient. My favorite band is The Beach Boys, so there will come some inspiration from there..

JON: I guess growing up with my dad owning a record store when i was a kid had an impact too.

OLIVER: Sometimes i consciously mix sounds for pleasure or to make some headspace. The Archies meets Augustus Pablo or Cluster… or something in that vein..

I am a big Beach Boys fan

JON: Now you mention it I can hear the sort of multilayered textures of albums like 'Holland' in your work
I always feel sorry for the rest of the band, because the accepterd wisdom is that they were only good when Brian was good, but actually albums like Sufs up and Holland and 20/20 are magnificent

OLIVER: Great! Always lovely to meet a fellow Beach Boys fan. Glad i saw them live two years ago.

Oh… Thank you. That is quite a compliment! I love Holland. So much variety.

I do feel sorry to for the rest of the band. I must confess to preferring the albums when they were searching for a direction. Friends is beautiful. I also think i kinda prefer Smiley Smile to Smile.. It`s admirable that they dared release such a lo-Fi version of that material.

All honors to Brian as i love his productions. He did great stuff in the late 60`s and 70`s too.
it is one of the things most noticeable about your music is the textures of the sounds

Bless you Jonathan for pointing that out. It is very interesting to work with frequencies and textures… It certainly takes its time. Often when i work with different sources which have been sent to me, i have to make them sound natural and not out of place.

JON: Considering the fact you are a primarily electronic musician, the effect is very organic

OLIVER: I started to work with tape on four track recorders and i have always loved the warmth of it. It`s probably those experiences which makes me work to make it sound organic…

JON: you record completely digitally now

OLIVER: I love Kraftwerk too as you mentioned Kraftwerk, but generally find Ralf and Florian more exciting…

Yes, i do record digitally at the studio. In fact i might try a bit of beats to move away from the Black Sails…

I`ve also written a few straight pop songs lately which i might give to other artists for recording. I do however record at home still with primitive equipment which is always nice. One have to make the best out of the resources. I am planning on recording some sitar sounds (well that is a Jerry Jones Guitar Sitar) for fun. I`d hate to lose the fun aspect of it. Sometimes one creates mistakes which might turn into something.

Being a rock and roll guitarist always attracts the birds

Jon meets Boltz

I first met Steve Bolton in 1990 or 1991. My first wife and I had finished a tour with Steve Harley and Cockney Rebel during which we had become particularly friendly with the soundman Roy Weard. A few days before the end of the tour he asked us whether we fancied going to a gig in London.

At the time we were publishing a magazine called ISMO which was very much a precursor for Gonzo Weekly, except for the fact that it had nothing to do with Gonzo and it wasn't weekly.

However, it had much the same mix of music, humour, anarchism and general malcontendedness as this current organ (oo-er missus) and only goes to show that either I was a rather prescient man in my late-20s, or that I am totally socially retarded now I am in my mid-50s. It so happened that we were going to be in London doing something completely different on the days that Roy mentioned, so we agreed.

It was only then that Roy explained that the lead singer and guitarist of this band called 6foot3 was a bloke called Steve Bolton, who had been Pete Townshend's chosen amanuensis during the tour in the late 1980s when – due to his ever-increasing tinnitus – The Who geezer was unable to play electric guitar on stage. He spent the tour standing in a weird acoustic beehive affair strumming away at an acoustic guitar whilst doing an extremely funky thing on lead was none other than Roy's mate Steve.

We went along to a venue in Greenwich and I can truthfully say that I don't think I've ever been in such a loud concert.

My ears have since gone the way of Pete Townshend's, and whilst I think it would probably be most unfair to try to blame this circumstance upon the first time I saw 6foot3, they were truly the loudest and most brutal noise that I have ever heard on stage since.

Brutal, yes. But elegantly brutal as well. I think that one of my favourite memories of them was their exceptionally stylish, guitar-led version of Jacques Brel song Jackie, as sung most famously by Scott Walker. Here I will make another admission. Whilst I had vaguely listened to Scott Walker before this, I was so impressed by 6foot3's rendition that I went to listen to Walker's version again and so discovered the man who to this day the man who is my favourite male singer.

Totally by chance I met Roy Weard again last year at one of the last concerts that Mick Farren played with The Deviants, and we soon picked up where we had left off 20 years before. It also happens, that a year ago, I met one of my favourite authors – C J Stone – and published a book of his through Gonzo Publishing. Stone is also a friend of Steve Bolton's, and through the agency of one or another of these good fellows, Steve contacted me on Facebook.

We have been chitter-chattering for some months mostly because again after an unfeasible length of time he has reformed 6foot3, and I have mentioned the fact on a number of occasions in these pages.

The obvious thing to do next was to interview him, and I really had no idea why it took me so long to realise this.

However, on Wednesday afternoon this week I gave him a ring and we had a fascinating conversation about 6foot3 and just a few of the other things that he has done in a remarkable career. Would you believe that we didn't actually have time in our conversation which was interrupted by my various recalcitrant hounds, to even mention The Who, but that will keep for next time.

http://www.gonzomultimedia.co.uk/radio/player.php?id=309

The Gonzo Annual 2015

Felix Dennis died earlier this year. He was a remarkable man and one of the most important people to have come out of the counter-culture of the late-'60s and early-'70s. Indeed he can probably be described as being the person who came out of said counter-culture who had the most successful publishing career of all. More importantly, unlike many of his peers, who will remain nameless, he continued doing projects – such as the Heart of England Forest, whose mission statement is: ""the plantation, re-plantation, conservation and establishment of trees for the benefit of the public, together with the education of the public by the promulgation of knowledge and the appreciation of trees"." which are totally inline with the ethos of the hippy movement then and now. According to Sean Coughlan, writing in 2006, Dennis told him: ""I've been busy for years, buying land, often under pseudonyms, and planting trees on it. All the money is going into it when I die - and in the end I'd like to think that it will be 20 to 30,000 acres.""

Later in the same interview he described how he still felt that need to stand up against the establishment where necessary: ""It's the bullying that annoys me... When I see something that's wrong, I just speak and act first and I'll take the consequences later.""

He was the youngest and arguably the most dangerous of the three Oz conspirators, and his death has left a very big gap to fill. The trial took place in the summer of 1971. Writer, broadcaster and film-maker Tony Palmer was in the court throughout the trial, and wrote an excellent book on the subject called 'The Trials of Oz'.

Some years ago I worked with Palmer on a new edition of this book which is now being reissued via Gonzo Publishing.

Palmer had this to say:

"Felix Dennis vowed revenge on all and sundry when, at the infamous OZ trial in 1971, Judge Michael Argyle sentenced him to a lesser term of imprisonment than the other two defendants, Richard Neville and Jim Anderson, "because he was obviously less intelligent."

The Wizard of Oz

Within a few years Felix was a multi-zillionaire who could easily have destroyed Argyle financially in a threatened libel case against the now discredited Judge. That he chose not to do so is symptomatic of the Felix I knew - a pussy cat, generous, funny and a very shrewd business man.

And a good poet, connoisseur of wine and collector of art - he had over 40 bronzes in his gardens. He adored the fine life and the pleasures it brought him. Nothing pleased him more than buying David Bowie's house in Mustique, not to mention the million (yes, a million) trees he planted around his house in Warwickshire as part of an educational scheme for children.

He gave away his money as fast as he earned it. It meant nothing to do him, except that it allowed to do those things which he hoped would give others pleasure.

This for him was happiness.

Incredibly, he still lived in the same house in London he bought soon after the Oz Trail. "Why move?" he asked me. "It's quite big enough for what I need."

He was a lovely, lovely man, only 67 when he died and, as he told me last year "so much to do, and so little time."

What a waste.
TONY P.

The new edition of *The Trials of Oz* on which I worked long and hard is now available both through Gonzo Multimedia and outlets such as Amazon. And just to see whether the world has changed much since 1971, here is the original picture of Rupert Bear with his cock out that caused all the trouble in the first place. In these days of widely available pornography, sexting, and the appalling revelations about the behaviour by once much-loved national figures it seems very tame indeed.

I first met Jaki Windmill in the spring of last year. My nephew Dave Braund-Phillips and I went up to Brighton to see, interview, and film the legendary Mick Farren in what turned out to be one of his final shows. As we all know, sadly, he passed away a few months later. Because of his rapidly failing health Mick didn't turn up at the venue until very shortly before he was up on stage, and so David's and my well thought out plans of interviewing him before the concert came to naught.

But as a happy result we had more time to spend getting to know the other members of the band. As these included two of the original members of *The Pink Fairies*, we spent a long time happily interviewing them, but it was Jaki, sitting quietly in the corner nursing a pint of lager with whom I became most friendly. It turns out that we have many interests in common within the Fortean world and both that evening, and on several occasions since, both in person and on the telephone, Jaki and I have happily chatted about all sorts of esoteric subjects.

Since our first meeting, and as a direct result of the untimely death of dear Mick Farren (and it may seem strange to you that I am describing the one time *enfant terrible* of the underground as a 'dear' but the notorious anarchist was one of the dearest and sweetest men I have ever met) the latest stage of the Jaki Windmill story has taken place.

The Deviants could never have continued without Mick Farren, so the remaining members did exactly what they had done after kicking Mick out of the band first time around back in 1970, and reformed as *The Pink Fairies*. Except that on *this* occasion they have a female member – Jaki Windmill.

I was just about to write that this was the first time that this band had ever had a female member but then, proving (as if any proof were needed) that the universe is far more

JON MEETS JAKI

complicated and peculiar than we believe, I ran across this piece of interesting information from Wikipedia:

> "Farren had, however, previously discussed the idea of a solo album for the second LP of three on the Transatlantic contract (after The Deviants 3), with the third LP to be an album by the other band members, potentially also featuring drummer Russell Hunter's girlfriend Jenny Ashworth as frontwoman - an idea with which the three sidemen had been toying around the time of the contract signing."

I include this snippet only because it's one of those little pieces of musical minutiae that keeps an old rock and roll archaeologist like me happy. It also turns out, for those of you interested in such things, that Jenny Ashworth appeared on the 1968 *Deviants* album 'Disposable'. And that at the Isle of Wight Festival in 1970 at which *The Pink Fairies* appeared, "Friend's arrive & start amazing festival bulletin which eventually led Miss Jennifer Ashworth, friend of percussionist B.R. Hunter, to the police tent to recover 'Sunshine', her pet poopsy-woopsy apple-dumpling & red-setter puppy."

But I am deviating wildly from the main path of what I am supposed to be writing about. So let's get back to the matter in hand, which is a pre-amble to my interview with Jaki Windmill rather than a complicated diatribe about everyone without a y chromosome that ever played with the *Deviants/Pink Fairies* family.

Jaki is also an author, with a children's book called *Fairy and Foul of St. Ives*.

It is always a pleasure to talk to Jaki and so it was with great pleasure that I rang her up at lunchtime on Friday just as she was preparing to record this week's episode of 'Sub Reality Sandwich' for Gonzo Web Radio.

Enjoy.

http://www.gonzomultimedia.co.uk/radio/player.php?id=322

I have written before how I am not a fan of Facebook. I dislike its facile approach and the way that it conveniently replaces so much of importance with a shallow analogue.

For example, people are convinced these days that they are doing their bit for social change, not by marching on a protest demonstration, manning the barricades or making Molotov cocktails, but by clicking 'I like this' on a Facebook petition.

There are also so many pictures of people's pet cats that one can possibly stand to look at in any given period, but I am the first to admit that I am becoming a curmudgeonly old sod.

However, as I have admitted on many occasions on these pages, Facebook is undeniably a very convenient way of keeping in touch with people, and the other day I sent an instant message to Andy Thommen and asked him if there was any news from the Clepsydra camp.

For those of you not aware, Clepsydra is a magnificently tuneful progressive rock band from Switzerland.

In 1991 Clepsydra released their first album Hologram, which was followed by the EP Fly Man in 1993. Clepsydra then signed to InsideOut, who released their second album More Grains of Sand in 1994.

This CD included the song Moonshine on Heights, which by many is regarded as neo-prog classic. 1994 also saw them performing two songs on national Swiss TV, a rare occurrence for a progressive rock band at that time.

Says Andy, "We had no idea that there was a progressive rock scene. In fact we never heard the expression progressive rock until about three months after the release of Hologram in 1991."

In 1998 Clepsydra released their third album Fears, the first album with Marco Cerulli on guitar.

In the wake of the album release Clepsydra had a 10-day-long European tour and was booked for a concert in Canada on the strength of this production. In 2001 the band released Alone with Nicola De Vita on bass. This album came with three different album covers: The Chicken, The Octopus and The Fish.

Following these four albums Clepsydra entered a state of hiatus. At this point they had established themselves as a popular entity among fans of neo-progressive rock, and they were often compared to the likes of Jadis, IQ and Fish-era Marillion.

In 2013 Clepsydra announced they

were reuniting, with Andy Thommen back on bass guitar, and a reunion tour scheduled for 2014. Says Andy about the reunion, "On Sunday June 23 we met and decided to go for the reunion. The day after we did one single post on facebook announcing the reunion, within 24 hours we had the first 3 concert offers!"

There have been whispers on the internet that the band's reunion has been so successful that they were planning to continue beyond this reunion tour. Andy began by saying:

> "We're approaching the end of the reunion tour, with the last three concerts to come ..."

And confirmed that the band is working on a live DVD recorded on a multi-cam at the RoSfest earlier this year in Gettysburg, USA, when Clepsydra shared a stage with the legendary Caravan. RoSfest, or to give it its full name, the Rites of Spring Festival, is an annual progressive rock festival in Pennsylvania. This was its 11th year, and as they say:

> "RoSfest has always been at the forefront of bringing new and upcoming progressive rock bands to an American audience, while also bringing in bands that were at their peak during the heyday of prog rock in the '70s."

John Lennon always said that were the Beatles ever to re-form he would want them to go into the studio and see what they could produce rather than just play a series of what are now known as heritage gigs. I have always taken this as a yardstick by which bands' re-unions work and are judged so I am very glad to hear that, as Andy told me:

> "We have started talking about the recording of a new album."

Although these plans are at a very early stage. I asked him whether they had written any of the material for the new album yet. He replied:

> "No writing, just ideas, concepts and the decision that we WILL DO IT!"

He told me that the release date for the DVD is planned for the end of this year, and that:

> "The DVD will contain the full uncut concert, which is about 100 minutes, plus a bonus tour backstage footage."

I am sure that all Clepsydra fans will agree with me that this is really exciting news, and that we are all looking forward to finding out what the 'pearl of Switzerland' does next.

The Gonzo Annual 2015

It's stylish, it's witty, it's subversive, it's free. It's everything you want from a music magazine

www.gonzoweekly.com

Well, boys and girls,

I hope that you have enjoyed this compendium of just a little bit of what *Gonzo Weekly* has brought its readers throughout the last year. In putting this book together we have tried to provide a snapshot of what the *Gonzo Weekly* experience is like.

This is the magazine that I have been dreaming of producing since I was a teenager—an intelligent, witty and subversive slice though the parts of pop culture that I find interesting and that I believe to be important. As I write, I am working on issue #107, and—regularly people ask me whether I find it difficult to fill the magazine each week. My answer to them is that the difficulty is in deciding what to leave out.

Working on this annual was even more difficult—there were no less than 52 front cover stories to fit in, and if I had followed my original idea then this volume would be nearly three times the size, and I would have probably had yet another nervous breakdown putting it together.

But I decided that discretion is the better part of valour. After all, if you want to read more, the last 106 issues are available for free at the Gonzo Weekly website, which is also the hub of a happy and interesting little community of readers, writers, musicians and activists.

Come in and join us, the water's fine

Love and Peace
Jon Downes (Editor)

www.ingramcontent.com/pod-product-compliance
Lightning Source LLC
LaVergne TN
LVHW081451070426
835512LV00015B/2623